CLOTHED IN READINESS

LESSONS FROM THE VINEYARD

BEN DISMUKES

WWW.CLOTHEDINREADINESS.COM

714 Enterprises, LLC

CONTENTS

INTRODUCTION
AN UNLIKELY HERO

In the spring of my junior year of high school, a small group of guys crowded into my baseball coach's office to witness first-hand the unthinkable. A friend had a VHS recording of a boxing match that had taken place just two days earlier, and we had snuck out of study hall to watch it, knowing that my coach was the least likely adult on campus to turn us in. Prior to this fight, it was widely held that Mike Tyson was the closest thing to invincible that existed in the realm of athletics, and he had faced a virtually unknown challenger, James "Buster" Douglas—a 42:1 underdog. Of course, we already knew the outcome, but we wanted to see it for ourselves. What we witnessed that Monday morning was the very thing that had sent shockwaves throughout the sports world just two days prior: *Mike Tyson had been knocked out for the first time in his professional career.*

In the following weeks, boxing pundits pointed to several factors contributing to his defeat. Success had softened him, and he no longer trained as hard as he had during his ascension to the top. He was prone to late night partying, drugs, and womanizing, all of which impacted his focus and his physical condition so much that just a month before the fight, he was a whopping 25 lbs. over his normal weight. In the remaining weeks leading up to the fight, he dropped all the extra weight, which had a devastating impact on his energy level. During the fight, Tyson was clearly out of rhythm, revealing a decline in fundamental boxing skills, due in part to his lax training regimen but also because he simply wasn't fighting as often as he had earlier in his career. If I were writing a screenplay, I would tell you that the champ had lost the "eye of the tiger," but to put it bluntly, he simply showed up unprepared. He admitted as much in an interview published in the LA Times shortly after the fight, during which he told a reporter that he never took his opponent seriously. In the end, his lack of readiness cost him.

Douglas took a much different approach to the fight. The largely unknown, unheralded, and unappreciated boxer was hungry for success, yet had none of the distractions that typically accompany it. He knew his fight with Tyson would be his greatest opportunity to prove his merit as a boxer, and he gave himself over to an aggressive training regimen. It showed in Tokyo that historic night. The ordinarily overweight boxer entered the ring lean, hard, and in peak physical condition. His focus during the buildup to the contest had been laser-like. He understood he was going toe-to-toe with the best, and he managed to put everything else out of his mind. That was no small feat. Just weeks before heading to Japan, Douglas lost his mother to a stroke. Yet he somehow was able to channel his grief and emotion into his boxing, later sharing in an interview that her death had been a source of motivation. In short, what Tyson had failed to do, Douglas had done remarkably well: he made himself ready physically, mentally, and emotionally. His preparation put him in the perfect position, not only to survive a 7th round knockdown from one of the greatest boxers of all time, but to go on to put Iron Mike down for the count.

As the famous saying goes, "Success occurs when opportunity meets preparation" (Zig Ziglar), and Douglas rose to the occasion simply because he was the better prepared of the two. This is a concept we readily embrace when applied to such things as sports, academics, or career choices. But what about our relationship with the Lord? Have you ever given thought to the inevitable truth that you will one day stand before the King of kings and be required to give an account for the life you lived on this end of eternity? Have you considered what success will look like in that moment when you face His fiery, piercing gaze? Are you living with great anticipation towards that day, putting your time and energy into the preparation that will be required on that day? Do you recognize the eternal implications of that extraordinary occasion, and are you bent on being made ready, just as Douglas was for his match with Tyson? Or will you coast into God's final judgment, clinging to the spoils of blessing like an overconfident champion, wrongly believing that your eternal reward is a done deal?

There was a time in church history—even in the church here in America—when readiness was a primary focus. The apostles recognized the temporal nature of life on earth and urgently proclaimed the Lord with eternity in view. Emphasizing both the crucified life and the denial of self, they willingly suffered the loss of all that the world had to offer in anticipation of an eternal reward. They were despised and rejected by those unwilling to join them on their spiritual journey. They were in the world but not of it (John 17:14), and they loved not their own lives, even to the point of death (Revelation 12:11). Understanding the fleeting nature of time, they made the most of what they were given, storing up treasures in Heaven, where moth and rust have no power (Matthew 6:19-21). And as much as they lived their own lives in such a manner, they fervently labored so that others could receive and walk in that same revelation. Today, they stand in heaven as heroes of the faith to whom we owe a tremendous debt of gratitude. The same could be said of countless others down through the ages, most of whom are largely confined to the realm of obscurity here on earth, while heaven refers to them as those "of whom the world was not worthy," (Hebrews 11:38). Such men and women held true to the gospel as preached by the Apostle Paul, laboring to make a bride ready for the Lord, understanding that, eternally speaking, the difference between success and failure has everything to do with the issue of readiness.

Perhaps the most familiar exhortation for readiness comes from the Lord Himself in Luke 12. Notice the warning to resist the temptation to fall into complacency:

> Be dressed and ready for active service and keep your lamps continuously burning. Be like men who are waiting for their

> master when he returns from the wedding feast, so that when he comes and knocks they may immediately open the door for him. Blessed (happy, prosperous, to be admired) are those servants whom the master finds awake and watching when he arrives. I assure you and most solemnly say to you, he will prepare himself to serve, and will have them recline at the table, and will come and wait on them. Whether he comes in the second watch (before midnight), or even in the third (after midnight), and finds them so [prepared and ready], blessed are those servants.
>
> But be sure of this, that if the head of the house had known at what time the thief was coming, he [would have been awake and alert, and] would not have allowed his house to be broken into. You, too, be continually ready; because the Son of Man is coming at an hour that you do not expect.
>
> Luke 12:35-40—AMP

In this passage, Jesus is speaking of His physical return to the earth—a subject which, for a myriad of reasons, many modern-day believers seem unwilling to discuss. Perhaps this reluctance stems from the plethora of false prophecies that have come down the pike over the years, and I can certainly relate. I was a high school sophomore in 1988 and vividly remember the terror that hit me when a friend informed me that Jesus would return within the month based on a "prophecy" given in the book, *The Rapture—Rosh Hashana 1988 and 88 Reasons Why*. Fear soon gave way to relief, as the specified date passed with no sound of a trumpet blast, and I went on to finish high school which, at the time, I wanted more than for the Lord to return. It should go without saying that I was not ready to stand before Him, hence the fear and selfish immaturity. (Incidentally, you can still buy a copy of this book on eBay for $100, even though it's both out of print and, clearly, out of touch with reality.) While the book merely alarmed and inconvenienced me, the stories of those who bought into its message—to the point of running up credit card debt, foolishly thinking it would never have to be repaid—are real and sad. Nevertheless, Jesus addressed His return head-on, knowing that there would be a great deal of confusion and "fake news" surrounding the timing of His coming (Matthew 24:26-27, 36). It is precisely on this basis that He appeals to His disciples to "stay awake," (Matthew 24:42) which is another way of telling us to be ready. We should, therefore, face this topic with resolve to heed His words and be clothed in readiness!

Regardless of how many times we've endured errant predictions or shown a lack of wisdom concerning the end, the Day of the Lord is an absolute for all believers. Whether He returns to the earth in our lifetime or not, each of us is guaranteed to one day stand before Him. How we deal with this inevitability will have, whether we realize it or not, a profound impact on the way we live our day-to-day lives. A wrong interpretation of what it will be like to stand before Him, or even a blatant disregard for that moment, will lead us to complacency and passivity, both of which are the exact opposite of the Lord's desire for us to be "dressed and ready for active service," (Luke 12:35 AMP). Such apathy towards Him will undoubtedly result in a rather rude awakening for those who cling to it. This was true of Mike Tyson when he faced Buster Douglas in 1990. Yet for the champ, his defeat was a wakeup call—an opportunity to get serious about boxing once more and make the necessary changes required to reclaim the title. But when we face the Lord on Judgement Day, it will be too late for second chances. Time will have run out, and there will be no rematches. Our choices in this life will have determined our eternal relationship with Him, or a lack thereof. Let's face it: as the body of Christ, we have failed to rightly divide the word of truth (2 Timothy 2:15) regarding the necessity of inward preparation. As a result, we are sinking increasingly deeper into half-heartedness, lukewarmness, and mixture. We are hardly ready for His coming, and the midnight hour seems to be approaching quickly (Matthew 25:6).

WE MUST BE TEACHABLE!

Last year, while driving past my old church home in Atlanta, the voice of the Lord broke into my spirit with an inaudible shout: "The message of readiness is no longer preached in My church and it's time to bring it back!" In that moment, I knew the Holy Spirit was asking me to write this book. Yet even as I share this, I want to be very clear. First, I am not qualified to write a book on this subject. When the Lord spoke to me, I was well aware of that fact. To be quite honest, I remember a twinge of argument with Him over this issue as I responded in my mind, "But Lord, I wouldn't even know where to begin! I should be reading a book on readiness, not writing one!" But if the Lord only worked with qualified people, nothing would ever be accomplished, and disobeying Him was not an option for me. So, I have written this book not as an expert, but as a student of the Lord and as one who will remain on this journey of preparation for the rest of my days. I am simply making available the instruction that He was faithful to give me with the hope that it will be a help to you in your own maturity.

Secondly, I am under no illusion that the Lord has chosen me to single-handedly restore a lost message to His church. None of this originated with me, nor is it about me. (I didn't even want to put my name on the book cover! I went so far as to attempt to think of a clever pseudonym, but the Lord wouldn't allow it!) Nevertheless, He is fanning the embers of an all but lost message, and I am hopeful that we are witnessing a move of the Spirit to awaken the wise virgins in our day, so that they may acquire the much-needed oil to light their lamps as the bridegroom draws near (Matthew 25:1-13). It is the Lord who is rousing His people from their slumber in a beginning way, and He is doing so on a global scale. Yet, He uses vessels of His own choosing, and He even once used a donkey to speak words of wisdom (Numbers 22:28-30). That didn't make the donkey wise, it only served to testify of the greatness of God. I relate to that precious creature in many ways, and I'm hopeful that God will use this book in a similar manner.

Bear in mind, reading a book is not going to make anyone ready for anything. But as I've stepped out in obedience to the Lord, I've discovered that I'm not so much writing a book as He is writing on the tablet of my heart. In seeking Him as to the message, He's been doing a deep, transformational work within me, spurring me on as I align myself with His instruction to be inwardly prepared to meet Him face-to-face. I believe He is so longing to make a people ready for His return that if we will simply give Him our "yes" and "amen," we'll be utterly astounded by what He'll do within us. My hope is that as you read what the Lord has prompted me to share, you will grant Him access to your innermost being and ask Him to do a similar life-changing work within you.

Some may balk at the premise of a book that beckons the church to readiness, thinking that it is the equivalent of "preaching to the choir." Sadly, too many have wrongly believed that the only true preparation necessary for eternity is praying the "Sinners' Prayer," thus experiencing the event often referred to as "salvation." But this line of thinking stems from an incomplete understanding of what God has purposed for humanity and severely limits the gospel proclaimed by the apostles. The good news of Jesus Christ goes far beyond a born-again experience. In saying this, I'm not diminishing in any way the importance of being saved. It is, without question, the necessary first step in the readiness process and one which speaks volumes concerning God's love toward a rebellious people. I am simply stating that salvation was never the full intent of God's plan concerning humanity. He has something far greater in mind: His eternal purpose, which is hidden in plain sight within scripture. The readying of His people is specifically and uniquely tied to that purpose!

Paul likens the process of preparation to a marathon: "Do you not know that in a race all the runners run, but only one receives the prize? So run that you may obtain it," (1 Corinthians 9:24).

In that light, being born again would be synonymous with the starting line and not the finish. The Great Commission, which was the charge that Jesus gave His apostles before ascending into Heaven, was to "make disciples," (Matthew 28:19) and not simply get people "saved." We have historically put much emphasis on leading others into praying a prayer and, comparatively speaking, very little on the process of discipleship. We must get back to an understanding of the distance race analogy with an emphasis on finishing strong. The prize that awaits us is not a participation trophy. It is a reward for those willing to endure to the end. Such an ongoing push toward the finish line is critical if we desire to hear the words, "Well done good and faithful servant," (Matthew 25:23). This is precisely why a return to the message of readiness is not only relevant but desperately needed in the church today.

Others have argued that a focus on the return of the Lord is counterproductive. Their rationale is that narrowing in on an event to take place at some unknown point in the future can all too easily render us useless or ineffective in living Godly lives today. Some point to a "doomsday thinking" that can emerge during discussions surrounding the coming of the Lord, suggesting that talk of end times is akin to fear mongering. While I would agree that we must guard against allowing fear into the equation, refusing to acknowledge and discuss the Second Coming has proven to be a colossal mistake, as evidenced by the present carnality in the western church. To live without our eventual face-to-face meeting with the Lord in view is like a runner who forgets about the finish line. When the going gets tough, he's likely to stop moving forward, back-peddle, or even drop out of the race altogether. Much of the church in our day has regressed into a state of moral confusion, and it would serve us well to remember the temporal nature of life on earth. The Lord's return was a major component of the apostles' teachings, and Jesus Himself referred to it on multiple occasions, both directly and indirectly. There is even an entire book of the

Bible devoted to the subject in the book of Revelation! Undoubtedly, it's important to Him, and therefore, must be a point of emphasis for us as well.

Readiness is vital to all believers, whether He comes in our day or not. We will all stand before Him, ready or not. For the prepared, it will be a glorious occasion indeed—far beyond the fame and accomplishment associated with winning a heavyweight boxing title or a gold medal in the Olympic marathon! But for unprepared unbelievers, that day will be one of great terror, leading to eternal judgment. And for unprepared believers, although they will be spared eternal damnation, it will be a time of great sorrow as they face the reality of having missed out on God's highest purpose for their lives. Jesus issued this call to readiness for all who have ears to hear and made sure it was included in the cannon of scripture. Therefore, we cannot… we must not… turn a deaf ear to it!

In recent years, I have increasingly become convinced that our lack of readiness is actually delaying His coming. For far too long, we've approached the day of His return as a fixed date in time, but a careful examination of scripture reveals something quite different. For many, this may seem heretical, but only because we tend to hold more tightly to doctrines, traditions, and other people's interpretations of the written Word than we cling to the Lord, Himself. Within the coming chapters, we will examine key verses together. As we do, I would simply ask that you listen to what the Holy Spirit would say to you in an attitude of humility and a desire to learn. In doing so, I'm confident you will come away with a different understanding than what is commonly taught in most churches. Please know, too, that I don't want you to merely accept what I've written at face value. Instead, I encourage you to seek the Lord as your Teacher. He alone is the embodiment of true wisdom and knowledge. We need to hear what He has to say, even if it is contrary to years of error and bad doctrine.

A COSTLY MESSAGE

The church in our day has become like an overweight, lazy, undisciplined boxer. Not only have we forgotten how to fight, but we prefer the intoxication of worldly pleasures over a life of inward readiness. Our present understanding of cheap grace has resulted in a false belief that we can just show up for judgment having put neither thought nor effort into being made ready for the Lord, yet fully expecting to be crowned with eternal authority, glory, and intimacy with Jesus simply because we profess to believe. We don't understand the fact that we've been entrusted, by God, with great wealth, in expectation of a return on His investment (Matthew 25:14-30). If we fail to learn specifically what that return is and live with it in mind, it is the equivalent of burying treasure in the ground, thus squandering it entirely. Please know that what I'm sharing here is not intended as criticism or judgment. It is, rather, an honest assessment of the present condition of the church. As the body of Christ, we desperately need the Lord to awaken us before it's too late!

Thankfully, we have a Trainer—the Holy Spirit—who is in the business of building champions. Romans 8:37 reminds us that "We are more than conquerors through Him who loved us." While we're all familiar with this verse, how many of us are truly inviting—or even allowing—Him to train us for battle? Don't fall into the hubris of Tyson, who boasted of his invincibility while failing to prepare for the challenge in front of him. Conquerors conquer because they've been sufficiently trained to do so. They have the scars to prove it. They are not self-indulgent, nor are they undisciplined. And they do not turn a deaf ear toward those whose job it is to both train and equip them for victory.

God's regimen is intense, and it is not for the fainthearted. But the good news is that His grace is sufficient, and His strength is perfected in our human weakness (2 Corinthians 12:9)! It's time for us to heed His Word and step out in obedience to our call to know Christ as life (Colossians 3:4). It's time for us to get back into the "gym," knowing that our greatest fight is ahead of us, not behind us. The Lord is looking for those who, like Douglas, hunger enough for true victory to endure the necessary pain and sacrifice to bring it forth.

He is asking you to take up your cross and follow Him (Mark 8:34-35). As you do, He will mold you into His champion, but He won't do so against your will. You must *truly* desire inward transformation, understanding that it's not temporal pleasures or earthly rewards that await you on the other side of eternity. *It is the Lord **Himself** and the fullness of intimacy with **Him** that He is offering you.* He alone is our exceedingly great reward. It's Christ as life as we have never even imagined (1 Corinthians 2:9), in a measure of fullness! The question before you today is simply this:

Are you willing to love Him with the same love with which He has loved you and abandon everything for His sake?

To do so is impossible on our own, but if we're willing to say "yes" to Him, He will cause a supernatural love to spring up within our hearts as a continuous fountain freely flowing back to Him.

IT'S TIME TO GET READY

About 15 years ago, while at a conference in our church in Phoenix, a well-known prophetic minister asked those in attendance to circle up around the auditorium so he could go around the room and give a personal word of prophecy to those whom the Lord highlighted. There were easily a couple hundred people there that night, so it took some time for him to make his way to where I was standing. As he drew closer, anticipation began to build in my soul as I fantasized about the spectacular, life-changing word that I just knew the Lord would speak to me, endowing me with both wisdom and power, thus opening the door to a world-renowned ministry where hundreds of thousands would come to know Jesus, while His glory would come to rest permanently and manifestly upon me, His humble servant. Needless to say, I was up to my eyeballs in flesh!

When he finally drew near, he looked me in the eyes, grabbed my hand and said almost in a whisper, "You better get ready," and then moved quickly on to someone else. I barely had time to get into prophetic-word-receiving mode before it was all over. Not only was I disappointed, I was devastated. Along with the visions of my humble—yet powerful and glorious—ministry, my religious façade began spiraling down the proverbial commode. "*I'm a man of God,*" I thought to myself, as I'm confident a scowl appeared on my face. "*Who does he think I am? Get ready? Does he think I'm not even saved? What a bunch of garbage! What a false prophet…*" This internal dialogue went on long enough for me to completely miss what I now believe was a direct and deeply profound word from the Lord. In my immaturity, I failed to hear and respond to His invitation. Thankfully, He was faithful to pursue me with the issue of readiness in mind. While I lament the wasted time, 15 years later I am now learning not only to heed that word but to obey as well. And as the saying goes, better late than never. I can now say with great certainty that as I've been intentional about pursuing readiness in the Lord, I have experienced more of Him in these past months than ever before.

The Holy Spirit reminded me of that story after giving me this writing assignment, revealing to me how my pride had kept me from hearing what He had to say in that moment. And while I realize I still have far to go on my journey, God has humbled me significantly since then. Now I am encouraging you to invite the Lord to deal with any pride that might keep you from embarking on your own readiness journey. The Lord's invitation for you to be made ready for Him is very real, and I do not want you to miss out on it! As you continue reading this book, please do so with a teachable spirit and humility towards Jesus. Bear in mind, God "opposes the proud but gives grace to the humble," (James 4:6).

For those of us who have become entrenched in a narcissistic brand of Christianity (an oxymoron if ever there was one!), we may need to be taken down a few notches before we have ears to hear what the Lord is saying to us. Much of the teaching we've accumulated over the years places man and his carnal desires at the epicenter of the gospel narrative, leaving the Lord on the periphery to diligently work to meet those desires in the form of one blessing or another. Sadly, this is more of the "American dream" than it is the good news of Jesus Christ, as presented in scripture. Paul's gospel, as he received it from the Lord, declares Christ to be the preeminent King of kings before whom every knee will bow and every tongue confess that He, and He alone, is Lord (Philippians 2:10-11). You and I were created for His pleasure, not the other way around. We are bit players in this story. He is both the main character and the hero. All things were created through Him and for Him (Colossians 1:16). The gospel message does not revolve around us. If He is saying get ready (and He is... repeatedly in scripture), then it would be wise for us to not only seek understanding regarding what this means to us personally, but also to fully cooperate with Him in the process as He faithfully leads us. This will demand humility on our part, as I've so painfully learned through experience.

Much of what I share throughout this book will challenge you. Some of it will be hard to receive—and possibly even offensive—if heard through the wrong grid. I was an athlete in my youth, and some of the best coaches I ever had were the ones who yelled the loudest when I wasn't putting forth my best effort. I easily could have taken offense, questioning their right to criticize my techniques, confront my attitude, and assess my effort. But had I responded in that way, not only would I have suffered athletically, but I would have fashioned myself into a permanent fixture on the bench. And no, I'm not your coach! I assure you I don't know more than you, and I promise not to yell at you. But I've been hanging out with the Coach a lot over the past few months, and He has been pushing, encouraging, teaching, rebuking, and even disciplining me. Not only am I growing to love the way He is calling me to maturity, I'm passing along to you what He's been sharing with me. "Blessed is the one who is not offended by me," (Matthew 11:6).

With that in mind, let's begin our journey together into becoming clothed in readiness!

CHAPTER 1

BEGINNING AT THE END

> In Him we have obtained an inheritance, having been predestined according to the purpose of him who works all things according to the counsel of his will, so that we who were the first to hope in Christ might be to the praise of His glory. In Him you also, when you heard the word of truth, the gospel of your salvation, and believed in Him, were sealed with the promised Holy Spirit, who is the guarantee of our inheritance until we acquire possession of it, to the praise of his glory.
>
> Ephesians 1:11-14

I am by nature a sloppy dresser. I get dressed simply to deal with the problem of nudity, and I do so with comfort in mind. If I had my way, I'd wear jeans and a tee shirt all the time, no matter what the day holds. But I have a wife and three daughters who have no problem making it known when my attire doesn't match the occasion, and they've taught me to "dress up" when the situation warrants it. In those instances, I am making myself ready for an occasion. I would never sit around the house watching a ballgame while wearing a button-down shirt, dress slacks, and leather shoes. When Jesus tells us to be "dressed in readiness" (Luke 12:35 NASB), He isn't just casually throwing out a general edification for us to be on our best behavior… just because. Rather, He is telling us to be prepared for something. And that "something" is the very reason we exist.

Going on a journey without an established destination is called wandering, which is a lot like dressing up for no reason. The pathway of readiness is not a walkabout. It leads to a specific destination. If we don't know where He intends to take us, chances are we'll be more inclined to resist Him as He leads us along the way, thinking either that we have a better destination in mind or that our desired end is His as well.

As a young man, I had the opportunity to spend a couple of weeks trekking through Europe, and, thinking I was cooler than all the tourists who flood the continent on an annual basis, I decided to see it without the help of a guidebook. The truth of the matter is, I was still a tourist, just one with no direction or clear sense of purpose. My desire to do things my own way turned out to be a huge mistake! After a week of arbitrarily jaunting about from one place to the next with little to no thought regarding what to see or do once I arrived, I grew so frustrated that I couldn't wait to get back to America! When I did, I discovered Europe second-hand as multiple people asked about the sights they assumed I had taken in, not realizing they were dealing with a hard-headed nincompoop! As the Author and Creator of the path that leads to life (Matthew 7:14), God has absolutely no desire for us to miss the point of the sojourn through this temporal life.

CREATED WITH PURPOSE

As human beings, we tend to project our human characteristics onto God. But His ways are not our ways, nor are His thoughts our thoughts (Isaiah 55:8). Though we can be quite sporadic in our thinking and behavior, He never is. We tend to choose our words and actions without much thought or intentionality, but God does not. Everything He does is carefully and strategically calculated. The Bible tells us that every word He speaks, as it is released, does not return to Him void, but it accomplishes all that He purposed in sending it forth (Isaiah 55:11). If God is that intentional over the words He uses, then doesn't it stand to reason that His actions are just as pregnant with meaning and purpose? I assure you, He didn't just decide on a whim to make a creature in His own image, only to plop it in the midst of a garden so that it could autonomously go about determining its own destiny. Just as every word God speaks is held to account regarding its effectiveness in accomplishing what it was sent out for, so, too, will you and I be required to give an account for whether or not our lives were lived according to His purpose in creating us.

Life is a gift of His kindness and generosity towards us, yet we often approach it as if we're entitled to pursue our own end rather than His. When He created us, He did so with a specific destiny in mind, which has nothing to do with our hopes, dreams, wants, or interpretations of scripture, and everything to do with His predetermined plan. In His infinite wisdom, He assigned a specific, unique, and well-defined purpose for humanity long before He ever began the process of creation. That purpose is our very reason for existence and, therefore, is of utmost importance. Oddly enough, few believers, including myself until about seven years ago, have ever been taught a scriptural understanding of God's eternal purpose for humanity. Furthermore, few, even within the church, think to ask Him why they were created. To no small degree, keeping people ignorant of God's plan for us is a strategy of the enemy. He has intentionally made this underlying foundation a point of attack, both by introducing false doctrines meant to deceive us regarding our created purpose and also by downplaying its significance to such degree that we simply don't consider it relevant. The church's ignorance in this arena has resulted in the muddying of the waters regarding the Lord's design for life. Perhaps even more importantly, our ignorance has robbed us of the necessary motivation to cooperate with the Holy Spirit as He seeks to prepare us for eternity.

In the Genesis creation account, nothing was done randomly. God—who doesn't speak a word without focused intention—had a unique, preassigned purpose for every "thing" He created. The sun, for example, was placed in its exact position in the heavens at a precise distance from the earth. It was formed with a unique composition of matter and gases to emit a particular amount of heat and light. The earth was set in a fixed orbit around the sun at specific, predetermined distances throughout its trajectory, and by its rotation is exposed to the sun's heat and light in regular, 24-hour intervals. We can safely say then that the purpose of the sun is to provide the energy necessary for physical life on this planet, as well as for marking the passage of time and establishing the seasons. The sun carries a specific purpose, and the same could be said of the moon, the stars, the dry land, the waters, and all the rest of creation. Nothing within the physical universe that God created is arbitrary.

Whether we acknowledge it or not, we accept this "principle of purpose" about most things, however we may never even have considered that this same principle applies to us. In Ephesians 1, Paul mentions God's purpose for humanity three separate times (Ephesians 1:5, 9, and 11). Twice he tells us that the Father has predestined us according to His purpose (vv. 5, 11), and in verses 7-9, he declares that God has lavished His grace upon us according to that same purpose. Clearly, the truth that He desires something very specific from humanity is a point of emphasis here. The Greek word in all three instances is *prothesis*, which literally means "a setting forth of a thing, as to place it in view."[1] In other words, our Creator has set forth a destination for mankind. He not only created us with this end in mind, but as Paul declares in this passage, He is continuously lavishing His grace upon us, toward that ultimate goal. Grace, from the Greek word *charis*, means kindness or favor,[2] but it is often used scripturally to reflect the truth that God has extended Himself toward us in love to do what only He could do. This is typified in Zechariah 4:6-7, where God's word to Zerubbabel was that the temple would be rebuilt—not through the efforts of man—but by His Spirit with shouts of "grace, grace

---

1 Strong, J. (1890). Strong's exhaustive concordance of the Bible. Abingdon Press.

2 Strong, J. (1890). Strong's exhaustive concordance of the Bible. Abingdon Press.

to it!" Thus the Lord, as communicated in Ephesians 1, continually offers Himself to us, that He might do what we could never accomplish: bring us into His predetermined purpose. Our eternal purpose is always on His mind and in His view—it is literally that important to Him—and He's continuously laboring toward its realization!

Also worth noting is that the Greek word, *prothesis*, is the same word used to reference the showbread in Matthew 12:4, Mark 2:26, and Luke 6:4. In scripture, bread often symbolizes God's provision, which is made clear in the abundance of manna in the wilderness—a supernatural gift that only the Lord could have provided. The Lord has provided us, then, with meaning that only He is capable of assigning. Just as He alone was able to rain bread down from heaven, so, too, is our purpose defined by Him. It has not been left up to us to determine! If we walk within the parameters that He has established, we will experience joy and true fulfillment, but if we choose our own destiny, we'll only arrive at emptiness.

The showbread was a special kind of bread pointing to Christ in type and shadow. Located in the Holy Place, it was set out on a table opposite the lampstand, the light from which illuminated the showbread causing it to be within view of the High Priest. Jesus specifically referred to Himself as "the bread of life" that came downfrom heaven (John 6:48-51). Thus, our purpose is 100% rooted in the person of the Lord Jesus and cannot be accessed through any other means. He must remain in view, spiritually speaking, for us to realize our God given purpose. It is also important to recognize that even the uncreated Son of God carries a predetermined purpose. That said, to reduce Christ to a single purpose would be a gross underestimation on our part. However, regarding God's intent toward humanity, the Son was and always will be the means by which He brings His eternal purpose about. Not only so, but Jesus also demonstrated what that purpose looks like. He is the blueprint! So, in the wisdom of the Godhead, it was determined that the Son would carry great purpose in fulfilling the Father's plan for humanity. I will come back to this later, but for now, know that is it absolutely significant that the same word is used to refer to God's plan for mankind and to point to the Son! I am simply saying that the Son—the true Showbread—speaks both to our purpose and the means by which the Holy Spirit is laboring to bring it about. As for His specific purpose toward us, He fulfilled it in totality, uttering the words, "It is finished," while hanging on the cross (John 19:30). This doesn't mean He's no longer relevant or active in our journey, it is simply to say that He has done His part in making a way for us to come into our true purpose in Him.

When we live outside of the boundaries of God's purpose for our lives, we have a serious problem. This is a principle that is clearly demonstrated in the natural. When an object is used in a way that's not consistent with the intent of its designer, it can be quite destructive. I remember when I was about three years old, I was left in the care of my older siblings, who were 9, 11, and 13. My brother, who was the nine-year-old, was arguing with my 11-year-old sister, which was pretty common in those days. In a fit of rage, my brother picked up an LP record and threw it across the den like a frisbee, aiming for my sister. The thin edge of that hard vinyl album could have seriously hurt her, but thankfully, it veered to one side and smashed into the wall. What a potentially devastating use of that record! Vinyl albums are meant to be listened to, not flung through the air at top speed toward other people. Using it in a way that was inconsistent with its intended purpose resulted not only in a broken record, but it could have done serious harm to someone.

When we attempt to live our lives outside the boundaries of His assigned purpose, we end up much like that vinyl album, reaping the pain and destruction associated with our choice to live randomly according to our self-centered whims. Tragically, far too many people pass their appointed time here on earth completely beyond the boundaries God has established. We accept this to be true of those who never come into a salvation relationship with Jesus, but as believers, many of us have wrongly believed that our created purpose is tied up in salvation. It isn't. We can know the Lord as Savior and never enter fully into His eternal plan and purpose for our lives.

A SPECIFIC KIND OF SON

If we've spent any time in the church, this most likely flies in the face of much of what we've been taught. Countless sermons, Bible studies, devotionals, Sunday School lessons, and Christian books have helped drive us to the conclusion that salvation is our very reason for existing. And because we've not received the revelation of God's eternal purpose, we've simply accepted this as a logical conclusion. But the idea that God created man solely to save him from sin—and thus revealed the depths of His goodness toward an undeserving creation—is simply not true! Sure, in His foreknowledge of man's fall, He made a provision for salvation. But it's quite the slippery slope to assume that salvation was His entire reason for creating man in the first place. If that were true, this would have put God in the position of needing sin and death in order to accomplish His ultimate objective. Would God—who is not only the personification of holiness, but who also commands us to walk in that same holiness—ever put Himself in the position of needing sin to accomplish His desired end? Would God have commanded Adam and Eve not to eat of the tree of the knowledge of good and evil, only to pin His entire reason for creating them on their doing precisely that? The answer to that question is a resounding no!

God's predetermined purpose preceded not only the fall but even the creation of man himself. When God conceived the idea of humanity, sin was not yet even in existence. Yes, God knew that man would choose poorly and thus fall into rebellion, and He accounted for that poor choice within His amazing plan. But whether man had fallen or not, God's intent would have remained the same, and, in fact, it has never changed. Even Adam and Eve, prior to their fall, were not walking in the fullness of created purpose. In fact, if we think back to the analogy of the race from the introduction, they were merely at the starting line. The full realization of God's assigned purposed is the prize at the end of the race, and even they had a race to run! The journey of readiness is a progression towards maturity, and Adam and Eve, as they existed prior to the fall, were not mature. And while they carried the potential for purpose, it was merely that: potential. When they fell into sin, the need for getting back to square one was immediate and pressing, not just for them, but for all of humanity. However, square one is not our ultimate destination. If you have accepted Jesus as Savior, that's wonderful news! But being saved simply means that you now carry the potential for walking in the fullness of His purpose, whereas, apart from Christ, even that potential is out of reach. And just as there was a choice to be made in the Garden, so, too, do we face choices on a daily basis. The good news in all of this is that even sin and the rebellion of man cannot alter God's purpose for creation. But to realize it, we must accept the fact that simply praying a prayer and asking Jesus to be your Savior and Lord does not equate to the fulfillment of God's plan for your life.

Let's jump back into Ephesians 1. Remember that God is continually giving Himself toward the fulfillment of His purpose in us. If salvation were that purpose in entirety, then what remains to be done once we're born again? Why the need for the ongoing lavishing of His grace in our lives? Evidently, salvation is not the purpose that is being spoken of here. So what is? For some of us, our minds immediately gravitate toward a vocation, a ministry, or some other "calling," but Paul is not talking about a vocation or calling. In fact, he's not even addressing us at an individual level. He's referring to a corporate humanity, and within that context, he mentions a singular purpose—not many different purposes for many different people. God's design for all humanity—not just a select few—is that each of us would come to walk fully in His singular purpose. Failure to allow Him to teach us how to do so will yield similar results as a vinyl album violently hurled across a crowded room.

A key to our understanding lies in verses 4-5:

> "...even as He chose us in Him before the foundation of the world, that we should be holy and blameless before Him. In love He predestined us for adoption to Himself as sons through Jesus Christ, according to the purpose of His will..."

Did you catch that? Here we see that God's purpose for humanity is a relationship which, in verse 5, is compared to a father/son relationship. But before examining the biblical and historical concept of sonship—which is quite different than our modern understanding—I want to take a step backward and look at the bigger picture. God's purpose for humanity isn't primarily in the realm of behavior modification or activity. He didn't create us just so we could do something for Him. He made you for a relationship with Him. Scripture shows us that the Almighty is driven by a desire for intimacy with humanity in all that He does. Jesus tells us in Matthew 22:37-40 that the entirety of the law and the prophets—which is another way of saying the Old Testament—hang on two commandments: loving God with our whole being and loving others just as we love ourselves. Not only is this true of the original 39 books of the Hebrew scriptures, but it's also true of the New Testament, which brings even greater clarity to His desire for relationship with us. From cover to cover, the Word of God affirms that He is after our hearts. And it's for this friendship with Him that we were created. Furthermore, this isn't a random relationship, but a unique one that is framed within the specific context of sonship.

The Greek word translated as "sons" in verse 5 is incredibly significant. In the New Testament, there are three primary Greek words translated as son or sons: *nepios, teknon,* and *huios. Nepios* speaks of an infant or baby,[3] *teknon* generally indicates an immature child,[4] and *huios* refers to a mature son.[5] In Ephesians 1:5, Paul is specifically using the Greek word *huiosthesia*, which is the adoption or legal placement of a son.[6] In Ancient Rome, fathers with no male children of their own often would adopt male sons, who, upon the father's death, would be trained to oversee and manage his estate. The child, though legally considered the heir upon his adoption, was not immediately entrusted with the authority of oversight. Instead, he was placed under the care of a *pedagogue*—the primary caregiver responsible for both the instruction and discipline necessary for preparing the child for his eventual role as overseer of the estate—until he reached full maturity. When that time came, as determined by the father, there would be a formal placement ceremony, or *huiosthesia*, in which the child would be entrusted with full legal authority. This was symbolized through the putting away of a crimson toga worn by a child (*teknon*), in favor of a white toga, signifying maturity (*huios*).

Paul calls upon this imagery in several of his epistles, perhaps most notably here in Ephesians 1:4-5 and also in Galatians 4:1-5 and Romans 8:12-23. In Romans 8, he reveals that while those of us who are in Christ have already received the "Spirit of adoption as sons" (8:15), we are still "wait[ing] eagerly for adoption as sons, the redemption of our bodies" (8:23) In other words, while we have been adopted into the family of God, we are awaiting our formal placement, whereby we will be entrusted with the full legal authority to oversee the Father's business. In the meantime, we have been put under the tutelage of the Holy Spirit, who is actively training us toward that day when the Father allows us to shed the "old toga"

---

3 Strong, J. (1890). Strong's exhaustive concordance of the Bible. Abingdon Press.

4 Strong, J. (1890). Strong's exhaustive concordance of the Bible. Abingdon Press.

5 Strong, J. (1890). Strong's exhaustive concordance of the Bible. Abingdon Press.

6 Strong, J. (1890). Strong's exhaustive concordance of the Bible. Abingdon Press.

of corruptible flesh and put on the new, resurrected bodies that will signify full maturity.

In scripture—with the exception of a few instances in the Gospels—Christ is referred to as the *huios*, or fully mature, Son of God. Yet the writer of Hebrews teaches us that even Jesus endured a process of preparation toward a more complete expression of sonship. Hebrews 5:8 says, "Though He was a Son (*huios*), yet He learned obedience by the things which He suffered," (NKJV). It is this process of learning obedience to the Father's will that is so key to understanding our own journey of readiness. From the Father's perspective, sonship, is not in name only. There is a function attached to it, and that function requires that we have a "not what I want, but what You want" (Mark 14:36) posture before God, which goes far beyond lip-service and into cheerful obedience to all that He commands. Philippians tells us that because Jesus "humbled Himself and became obedient to the point of death, even the death of the cross" (2:8 NKJV), God has given Him all authority, making His "the name which is above every name (v.9)." The mature sonship of Jesus Christ was expressed completely throughout His time on the earth, and it has never stopped. In obeying His Father to the uttermost, He gave us an untainted picture of who the Father is, fully carrying out the Father's will in all things. This is why the writer of Hebrews called Jesus, "the exact representation and perfect imprint of His [Father's] essence" (Hebrews 1:3 AMP), and it is precisely what Jesus meant when He said to His disciples, "Whoever has seen Me has seen the Father," (John 14:9). In all things, He submits to His Father's will, being led by the Holy Spirit even to the point of death on the cross. He obeys the Father perfectly, and so has been placed over the Father's estate with full legal authority, so much so that at His name, every knee will bow and every tongue will confess Him to be Lord of all (Philippians 2:10-11)! This is the full picture of mature sonship given to us, and it is the very relationship into which He's called us.

The demeanor of the mature son is captured quite clearly in John 5, when Jesus says of Himself,

> Truly, truly I say to you, the Son can do nothing of His own accord, but only what He sees the Father doing. For whatever the Father does, that the Son does likewise.
>
> John 5:19

This is *huios* sonship beautifully expressed, and it is the relationship that God pre-purposed for us—one in which we are to walk as our firstborn Brother does, wholly yielding to the will of God in every situation, never presuming to live independently of Him. It is not a sonship in name only, but one that is relationally demonstrated in our day to day living.

We will never become the Son of God, nor will we, in any way, be His equal. That should go without saying, but I must be clear. We must not fall into the trap of diminishing His significance or His preeminence in any way. He always will be the only begotten Son and the exalted King of the Universe. Yet in His love, the Father has invited us to know Him through the Son. His ultimate desire is that we should one day be conferred with the authority to represent the Son before creation in the same way that the Son has represented the Father. And while it's clear that, upon receiving His gift of salvation, we become His children and thus His heirs, there is still a process by which we must learn the way of *huios* sonship. Paul put it this way: "The heir, as long as he is a child (*nepios*—or baby) does not differ at all from a slave, though he is master of all," (Galatians 4:1 NKJV).

There is a necessary work of maturity that must take place in order for us to come fully into the relationship for which God created us. This goes far beyond simply being born again and comes right onto the ground of maturity or readiness, a primary emphasis in the New Testament epistles. And while there is much "identity" teaching circulating in the church calling believers to cling to a title of sonship, the Father was never interested in titles. It is the function of true sonship that He's after, and that comes through a process. If we fail to progress along the pathway of maturity, we remain immature babies in the Lord, which is precisely what Paul called the Corinthian church because of their carnality (1 Corinthians 3:1). Instead of instant inheritance, which is what many in the church are taught, training and discipline are needed to prepare us for the placement ceremony that awaits us—the "revealing of the sons of God," (Romans 8:19).

Whether or not we will cooperate and allow our Pedagogue—the Holy Spirit—to prepare us for the great responsibility that lies before us, however, is yet to be determined. There is a weight to Jesus' words in Luke 12, isn't there? Our full cooperation is necessary in order for us to be dressed in the readiness He desires, and our inheritance hangs in the balance. Being born again, though it carries the promise of eternal life, doesn't guarantee the full measure of the inheritance He has in mind. Readiness does.

That the Father could ever look upon us with such favor as to call us mature sons is a striking picture of His lovingkindness towards us. What an amazing gift He's offering us! John says it this way: "Behold what manner of love the Father has bestowed on us, that we should be called children of God!" (1 John 3:1 NKJV). And sonship is only one analogy given in scripture of both His eternal purpose and divine love towards us. There are others in the New Testament, namely, the bride of Christ (Ephesians 5:25-32,) and the Temple of the Holy Spirit (1 Corinthians 6:19-20). While each of these illustrations provides us with a unique perspective filled with additional layers of context and richness, they all point to one relationship with one God. Yet, regardless of the specific context in which it's framed, it is for this relationship with Him that we were created. The very purpose that God had in mind was an intimate, life-giving relationship with Him, whereby we become conduits of His nature, expressing His life in all we say and do. Incidentally, sonship applies to both men and women alike, as does bridal intimacy. Remember, in Christ, which is a relationship, there is no such thing as male or female (Galatians 3:28). Women are meant to be "sons," and men are meant to be "bridal" towards the Lord.

CHRIST—OUR ETERNAL DESTINATION

We could devote much more attention toward the exploration of God's eternal purpose, but that's outside the scope of this book. For now, I'm simply laying a foundation. But I must not talk about this divine relationship without emphasizing this truth: we will never become who God intends for us to be apart from Christ within us. Simply trying to be a good son for the Father or a faithful bride to the Son ultimately will result in failure every time. What is needed isn't our best efforts or our own wisdom. Only Christ could ever be the mature Son. The Holy Spirit's job is to conform us to the image of the Son, reproducing the life of Jesus in and through us (Romans 8:29). Think of this: He's already demonstrated perfect sonship once before, and He's fully capable of producing it again—through His mature sons. Likewise, only Christ is worthy to be joined in unity with One so perfect and beautiful as Himself, and He will be that within us, if we'll allow the Spirit to take us on the journey of readiness. In the same manner, only Christ was capable of living as a perfect temple, being led of the Spirit in all things, and it is the very Spirit of Christ (Romans 8:9) that is working within us to make us His temple. We're not just being made ready for the Lord: we are being made ready in Him and through Him and by His life coming to a place of dominion within us.

Paul affirms this in Ephesians 1:9 by telling us that God has "[made] known to us the mystery of His will, according to His purpose, which He set forth in Christ..." This means that God's purpose for us does not exist outside of Christ. If we want to walk in true fulfillment of the Father/mature son relationship, we must be "in Christ," which is a relationship whereby the Son's life is becoming my own. The same is true of the bridal dynamic and the temple analogy, both of which are impossible outside of a true and complete reliance upon the Spirit of God, who takes up residence within us the moment we're born again. Only He can walk in true holiness. Only He can be fully obedient to the Father, yielding to His command at all times. Only He can manifest the fruit of the Spirit, fully expressing His divine life, which truly is the Light of the world (John 8:12; 9:5)! If we are to live as the Father intends, we only will be empowered to do this through the life of His Son! We have been predestined to be clay jars filled with the very life and nature of the King (2 Corinthians 4:7)!

And let's be clear about the use of that word "predestined." This word tends to get theologians riled up and ready for battle, but it is often misapplied. The Greek word used here is *proorizo. Pro* means "before," and *orizo* is the same word from which we get the English word "horizon." Combining the two gives us a "pre-establishing of boundaries, limits or a horizon."[7] Predestination doesn't speak of a controlling God who dictates every situation, herding us like cattle into a fixed outcome. Rather, it reflects a loving God who has put His purpose within our "horizon" while allowing us the freedom to choose it or to reject it. Throughout our lives, He is constantly working behind the scenes in every circumstance, pointing to and leading us towards that horizon if we'll take notice of and yield to Him. But He never forces it upon us. The same horizon, or destiny, has been available to everyone who has ever existed, so that we're all without excuse (Romans 1:20). Whether or not we choose to pursue it is up to us. Remember, His purpose for us is a love relationship, and love cannot exist outside of free will.

The sovereignty of God does not mean that He always gets what He wants. Such thinking demonstrates how prone we are to projecting our weak, human qualities onto Him. Self-centered man would use omnipotence to get what he selfishly desires, and thus we associate sovereignty with having one's way. But our selfless Creator restrains His great power, desiring that we would choose

---

7 Strong, J. (1890). Strong's exhaustive concordance of the Bible. Abingdon Press.

to love Him as a function of our own free will. His sovereignty is expressed in His ability to work within the choices we make, keeping His purpose on the horizon.

Picture yourself in a desert landscape with nothing but parched earth stretching far off into the distance. As you survey your surroundings, you notice an oasis, teeming with life, off on the horizon. The oasis is within view, but in order to drink from it, you have a choice to make: stay in a place where water, though on the horizon, is not available to drink or make the journey toward the oasis. Without a wise choice, your predetermined horizon does you no good! Such is the nature of God's predetermined purpose for humanity. He won't force you into the oasis of His love, manifested in the person of Jesus Christ, but for as long as you have breath, He will always be within your view. He preordained this. Your role is simply to choose. You can come to Him or go your own way, and only the former will truly satisfy you.

I'll conclude this brief, but dense, chapter with a story that beautifully illustrates what has been covered in these last few pages. The children of Israel were freed from the bonds of slavery in Egypt, but their purpose for existing had nothing to do with either their oppression or their Exodus. God had long before determined that Israel would be to Him a priestly nation through which He would bless the entire earth. This was fulfilled in the coming of Christ the High Priest, from among Israel. But before that could take place, this ragtag bunch of slaves, who didn't yet exist as a nation, had to become one. God gave them a homeland, and their purpose in the natural was tied up in the Promised Land. Their wilderness journey was to be a journey of preparation during which they could learn how to live as sons of the Most High God. Within this relationship of sonship, they were to go into Canaan and fight for the very land that symbolized their purpose—a land that the Father promised to give them. As they drew closer to that land, some of them decided they didn't want to live within the boundaries God had set for them (Numbers 32:5). They therefore rejected His purpose for their lives, and God honored their choice. As a result, they were exposed to the enemy and were eventually among the first taken into captivity by the Assyrians, several years prior to the fall of the northern kingdom of Israel.

My friend, we must see ourselves in this story, because we most assuredly are in it. If we've chosen Jesus to be our Lord and Savior, then we no longer live in a spiritual Egypt under the tyranny of sin and death. Yet while we have been set free, we are not yet dwelling in Canaan. Our Promised Land is not a place called heaven, but a spiritual relationship called sonship, whereby we learn to abide fully in Christ, and He abides fully in us. We are being prepared for this destination in the wilderness of life, and we must never become passive or apathetic in the journey. It is not a foregone conclusion that we'll go in and possess the ground He would give us. To arrive at our glorious inheritance in Christ, we must choose daily to pursue Him! We must be willing to suffer the loss of all things in favor of gaining Christ (Philippians 3:8), and we must guard against becoming enthralled with the trappings of the wilderness. If we choose not to, He will honor our choices just as He honored those tribes that refused to make His Promised Land their home, and the consequences will be with us for eternity.

So, my friend, what will you decide? Will you choose to set your eyes on the spiritual ground God has promised to give you? Will you choose to endure the process of preparation necessary to go in and possess this divine relationship He is offering? Will you choose to clothe yourself in readiness in anticipation of meeting Him face to face? If so, then read on!

CHAPTER 2

A BEAUTIFUL DRESS IN DEED

> Then I heard what seemed to be the voice of a great multitude, like the roar of many waters and like the sound of mighty peals of thunder, crying out, "Hallelujah! For the Lord our God the Almighty reigns. Let us rejoice and exult and give Him the glory, for the marriage of the Lamb has come, and His Bride has made herself ready; it was granted her to clothe herself with fine linen, bright and pure"— for the fine linen is the righteous deeds of the saints.
>
> Revelation 19:6-8

In the previous chapter, I introduced eternal purpose as defined in scripture and discussed it through the lens of a sonship relationship. In this chapter, we'll delve deeper into this subject and talk specifically about how it ties in with the issue of readiness, but we'll do so through the grid of the "Bridal Paradigm." Though we touched on this previously, I want to reiterate to be clear: We have one relationship with God, but it's illustrated through three distinct biblical, relational analogies. God is one, although He has revealed Himself to us through three distinct persons—Father, Son and Holy Spirit—and we are called to relate to Him through each of these unique contexts:

- The Father longs for a family of sons conformed to the image of Christ.
- The Holy Spirit seeks a temple who is easily and readily led by Him in all things.

- The Son desires a bride worthy of His eternal devotion, with whom He will share His throne.

THE BRIDE OF CHRIST

The Bridal Paradigm is referenced throughout scripture, from the Song of Solomon to the prophets in the Old Testament and from John the Baptist, the parables of Jesus and the teachings of the apostles in the New Testament. It speaks of God's incredibly kind and generous nature in desiring to share Himself in the most intimate form of fellowship with man. Perhaps the clearest mention of the bridal dynamic comes from the Parable of the 10 Virgins in Matthew 25:1-13. In this passage, Jesus likens His second coming to a bridegroom returning for his bride at midnight. There are 10 virgins betrothed to be married, but only five are prepared for his midnight arrival. Those five are allowed into the wedding feast, which represents both the consummation of this divine relationship and the fulfillment of God's eternal purpose for humanity. The remaining virgins are shut out of the celebration altogether, and so are unable to enjoy the intimacy offered them by their would-be husband. Some have interpreted this parable as a contrast between the saved and the unsaved, but I believe that to be inconsistent with the whole counsel of scripture.

As I mentioned in the previous chapter, God chooses His words carefully and with great intention. The symbolic imagery He uses throughout the Bible is consistent. Virginity is always synonymous with right standing with God, and sexual immorality is always synonymous with unfaithfulness towards Him. The idea that the five foolish virgins represent those who do not have a relationship with Christ is incompatible with the scriptural representation of sexual purity. They clearly have been washed in the blood of the Lamb, by virtue of the fact that they are virgins. In the same way, all ten had at least a measure of oil in their lamps. In Matthew 25:8, the foolish virgins plead with the wise virgins to share their oil stating, "...our lamps are going out." Oil, which is symbolic of the Holy Spirit, would not be available to an unbeliever. Therefore, the distinction in this parable is not between the saved and unsaved; rather it is between whole-hearted and half-hearted believers. What happens to the foolish virgins who are shut out of the wedding feast is not indicative of eternal judgment. It is, rather, a sealing of their choice not to have the deepest level of intimacy offered by the bridegroom. His response, "I do not know you" (Matthew 25:12) is a bit of a play on words, as the Greek word *eido* can mean both "to know" and "to see."[8] These unwise virgins could not be seen because the light of their lamps was dim, and there was no level of shared intimacy between them and their Creator. They are, therefore, unable to enter into the bridal chamber. This important parable, then, leaves us with the critical takeaway that not all who are born again will choose to be made ready for the bridal intimacy that Jesus offers us. Readiness on our part is a necessary process towards the acceptance of His invitation.

Marriage is, without a doubt, the most frequently and vehemently attacked institution in our day. This is a direct strategy of the enemy designed to distort or minimize the revelation of the mystery of the Bridal Covenant of which we are invited to partake. This beautiful, God-given institution represents the divine union that He has initiated with us, a truth that Paul made clear in Ephesians 5:32 when he called marriage a "profound mystery" referring to Christ and His church. All of God's people are meant to come into this mysterious union, and yet a lack of understanding can cause us to miss it entirely, even after we're born again. In Genesis 2:24, we are told that "a man shall leave his father and mother and hold fast to his wife, and they shall become one flesh."

When a husband and a wife make this commitment to one another, they are choosing to leave their former lives behind them, vowing to live as one from that day forward. While we rightly

8 Strong, J. (1890). Strong's exhaustive concordance of the Bible. Abingdon Press.

rejoice in the love that binds a couple together as one in the marriage ceremony, there is actually a death that is taking place simultaneously to the new union being formed. That death is a death to self-centered independence, and it is absolutely critical to walking in the fullness of becoming "one flesh" with another.

When I said "I do" in 1997 while standing at the altar with my bride, Heather, I was actually committing myself never to live with just my own concerns in mind, for as long as we both should live. The phase of my life known as "bachelorhood" was, as of that moment, forever gone and done away with. Of course, the realization of that commitment would play out in an ever-deepening way over the ensuing years as the Lord worked out the cross within both of us. In fact, it is still being "worked out." But without understanding this necessary death, we are likely to resist His attempts to lead us into the fullness of what it means for husbands to "love their wives as Christ loved the church," (Ephesians 5:25) and for wives to submit to their husbands as unto the Lord (Ephesians 5:22). Both require a death to our old way of living. If marriage, then, is a symbol of our relationship with the Lord, how much more so is there a need for a death of our "old self" in order to come fully into the matrimony He's invited us to partake of? Paul says precisely this earlier in the book of Ephesians: "...put off your old self, which belongs to your former manner of life and is corrupt through deceitful desires, and [be] renewed in the spirit of your minds..." (Ephesians 4:22-23). Without such cooperation with the Lord, we will never be able to enjoy the privileges that come with divine marriage to Him.

Please know this: I am not preaching perfection as we've come to understand that word. I am emphasizing, however, cooperation with Him as He makes us ready for eternal union with Him. There is a significant difference. In our struggle to achieve sinlessness through our own efforts, we attempt to measure what only God is capable of measuring, only to repeatedly fail to make any progress toward our desired end. In contrast, cooperating with the Spirit of

God requires us to yield to Him, determining not to get in His way and to trust Him to accomplish what only He can bring about. The Lord is simply looking for a heart that desires to be wed to Him in faithful intimacy and one who is willing to endure the necessary and sacrificial death to our old way of living. Said another way, He is desiring mature love. We would never expect that the Lord would take a child for His wife, and by the same token, He has no intentions of taking on a companion who clings to childish, self-centered independence. He longs to give Himself to one who is immersed in selfless devotion towards her bridegroom.

In Revelation 19, we're given a glimpse into a "fullness of time moment," when the bride of Christ is presented in full readiness, dressed in a wedding gown, coming out to celebrate her eternal marriage to the Lamb of God. As she does, a tremendous sound erupts from a great multitude crying out,

> Hallelujah! For the Lord our God the Almighty reigns. Let us rejoice and exult and give Him the glory, for the marriage of the Lamb has come, and His bride has made herself ready; it was granted her to clothe herself with fine linen, bright and pure..."
>
> Revelation 19:6-8

The language used here is significant. The bride of Christ, of her own choosing, has made herself ready. This statement alone is an irritant to those who cling to a grace message that negates the role of personal responsibility, and yet it is right there in black and white in the scripture! Incidentally, if the Bible is incompatible with our doctrines, it is not the scriptures that need to be reworded.

AN INTIMACY OF HER OWN CHOOSING

As we unpack this truth, I want to be clear from the outset that I am not, in any way, directing us backward toward a works-based relationship with God, whereby we are left to fend for ourselves to manufacture holiness. Scripture is crystal clear:

> For by grace [we] have been saved through faith. And this is not [our] own doing; it is the gift of God, not a result of works so that no one may boast.
>
> Ephesians 2:8-9

The salvation that Christ offers to us comes only through faith in Him, by the grace of God. You and I freely entered into a relationship with Jesus of our own choosing. We said "yes" to Him and when we did, His grace was enacted within us. Had we failed to assert our will in choosing Him, all of God's grace towards salvation would have been of no value to us. It would simply have remained "on the horizon." This is a spiritual truth that repeats itself throughout the Old Testament. God made many promises, but there was always a requirement for obedience on the part of the recipient. Such an "action," by the recipient doesn't equate to a works-based relationship. Quite the contrary, it is the very means by which God's grace is set in motion. This is precisely what James meant when he wrote, "...faith apart from works is dead" (James 2:26). Simply believing Him without acting on that belief in a way that produces obedience to His Word is useless. True faith always demands action on our part.

Let's once again consider the children of Israel as an example. God promised to deliver them from Egypt, and He followed through on His part. But the Israelites had to choose whether to pack up and leave or to stay put in the land of Goshen. There's no record of anyone remaining in Egypt, but a choice still had to be made, and upon choosing to leave, they became recipients of His grace, manifested in their deliverance from the bondage of Egyptian slavery. But as we all know, the story doesn't end there. The Lord also promised to give these former slaves the land of Canaan, but once again, He required an act of obedience. This time, not only did they have to choose to receive the land He had determined to give them, but they had to take up arms and fight against a powerful foe in order to activate His grace. Again, God allowed them the freedom to choose whether or not to obey. With the exception of two men, an entire generation chose to disobey, thus nullifying His grace towards them. The subsequent generation, however, received His gift of land, by obeying the command of the Lord to take up arms against the Canaanites.

Our "Egypt" is the dead spiritual condition into which each of us was born. But receiving His grace for salvation requires a choice on our part. When we choose Him, we grant Him access to wash us in His precious blood and cleanse us from our sin (1 John 1:7). He has accomplished a great spiritual work for us, but the journey is not meant to end at freedom from captivity. Like Israel, we were freed for something, and that something is an eternal relationship of abiding in Christ (John 15:1-7). Our story is not meant to end in the wilderness. Canaan, which represents the fullness of the union with the Son for which we were created, is on the horizon, and it is a good land. The scripture says it's a "land flowing with milk and honey" (Exodus 3:8), speaking of the richness of provision and blessing that comes from being joined together with Him in intimacy.

If we want to move beyond our present wilderness experience and into the "Promised Land" God offers us, then we must understand some things about the nature of the work that the Lord has accomplished for us and the need to allow Him to make it manifest. Earlier we spoke of the necessity of enduring a "death to self" in order to be wed to Him. At the cross, Christ has already put the old self to death (Romans 6:6), but that is a spiritual work He's accomplished on our behalf. He never intended for it to be a spiritual work alone. He requires it to be "worked out" (Philippians 2:12) into the arena of our souls. I'll go a bit deeper into the distinction between soul and spirit in a later chapter, but for now, please understand that the soul is comprised of our mind, our emotions, and our will. If we keep the regenerative work of the cross confined to a spiritual reality alone, it will have no impact in our thinking, our feelings, or our choices within the context of our day to day lives. It is in the wilderness of life—the time between salvation and death—where we have the opportunity of cooperating with the Holy Spirit as He seeks to make the grace of God accomplished through the cross a manifest reality within His people. Such cooperation is necessary for laying hold of the Canaan called "abiding in Christ" (John 15:4), which is a relationship, not a doctrinal position.

Bear in mind, you cannot work out your own salvation apart from the Holy Spirit. Paul tells us, "…it is God who works in you, both to will and to work for His good pleasure" (Philippians 2:13). Simply trying to make ourselves better through our own efforts is fruitless and will never result in any measure of transformation. Only the Spirit can transform us, and He will as long as we learn to cooperate with Him. He will not force us into maturity, much as He did not force the children of Israel to go into Canaan. Readiness comes as we make the choice to cooperate with Him, and we must make it daily. A refusal to do so could mean an eternal dwelling "east of the Jordan" (Joshua 22:4 AMP).

The bride revealed in Revelation 19 is all in with the Lord. She has chosen to cooperate fully with the Spirit of God in preparing her for Canaan, and she has maintained a life of submission towards Him right through to the end. While she is grateful for her salvation from sin and death, she is not satisfied with it, nor is she okay with spiritual realities not yet manifested in the natural world. Instead, she recognizes that while Egypt is a distant memory, something beautiful is on the horizon: a glorious inheritance of eternal union with Christ, her Beloved! But to be with Him as she desires, she must endure the necessary wilderness preparation. And, although she has received a measure of Christ in her spirit, she knows that this spiritual deposit is meant to spring forth like a mighty, rushing river, flooding all the realms of her spirit, soul, and body, thus transforming her from within until she manifests new creation life. She recognizes that while she is in right standing with God because of the blood of the Lamb, there is a deeper reality of expressed holiness in which she is meant to walk because Christ, the Holy One, is within her. And so, because she longs for this experiential reality she has chosen to cooperate with Him to that end.

MANIFESTED, NOT IMPUTED

Let's look back at the Revelation 19 passage, and as we do, notice that the garments that she's wearing: "...fine linen, bright and pure—for the fine linen is the righteous deeds of the saints," (Revelation 19:8). This is a very significant description and one that requires a deeper understanding of what takes place within us the moment we're born again.

In Romans 4, Paul writes about something called "imputed" or "credited" righteousness. He stresses the fact that Abraham was not justified through the things he did, but rather through his belief in God, going so far as to say that he became "fully convinced" (Romans 4:21) that the Creator would fulfill His promises to him. Thus, because Abraham had faith in God, "it was credited to him as righteousness" (Romans 4:22 NASB). Paul continues by revealing that this spiritual concept applies not just to Abraham, but to us as well. When we put our faith in Jesus Christ choosing to trust in His grace, we are credited with righteousness. In other words, through faith in Him, we become spiritually righteous. How? Because He credited our account with His righteousness. The moment we come to believe in Him who raised Jesus from the dead, we are spiritually in right-standing with the Lord (vv. 23-24). He exchanges our old, filthy, spiritual rags for a garment of purity (Isaiah 1:18).

This idea of imputed, or credited, righteousness can be illustrated this way. Imagine you are poor with not a single dime to your name. (Some of us may not have to exercise much imagination for such a scenario!) You've tried a number of things to escape poverty, yet no matter what you do, nothing seems to work. You are utterly trapped—enslaved, even—in your destitution. Then you meet a man who promises to make you so wealthy you'll never have to worry about money again if you'll simply trust Him with your finances. You agree to do so, and the moment you do, He deposits billions into a bank account in your name. At that precise moment, you came to be numbered among the wealthiest people on the planet because you were imputed a great deal of wealth. Your bank account was credited, and the money belongs to you. However, you will only realize that wealth as you learn to draw upon that bank account. A failure to do so will nullify the value of your wealth in the context of your day-to-day life.

The moment we are born again, we are in right-standing with the Lord, because He has imputed righteousness to us. Eternally speaking, we will live with Him forever, so long as our faith rests solely in what He has accomplished on our behalf. But He never intended to make a deposit into a bank account from which we don't know how to make a withdrawal. His great desire is that we not simply rest in the knowledge of our wealth of credited righteousness, but that we would learn to apply it in our day-to-day living, under the leadership of the Holy Spirit. Remember, we are not talking about a salvation issue. Egypt is behind us, and nothing short of a willful choice to turn back can enslave us to its tyranny again. We are, however, talking about the promise of an abundant life that He has created us for: bridal intimacy with Him. In order to lay hold of this, we must move off the ground of credited righteousness and onto the ground of manifested righteousness.

This is precisely what is meant in Revelation 19:8 by "the righteous deeds of the saints." The bride of Christ is not satisfied with credited righteousness. She has learned how to draw upon her spiritual bank account and now is fully clothed in a gown of outward, righteous works. The spiritual reality of right-standing with God has been worked out in her… so much so that she's now manifesting Christ in her life and walking in His nature in an externally visible way. She has submitted to the leadership of the Holy Spirit, and He has filled her full to overflowing, working out His salvation within the arena of her soul in such a way that she is now demonstrating obedience to Him in an unprecedented way. She's no longer a child, but rather a mature bride, ready for the consummation of the love relationship she has with her fiancé. She is not the same person who set out on this journey. That self-centered, self-consumed, independently minded creature has died. She now lives for her Beloved and has become His full possession!

The bride doesn't accomplish any of this by her own efforts. Only the Spirit of God can do what must be done in her. But unless she chooses Him of her own free will, she will never stand before Him as a fully mature bride. She will, instead, flounder about in the wilderness, going around and around the same old mountain, day after day, stuck in a veritable no-man's-land of being free from something but never attaining what she was freed for. She will remain in a childish, immature state. Tragically this cyclical loop is where the vast majority of the western church is today.

We love Jesus as Savior, but we've failed to come fully into the depths of what it means to be His betrothed. We celebrate the fact that the Egypt of sin and eternal judgment is behind us; however, the seemingly impossible task of fully manifesting His nature has led us to grow comfortable in the wilderness, even going so far as to develop doctrines suggesting that Canaan is both unattainable in this life and instantaneous for all believers in the eternity to come, regardless of our present choices. Because of this, we see little value in preparing to go in and possess the land and instead, have become enthralled with all that the wilderness has to offer us. And while it may not be much in light of the promise of continuously flowing milk and honey off in the distance, at least we're in control of our own destinies as we choose to sojourn in this dry and weary land. We have failed to see that this arid landscape, full of pain and sorrow and brokenness, is meant to prepare us for what lies ahead and not simply a place in which we attempt to live our best lives now.

Think back with me to the initial illustration of the heavyweight contender. Before he ever became "Buster" Douglas the heavyweight champ, he was simply James Douglas, an unknown kid from Columbus, Ohio, who possessed a raw, undeveloped capacity for boxing. He was nowhere near the man who would one day knock Mike Tyson down for the count. He had athletic ability, good size, and long, rangy arms combined with great potential for toughness and endurance. However, as a child, all this was yet undeveloped and untested. The raw ability was present, though very much unrefined and hidden. It needed to be developed... matured... made ready. Like the funds in the bank account in our earlier illustration, Douglas' capability needed to move out of the realm of potential and into the realm of realization in order for him to become the championship-caliber boxer the world would later come to see.

Douglas' athleticism and desire to win was developed over many years of playing competitive sports. In the process, he learned the value of pushing his body to its limits in order to strengthen and toughen it. When he decided to enter the boxing ring, his father taught him how to fight. Then, as he began competing, he learned not only how to be tough physically, enduring blows and knock downs from his competitors, but he also developed a mental resilience that comes from experiencing defeat. In the process, Douglas suffered, not only through the physical beatings endured by any aspiring boxer, but also through the strict training regimen that he faithfully followed. In addition, he had to overcome great personal adversity and the ensuing emotional toll after walking through a fallout and eventual split with his father and then once again when his mother died just days before his face-off with Tyson. Through it all, the tremendous personal adversity he faced only served to drive him into a realm of strength, ability, and stamina that manifested on February 11, 1990.

Sure, Douglas possessed God-given ability which was deposited into his physical, emotional, and mental "bank account" at birth. But had his potential never been developed, it would have remained just that—mere potential. Had there been no competitive sports in his life, no training regimen or strength development, no adversity to overcome, and no defeats to bounce back from, I daresay the world would have never heard of James Douglas. "Buster Douglas" the fighter would have never existed. He had to choose a readiness process in which his potential could be manifested, tested, and strengthened. This came at great personal cost to him, and he knowingly accepted it.

Imputed spiritual truths are much the same as potential. They speak of the Lord's desire to manifest something of Himself in and through us. However, if we won't cooperate with Him and yield to His process of maturity, these truths will remain unrealized potential within us. We must choose to submit to the Lord's plan, allowing Him to train us, deliver us, instruct our hearts, and discipline us, all while "[pressing] on toward the goal for the prize of the upward call of God in Christ Jesus," (Philippians 3:14). This is precisely the readiness process. It is a work of maturity that takes us from a little acorn bearing the potential for life to the mighty oak tree, expressing the life contained within in fullness and maturity. This is the very training regimen we must endure in order to go from being an unproven boxer to a tested champion who has fully overcome.

Such is the great pressing on that Paul writes of in Philippians 3:12—a leaning into the Lord so that we may "take hold of that for which [we were] even taken hold of by Christ Jesus" (NASB). This requires an intentionality on our part regarding the much needed preparation for our eventual face-to-face meeting with Jesus. Again, if salvation alone is the end goal, then we've nothing to prepare for. But scripture is brimming with the Lord's edification unto readiness, which does not come about through osmosis any more than the Israelites received their Promised Land passively. They had to go in and take the land, recognizing that it was God Himself who promised to give it to them. But a fight was involved, and the same will be true of you and me if we are to lay hold of His eternal purpose.

A MESSAGE FOR THE END TIMES

Revelation 19 specifically addresses an end-time bride, whose readiness will signal the end of the age. Her state of readiness is one and the same as the maturity of the *huios* sons of God, discussed in the previous chapter. This corporate vessel of the Lord is one, in whom, the Lord will have come to abide in fulfilling His eternal purpose, reigning with Him in the age to come. She transcends time, meaning there have been those throughout history who are part of the bridal company. Yet in the end, there will be a corporate bride who will emerge, and she will exude the life of the King in a way that is glorious in the midst of great chaos on the earth. What we see in Revelation 19 is a fullness-of-time moment, when the full measure of the bride of Christ comes into full maturity. By that, I mean that at some point, the invitation for all to say "yes" to union with the Son will either have been accepted or rejected, and the grace for choosing will no longer be available. The die will have been cast for eternity, and it will be too late to undo the choices of the past. Only the Father knows when that is, and only the Father knows the full number of those who will respond favorably to Him. Knowing ahead of time who will and who won't, He sees the exact measurement of the bridal company in a way that we're not meant to.

I've known far too many people who avoid talking about the return of the Lord like they would avoid exposure to sickness. Too often, their rationale is a belief that it's irrelevant to the way we live our lives in the here and now. I could not disagree more vehemently. How we deal with the coming of the Lord, and thus face this issue of readiness, has everything to do with the way we live our lives today. Our problem is not that we spend too much time focused on His return, but that, all too often, we live as if He's never coming back! We're going to meet the Lord face to face, whether that moment comes as a result of our death or His return. Each of us will be required to stand before Him and give an account of our life (2 Corinthians 5:10). This is more certain even than the rising and setting of the sun. And in that moment, when the righteous stand before Him, He's going to demand an accounting as to the multiplication of what He entrusted us with as in the Parable of the Talents in Matthew 25. To simply rest in imputed riches with no return in the realm of the soul will be akin to burying the eternal life of Christ within us in the ground (Matthew 25:25). But those who allow the spiritual realities accomplished at the cross to be worked out into their souls and fully manifest His life in every arena will be like those who maximized the return on the Lord's investment. Great will be their reward (Matthew 25:21)! They will experience oneness with the Son of God.

Salvation determines whether you spend eternity with Him, but as we've seen, His purpose extends far beyond having a spiritual bank account that we don't learn how to draw upon in this life. Each of us will be held accountable concerning the issue of readiness. During your time here on earth, are you learning how to submit to His hand as He seeks to mature you into a disciple? Are you moving increasingly onward from a mere salvation experience into a depth of relationship with Him that leads to an expression of His life coming forth through you? Or are you resisting His efforts to fashion you into a mature bride, choosing instead to remain in a spiritual wilderness? The answers to these questions must be proven in life and tested in the storms. And while they may not effect your salvation, they certainly have a bearing on determining your role in eternity. Only the bride will rule and reign with Christ (Revelation 2:26-27; 3:21). Whether or not you are alive on the day of the Lord's return is largely irrelevant regarding your participation in bridal preparation. The bride transcends time, as the bridegroom's invitation for marriage has eternally been God's intention. Throughout history, there always has been a remnant of those willing to go all the way into full obedience to the Lord.

We should also re-examine scripture pertaining to the timing of the Lord's return. I am convinced that most believers have a wrong understanding of that day. From the time I was a boy, I was taught that there was a particular date somewhere off in the future, which the Father had determined to be the "Day of the Lord." However, this is not consistent with scripture. In Galatians 1:4, Paul speaks of a "present evil age," and in 1 Corinthians 10:11 he explicitly tells the Corinthians that the "ends of the ages have come" in their day. In 1 John 2:18, John tells the church, "…it is the last hour," and in Revelation 3:10, he quotes the Lord referring to an "hour of testing which is about to come upon the whole world." The writer of Hebrews encourages the church not to forsake the meeting together of the saints, especially, "as you see the day drawing near" (Hebrews 10:24-25). Without question, Jesus's followers were convinced that His return would occur within their lifetime. However, the fact that He didn't does not make them wrong regarding the plan and intentions of God.

One of the most striking references to the timing of the Lord's return is found in 2 Peter 3:11-12: "…what sort of people ought you to be in lives of holiness and godliness, waiting for and hastening the coming day of God." Did you catch that? Hastening the coming day of God! Why would Peter, or for that matter, the Holy Spirit, encourage us to hasten the return of the Lord? If the timing is fixed by God the Father, how could we possibly influence or change it? Doesn't the mere fact that we're encouraged to do so mean that we can, in fact, impact its timing? And if we can hasten it, could we then not also delay it?

My friend, the Lord does not choose His words foolishly or randomly as we are so prone to doing. He means what He says, and He says what He means. With that in mind, it should be clear to us that absolutely we have the power to hasten or delay His coming. He planned it this way. It is scriptural. Christ's return is centered around the issue of readiness. If His people will come forth with bridal determination to make themselves ready for Him, He will not delay any longer. This is precisely what the Holy Spirit, through the apostle Peter, was getting at. Every generation has had the opportunity to be among those who receive Him as King on the earth, just as every generation of the children of Israel had the opportunity to choose to go up into Canaan and possess the land. Imagine what would have happened if the second generation had refused, just like the previous generation. Would God have forced the second generation in a way that He did not force the first, simply because He was tied to a specific date? Or would He have waited for the generation who would finally trust Him? There has yet to be a generation of believers who would choose to lay hold of the fullness of His promise of marital union, setting its eyes wholeheartedly on being prepared to receive Him as their beloved bridegroom, and this is why He has not yet returned. It has nothing to do with a predetermined date! Isn't it amazing how quickly we pass judgment on the Israelites, who wandered in the wilderness for 40 years because of their lack of faith, yet fail to make the connection between the bridegroom's delay and our own faithlessness? How many more generations must pass before one is willing to go in and possess the land He has offered us?

You and I could be a part of that generation! What an exciting thought—that we could see the conquering of evil once and for all on the earth, and the final and eternal putting away of the accuser of the brethren (Revelation 12:10, 20:3, 20:10)! I know this may be challenging to hear, and many may not receive it. I simply ask you to allow the Holy Spirit to teach you as He desires. I have no agenda. I'm simply trying to obey Him and rightly steward what He's given me.

A CHOSEN DESTINATION, NOT A DESTINY

Not incidentally, it is the bride who will share Christ's throne, ruling and reigning with her Beloved, and not those who simply trusted in Him for salvation alone. Revelation 3:21 promises us that.

> To the one who conquers, I will grant him to sit with me on My throne, as I also conquered and sat down with My Father on His throne.

Trusting in the salvific love of God to forgive us of sin and to create a new heart within us is not akin to conquering. However, enduring God's readiness process—and resisting all that our enemy throws at us to keep us from doing so—is precisely what makes us more than conquerors (Romans 8:37). In fact, if we want to see what true overcoming looks like, we need look no further than the Lord, Himself.

How did Jesus overcome? What did that look like? Let's look again at Philippians 2.

> "...though He was in the form of God, [He] did not count equality with God a thing to be grasped, but emptied Himself, by taking the form of a servant, being born in the likeness of men. And being found in human form, He humbled Himself by becoming obedient to the point of death, even death on a cross."
>
> Philippians 2:6-8

This is overcoming: obedient submission to God, even if it results in losing our lives for His sake. If this process was required even of the Lord Jesus, our eternal bridegroom, then most assuredly it must be endured by His bride as well. Again, it has been imputed to us to be "more than conquerors through Him who loved us," (Romans 8:37), and this spiritual reality is meant to be manifested in our daily lives. Any believer who refuses to engage in warfare against the enemy's onslaught—who wars against us unceasingly to keep us from fulfilling our eternal purpose—will not be numbered among the overcomers in the ages to come any more than Buster Douglas would have been the heavyweight champ if he had refused to go toe-to-toe with Tyson. Too many believers treat the words "more than conquerors" as a foregone conclusion rather than an edification to stand strong against the enemy, particularly as it comes to laying hold of the fullness of His purpose towards us. God hasn't randomly thrown about a title of "conqueror" any more than the various boxing associations throw out championship belts.

Conversations like this tend to provoke strong reactions, and more than once I've been accused of preaching elitism. But nothing could be further from the truth. The Lord's invitation to bridal intimacy is extended to everyone, not just a select few. However, the difficult reality is that not everyone is willing to be made willing. And if it's elitist to suggest that the bride of Christ is comprised only of those believers who have been sufficiently prepared, then it's just as elitist to suggest that salvation is only for those who believe and trust in Him to that end, which would be a ridiculous assertion, indeed! It only seems elitist, because we…

- Have strayed from the biblical mandate of making ourselves ready, opting instead for a false understanding of grace that suggests no further preparation is necessary for bridal intimacy with Jesus.
- Are unable, in our present immaturity, to discern between the voice of the Holy Spirit, who is beckoning us to buy oil for our lamps, and the bleating of counterfeit shepherds who offer false assurances that we can live as we please in this life, yet still receive God's full reward in the next.

- Are unwilling to endure the sacrifices necessary to be presented to Him as His Beloved, clothed in a selflessness that only can come through the power of the cross.
- Have succumbed to the same seductive spirit that took hold of the believers in the Corinthian church, who demonstrated a similar disregard for readiness and in so doing drew Paul's righteous indignation time and time again. Yet he remained faithful to his call, continuing to edify them in the midst of their poor choices:

> For I feel a divine jealousy for you, since I betrothed you to one husband, to present you as a pure virgin to Christ. But I am afraid that as the serpent deceived Eve by his cunning, your thoughts will be led astray from a sincere and pure devotion to Christ.
>
> 2 Corinthians 11:2

I urge you to ask yourself this question: If they were all destined to be wed to the Lord in the very ceremony that we just read about in Revelation 19, why was Paul so riled up? If it was inevitable that they would one day stand before Jesus as His bride regardless of their daily choices, why the indignation in Paul's voice?

Think with me just for a moment about the weddings you've attended. Is it not true that, for the most part, a young lady will put more planning into her wedding day than for any other day of her life? From the wedding gown to the bridesmaid dresses, from the reception menu to the music that will be played as her daddy walks her down the aisle, no detail is left to chance! All of the daydreaming when she was a little girl... the endless hours perusing bridal magazines... the planning with her mother and friends... all of it culminates in that one memorable, once-in-a-lifetime occasion. She will endure the discomforts of dieting, the despair of ever finding the right dress, the burns of lying in the sun too long, and countless hours spent putting on makeup, painting her nails, and fixing her hair. Why? Because this is the one day she has looked forward to for the better part of her life, and she will make every effort to ensure that she looks her best for her groom.

And if this is true in the natural realm, should it not also be true in a spiritual sense?

Would the Father sanction a marriage between His Son—who paid the highest price for His Beloved—and a bride who resisted the Holy Spirit's attempts to present her in holiness? We've not thought this through! Salvation is the reward for those who trust in Jesus Christ, but marriage is the reward for those who overcome through His life. There are foolish virgins and wise virgins, and the foolish ones will be shut out of the marriage feast (Matthew 25:10). And while they do not lose their "virginity"—meaning they won't lose their salvation—they will not be permitted to participate in the beautiful union of Christ and His bride, nor will they sit with Him on His throne.

I'm asking the Lord to awaken us to the reality of the invitation He has put before us and the necessary readying that must take place within us. I'm praying that He will shake the spiritual slumber off of us, which has led so many in the body of Christ to become enthralled with false teaching, prisoners to passivity, and intoxicated by the delights of this world. **NOW** is the time for us to "trim our lamps" and be filled with the oil of the Holy Spirit, who will prepare us for the return of the King. **NOW** is the time for His bride to be made ready. There is a wedding for which we must prepare! And the wedding dress He would clothe us in is the very life of the Son, outwardly visible to the world around us. And that dress is a beautiful one, in deed!

CHAPTER 3

SOULISH CHRISTIANITY, CROSS-COUNTRY, AND FINISHING WELL

> But understand this, that in the last days dangerous times [of great stress and trouble] will come [difficult days that will be hard to bear]. For people will be lovers of self [narcissistic, self-focused]... holding to a form of [outward] godliness (religion), although they have denied its power [for their conduct nullifies their claim of faith]. Avoid such people and keep far away from them.
>
> 2 Timothy 3:1-2, 5 AMP

> "There is a difference between knowing the path and walking the path."
>
> – Morpheus, "The Matrix"

We have a pastor friend from India whom we've grown to love very much over the past several years. He comes to America often and has had the opportunity to share the Lord in a number of churches, including the small fellowship I pastored in Georgia. We've often joked about one of the responses he frequently hears after speaking: "Oh, pastor! Thank you for your message. I enjoyed it very much!" While we both understand the heart of what's being communicated, we also agree that if a message is enjoyed, there's a high probability that the Word of the Lord was either lost in translation or not shared at all. While God is certainly an encourager, He often confronts things that are out of alignment to His will, and He always demands a response. He's not looking for a passive mental assent to a message, rather, He desires the sacrifice of obedience (1 Samuel 15:22). And if the Lord is being proclaimed through this book, then know that He is demanding action on our part.

Remember, the fully mature bride of Revelation 19 is clothed in righteous deeds. This is vitally important. She isn't clothed with good intentions or sound doctrines or great sermons. She doesn't view truth as a set of principles that she claims to believe while bearing no fruit of true faithfulness. Instead, she desires to be fully married to the Truth, who is a person, persistently walking in submissive obedience to all He asks of her. By every estimation, she has chosen a life fully laid down to the One her heart most desires. She isn't passively daydreaming of her wedding day or studying books on marriage. She is actively cooperating with the Holy Spirit, allowing Him to do a deep, transformational work within her, understanding her responsibility in the process.

An honest assessment of the western church will reveal that we have exalted information to a place of prominence it was never meant to occupy. A Greek mindset that craves knowledge and makes the pursuit of data a primary focus has heavily influenced the church, leaving many to think that the path to becoming a "better Christian" lies in the next conference or another sermon or a good Christian book. Please know that I'm not against any of these. But to be clear, the Lord is not in the business of peddling information. Instead, He invites us into revelation. To the natural mind, there is little difference between these two, but to God, they are profoundly dissimilar. In order to bring clarity, we should start by examining the distinctions between soul and spirit.

THREE-PART BEINGS

God created man in His image (Genesis 1:27). This statement is rich in meaning well beyond the scope of this book, but one of the truths contained in this verse is that our Creator, who is a three-part Being, created us to be three-part beings as well. In other words, God, who exists in three distinct persons—Father, Son, and

Holy Spirit—created man with three distinct parts: body, soul and spirit (1 Thessalonians 5:23). Just as each member of the Godhead carries out a unique and separate function, so too does each of our "parts."

The body is a physical shell that houses both the soul and the spirit. It is, perhaps, the easiest part of us to understand because it can be observed with our physical senses. Through our bodies, we are conscious of and interact with the physical world. With my hands, I can manipulate physical objects. I can move them around, combine them in such a way as to make something new, or even to destroy. With my eyes and ears, I can observe God's creation, taking in a sunset while listening to the chirping of birds and feeling the soft breeze from the wind in the trees. I also can observe something unpleasant, such as the barking of my dog Ginger, who presently is chasing my daughter around the house while I sit directly below them in my basement, wishing I had a quieter place in which to write. The same is true with the rest of our senses. Our bodies are necessary for life in the physical dimension, and without them, we wouldn't be able to interact with the natural world. My body is not my life in its entirety, but rather a necessary component of life here on earth.

The soul, as Watchman Nee describes it, is the "organ of personality"[9] and is comprised of the mind, the will, and the emotion. It is the part of us that makes us conscious of ourselves—both in an individual context and in a corporate one as well. With our soul, we interact with our own self in the form of thoughts, feelings, and choices, and it is also through the soul that we primarily interact with others in the same manner. According to Nee, the mind is the "organ of thinking and intellect,"[10] the will is the "organ of deliberation, with which we make judgements and choices regard-

---

9 Nee, Watchman. (1977) The Spiritual Man (New York Christian Fellowship Publishers)

10 Nee, Watchman. (1977) The Spiritual Man (New York Christian Fellowship Publishers)

ing what we want, what we think, and how we choose to act."[11] Likewise, our emotions are responsible for our feelings. Through them, we experience sentiments such as peace or anger, love or hatred, happiness or sorrow. The soul was first birthed when God breathed His breath into Adam's body. Scripture tells us that when that took place, "man became a living soul," (Genesis 2:7 KJV). God's breath is not soul; it is Spirit. The Hebrew word *ruach*, which is often translated as the "Spirit of God," literally means "breath" or "wind."[12] When the Spirit of God came into the body of man, the soul was created, and Adam became a living being. Without a soul, I have no capacity to think or feel, thus I cannot interact with others or be aware of myself. My soul is not the full extent of who I am, but it's a vital component of the three-part being God has created me to be.

The spirit is the part of us that is God-conscious. With it, we are aware of and able to interact with Him. God is Spirit (John 4:24), and without a living spirit, we cannot know Him or have a relationship with Him. It was the spirit of man that experienced immediate death resulting from the fall. God forewarned Adam not to eat from the tree of the knowledge of good and evil, telling him, "...in the day that you eat of it, you shall surely die," (Genesis 2:17). Though the process of physical death began the moment Adam disobeyed, his body did not perish on that day, nor did his soul. He still was able to think and feel and choose, as evidenced by the fact that Adam reasoned he was naked, felt shame in his emotions, and chose to hide from the Lord. His body and soul were still fully functional; however, his spirit immediately became disconnected from the source of all life—God. Thus, death set in immediately. That isn't to say that the spirit ceased to exist. It simply lost its awareness of, and connection to, God. And since our spirits were given to us so that we might interact with Him, they

---

11 Nee, Watchman. (1977) The Spiritual Man (New York Christian Fellowship Publishers)

12 Strong, J. (1890). Strong's exhaustive concordance of the Bible. Abingdon Press.

were no longer capable of functioning as God intended. Therefore, they died. In that same way, both the body and soul—which were still very much alive—came under the influence of death.

This spiritual death so impacted humanity that a few thousand years later, Paul tells us that because of Adam's sin, death entered the world and spread to all men (Romans 5:12). The result is that no one has the capacity to be conscious of or interact with God apart from Him breaking into the darkness of humanity and revealing Himself to us. We are cut off from fellowship with Him, hence the need for a Savior. And one of the many beautiful blessings that comes to us through the death and resurrection of our Savior is that He gives us a new and living spirit (Ezekiel 36:26), with which we can now interact with the Spirit of the Living God!

There is a great deal more we could explore about these three parts of humanity, but that's not the point here. I'm simply trying to convey that there is a profound difference between the functions of the soul and the spirit of man. The soul is not the primary organ of interaction with the Lord. We must understand this. As the soul is renewed (Romans 12:2), it can certainly become engaged in our relationship with Him, but the spirit is the specific part of us that God created to interact with Him. Bear in mind, God is not limited to the spiritual realm. He is powerful enough to cross over into the soul and speak directly to our minds and touch our emotions, and He does so as He deems necessary. Each of us has experienced this if we've accepted Him as Savior. When we were still without a living spirit and incapable of interacting with Him, He called to us in our souls and gave us enough understanding to see Jesus as the only Savior who can be trusted. Thank God for His mercy and grace, poured out in such a loving and powerful way!

God also is just as capable of breaking into the physical arena. I know a man who was raised as a Muslim and had never heard the good news of Jesus Christ who met Him face to face one day on the freeway in Los Angeles. While stuck in traffic, my friend turned towards the passenger seat just in time to witness the Lord descend into his car, feet first, through the roof and into the seat next to him! He then proceeded to reveal Himself as the King of kings to my friend. Can you imagine? Of course, having seen the Lord with his physical eyes and heard His testimony with his physical ears, he immediately gave his life to Jesus, and he's never been the same since! Thank God that He is neither limited nor constrained by the natural world which He created and is fully able to break through into the physical realm whenever and however He chooses.

After we're saved, the Lord can still communicate directly with our souls, and He's likewise just as capable of breaking into the physical realm. Obviously so. He is God, and He can do whatever He chooses, whenever He wants, and however He desires. At times, He may well manifest Himself in those realms, but His primary desire is to speak to us Spirit to spirit. Your spirit was designed for this function. The Bible tells us that God is Spirit (John 4:24), and He is the source of all life (1 John 5:12). True life doesn't come through oxygen or water or physical food, but "by every word that comes from the mouth of God," (Matthew 4:4). Jesus affirmed this in John 6:63 by saying to His disciples, "It is the Spirit who gives life; the flesh is no help at all. The words that I have spoken to you are spirit and life." Life comes from God, who is Spirit, and when He speaks, He addresses our spirit.

The spirit can hear and receive the Lord without input from the soul, and it's meant to do so. When He speaks, He is not appealing to our sense of logic or our emotions. This doesn't mean we can't have a level of understanding in our minds or be touched in our emotions as we hear Him in our spirit. It simply means He is not primarily interested in addressing our soul. That is the spirit's function. In 1 Corinthians 2:14, Paul warns us,

> The natural person does not accept the things of the Spirit of God, for they are folly to him, and he is not able to understand them because they are spiritually discerned.

In other words, the mind of man cannot ascertain the things of God unless that man has first received spiritual discernment as to what the Lord is saying. If we simply listen through the intellect, we cannot comprehend Him fully and will fail to come into full obedience to the directives of the Lord. But once the Holy Spirit gives us spiritual ears to hear, understanding can and will be imparted to our souls as an outflow of spiritual revelation. We then can choose to obey Him as He requires, acting upon His revealed word. As we do, our actions testify of His life within, giving creation around us an opportunity to witness the Lord through us.

This beautiful flow—from God, by the Spirit, to our spirit, through the soul, and into the physical realm—puts humanity in the rather unique position of being the only one of God's creatures that can act as a gateway between the spirit and physical dimensions. There is a prophetic picture for us in these words from Psalm 24:7 "Lift up your heads, O gates! And be lifted up, O ancient doors, that the King of glory may come in." Too many have associated this as being about physical gates and doors, but these words were written to beings not to inanimate objects. Mankind is God's gateway, and Jesus, being the firstborn among many brothers (Romans 8:29), is the "door of the sheep," (John 10:7). As we abide in Him, we too become a doorway through which God can reveal Himself in the natural world. If we're not abiding in Him, we become an open door to the enemy of our souls and a way for the kingdom of darkness to manifest all manner of evil. Why do you think Satan has such an interest in gaining a foothold in man? Man is a gateway for the spiritual realm to gain access to the physical world.

God's brilliant wisdom is demonstrated in His design for humanity. As we come to recognize that He alone is the source of life, we cultivate an ever-deepening dependence upon Him. This is precisely what He desires. We were created with an inherent need for Him. Maturity, then, is the pathway to greater and greater reliance upon the Lord in all things, and since our relationship with Him is spiritual in nature, it demands that we become more engaged in our spirit as we journey on with the Lord. As we become more spiritually engaged with Him, we discover that the Holy Spirit's primary language is not information. **It is revelation.**

INFORMATION VS. REVELATION

Information has to do with the mind, which is part of the soul. The work that God did in us at salvation was a spiritual work. And now it is the soul that must be conquered. One of the greatest battles in our walk with Jesus is learning to live by the Spirit rather than depending on our own thoughts, feelings, or judgments. The mind craves knowledge in the form of information. The world promotes and encourages this pursuit, viewing it as a source of personal empowerment. Think of the adage, "knowledge is power." However, Paul warns us that head knowledge "puffs up," (1 Corinthians 8:1) like leaven in a lump of dough. That is clear to us when considering the lost who have no connection with God, but Paul isn't writing to the world. He's speaking to the church. His warning is addressing our soulish tendency to relate to God as a function of our minds. But if we truly want to know Him, then we must know Him by the Spirit. In all things, He is relational, and He desires to share Himself with us, inviting us into a direct experience of Him. He has no desire whatsoever for us to merely accumulate information about Him. That is a cheap substitute for knowing Him first hand.

Let's pause here for a minute to illustrate the point. When I was a kid, I was a baseball enthusiast. I loved to play ball, watch major league games on TV and daydream of one day becoming a professional myself. I loved the game so much that when I didn't have friends around to toss the ball, I would spend hours bouncing a baseball off the wall of our house and into my glove, pretending I was fielding grounders. So it's no surprise that I picked a famous baseball player from the past as the subject of a middle school research paper on "significant historical figures." I read everything

I could find on Lou Gehrig, and in the process, I accumulated a great deal of knowledge about him. I learned that his real name was Heinrich Ludwig Gehrig—the impoverished son of German immigrants. I could tell you about his first baseball glove—a right-handed catcher's mitt given to him by a father who didn't know the first thing about baseball—forcing Lou, a lefty, to play first base with the wrong glove on the wrong hand. I could mention his unusual size and God-given athleticism and how that translated into a football scholarship at Columbia University. I could tell you that his first homerun at Wrigley Field in Chicago was a grand slam in the ninth inning of a high school all-star game. I could go on to spout off statistics from his baseball career, including his amazing streak of 2,130 consecutive games, his 493 career homeruns or his six world championships with the New York Yankees. I could also tell you about the quiet, gentle man who, at the tender age of 37, contracted a strange and relatively new illness that would come to bear his name in the years that would follow. I amassed a ton of information about a man, but none of it could ever translate into a relationship with him.

This concept is true of most anyone. It is impossible to build a relationship by collecting information about someone. Imagine a romantic relationship based on that approach. How far do you think you'd get if you attempted to collect second and third hand information about someone you were attracted to? We generally call such people "stalkers." The Lord doesn't want you stalking Him. He wants to give Himself to you and grant you the joy of fully giving yourself to the experience of Him.

When the basis of our relationship with God is head knowledge—doctrines, theologies, regurgitations of other people's teachings or writings—we are on dangerous ground. Like leaven in a lump of dough (1 Corinthians 5:6), we all too easily can become puffed up by our ability to throw out information about the Lord, yet with little structural substance supporting that knowledge. If you've ever baked homemade bread, then you are well aware that leavened dough, if left alone, will continue to rise until it eventually collapses under the weight of the excess gas it produces. In the same way, it is inevitable that our own religious hot air will eventually be exposed. The Lord will make sure of it! Rather than doing this to shame us or put us in our place, He mercifully and kindly exposes our lack so that we have an opportunity to repent of our soulishness and come onto the eternal ground of true and lasting intimacy with Him.

Revelation is vastly different from information and is translated from the Greek word *apokalypsis*, which means to "uncover or expose" (literally to make naked).[13] Paul's use of it in Galatians 1 is a clear depiction of what God desires with His children: "For I did not receive [the gospel] from any man, nor was I taught it, but I received it through a revelation of Jesus Christ," (Galatians 1:12). As a former Pharisee, Paul knew a thing or two about academic learning and the religious pursuit of head knowledge about God. Yet on the heels of his Damascus Road encounter with the risen Christ, his knowledge came from a different source: the spiritual unveiling of the person of the Son of God. Revelation is how God communicates to us, and it is a direct uncovering of Himself. It has nothing to do with the soul. Sure, Paul saw something with his natural eyes, but it was his spirit that had a direct encounter with Jesus as He revealed Himself to Paul in a spiritual way. This revelation eventually resulted in the impartation of understanding to Paul's mind, but it did not come through the pursuit of head knowledge. Do you see here the flow that we spoke of earlier? This created design was not meant exclusively for the apostles but is one that you and I are invited to partake of as well.

This doesn't mean that the Lord can't or won't use information at all. He can, and He does. But our ultimate goal must always be to know the person of Jesus Christ and not simply accumulate knowledge about Him. When the Holy Spirit is highlighting

---

13 Strong, J. (1890). Strong's exhaustive concordance of the Bible. Abingdon Press.

information to me, I often find that He's encouraging me to experience Jesus in a specific way that the information is speaking of. For instance, lately the word "joy" has been a recurring theme in my life. At "random" times and through "random" people, I'll hear it tossed about. And while I might otherwise miss half of what that person is saying to me, when they speak of joy, it's as though I'm hit with an electrical current, and I'm immediately and fully engaged. The same has been true of my time spent in the Word. When I come across the word "joy," it's as though the word leaps off the page at me. In addition, within a very short period of time, two close friends encouraged me to seek the joy of the Lord. On top of it all, I'm writing this chapter in the midst of allergy season and have been experiencing waves of exhaustion as my body reacts to the pollen. Yet every time this has happened in the past week or so, the line from the old praise chorus, "The joy of the Lo-oh-oh-ord is my strength!" pops into my head. These are all data points—mere observations processed in my mind as information. I could stop at a place of assimilating that data into the belief that says, "Joy is important, and the Lord gives us joy!" But if I do, it merely will become doctrine to me. On the other hand, if I recognize that the Holy Spirit is using that information to invite me into a deeper revelation of joy, then I can rightly pursue Him as my joy within the context of my prayer and fellowship with Him.

SOULISH CHRISTIANITY

We must understand that our souls—in their unregenerate, unrenewed state—are largely under the influence of the flesh. The flesh is the self-seeking, self-empowering, self-life that usurped God's government within us at the fall. In the partaking of the forbidden fruit, Adam chose what he coveted rather than obeying God. This tendency towards doing what seems right in our own eyes (Proverbs 21:2) did not go away at salvation. This is what Paul was referring to when he said, "nothing good dwells within me, that is, in my flesh. For I have the desire to do what is right, but not the ability to carry it out," (Romans 7:18). The flesh is in rebellion against the will of God, and we must not take it lightly. Its seat of power is the soul, and our unrenewed soul is governed by fallenness. The Lord's intention is to move us away from this seditious government and firmly establish the government of His Spirit within us. When we rely on our soul instead of seeking Him in the spirit, we are rebelling against His government. This may seem harsh, but it is precisely what is taking place within us. The soul, under the government of the flesh, is hostile towards God. It will not and cannot submit to His command (Romans 8:7). The flesh's thirst for power is unquenchable and its hunger for doing what it wants is insatiable. It is incapable of bowing to another, even the King of kings. As such, the flesh, or self-life, is quite irredeemable. The only remedy for it is death, which is precisely why Jesus tells us that if we want to be his disciples, we will have a cross to bear (Luke 14:27). This doesn't mean that our souls are meant to be crucified, but rather the self-seeking government of our flesh, which still is very much in control of our souls.

But the good news is that as we welcome the Lord to deal with our flesh, our soul is set free from the dominion of self and comes more fully under the governance of the Lord. In this way, we are becoming the people He intends for us to be. This is an ongoing process of death to the self-life and the increase of Christ's life within us. **This is the process of readiness.**

We must decide whose side we are going to take in this ongoing battle regarding readiness: the Lord's will or our own self-centered desires. As long as we are heeding the voice of our unregenerate soul, thoughts, emotions, and judgments according to the flesh, then we are actively resisting God's will in the crucifying of our flesh. The better way in this journey is to learn how to walk—or live—according to the Spirit (Romans 8:12-13). Sadly, my experience in the church is that we frequently place much too high of a value on what appeals to our soul, such as the dispensing of information and emotional experiences. In the process, we've often forsaken the absolute necessity of learning and then teaching others how to live by the Holy Spirit. The end result is a soulish form of Christianity that looks little to nothing like His bride as He intended. We have a "form of godliness," but we deny the very power of the Spirit to transform us (2 Timothy 3:5 NKJV).

As we continue to grasp for what our soul craves—information and tickled emotions—we cannot be truly set free. Instead, we simply feed the beast known as our flesh, which is now trying to emulate—or imitate—a Spirit-filled life. Our soul only receives true freedom as we encounter the Lord intimately in the Spirit. Then, as we increasingly enjoy fellowship with Him, we willingly and gladly grant Him the access He requires to arise within us as the Deliverer to destroy our self-life. This journey of preparation requires the gradual breaking of our dependence on soulish tendencies and desires. Until the soul has been sufficiently broken and humbled, it is incapable of being set free of self-government. When we approach God through our mind and emotions, not only does this do us no good, but it also potentially devastates His maturation process within us.

Paul speaks of transformation this way: "And we all, with unveiled face, beholding the glory of the Lord, are being transformed into the same image from one degree of glory to another. For this comes from the Lord who is the Spirit," (2 Corinthians 3:18). As we witness His transformation in our lives, we can be assured that this directly corresponds to the inward revelation of Christ in our inner man. However, if we aren't consistently experiencing personal transformation within us, there is a high likelihood we are stuck in the realm of our soul. Yet as we faithfully pursue Christ, our Living Word, and our true spiritual food (John 6:51), over time, we will witness the Lord getting ahold of us in such a way that He faithfully and consistently brings about a greater degree of inward readiness. Is this a foreign concept to you? If so, that's OK. Simply ask Him to lead you in faithfully walking out this journey, according to His Spirit. He is eager to give us revelation and trustworthy to fulfill His promises in all that He desires for you!

We also must recognize our own soulish tendency to become increasingly content with keeping our relationship with the Lord on an informational level. Doing so can result in an appearance of godliness with no power to transform us. Only revelation can transform, and it will do just that. Simply reading a book or listening to a teaching on readiness can easily become a religious exercise that allows us to feel as if we've truly invested in our relationship with the Lord, but without the hassle of having to yield our will to His. Again, I'm not against teachings, and clearly, I'm not against books. However, these tools are only valuable if they lead us into a deeper, inward knowledge of the person of Jesus Christ, thus bringing about the subjugation of our souls to His will. Said another way, the true measure of our intimacy with Him is the measure of His life that flows forth from within us.

Please understand that I'm not just talking about when we're at church and putting on our "Jesus face," nor do I mean when everything is going well and it's easy to be kind or joyful or loving to others. No! Instead, I'm referring to what comes out of us when the wheels come off the bus and nothing seems to be going our way. This is the most accurate picture of who's living in us. If what comes out of us is nasty, ornery, fearful, sorrowful, unbelieving, hopeless, critical gunk, then we are still very much in need of transformation. As the body of Christ, each of us must position ourselves before Him in the Spirit, setting aside our soulish tendencies so that we might know "the love of Christ that surpasses knowledge that you may be filled with all the fullness of God," (Ephesians 3:19).

God desires humility, not a religious knowledge that inflates our ego. He is attracted to true brokenness, not self-sufficiency. He resists the proud but responds favorably to those who are teachable in spirit. He cannot use those who satisfy their bellies on the pleasures, ways, and wisdom of this world, but will absolutely fill those who truly hunger and thirst for Him. It is not strength that He's looking for in us; it is weakness, which becomes the open door to His grace:

> My grace is sufficient for you, for my power is made perfect in weaknesses. Therefore, I will boast all the more gladly of my weaknesses, so that the power of Christ may rest upon me. For the sake of Christ then, I am content with weaknesses, insults, hardship, persecutions, and calamities. For when I am weak, then I am strong,
>
> 2 Corinthians 12:9-10

If our hearts are hungry and we are willing, the Lord will move us far beyond information and onto His ground of total heart transformation.

FINISHING WELL

Please don't let this be just another teaching that gets filed away in your doctrinal repertoire. Instead, test the scriptural soundness of what is being proclaimed, even while recognizing the urgency of the hour! The one limited resource we have—which God absolutely will not replenish—is time. None of us is guaranteed tomorrow.

While pastoring a church for eight years in South Georgia, I pressed our little congregation to go after the Lord wholeheartedly and learn to partake of Him as our life (John 6:53-54). As any good shepherd would, I eagerly desired for our entire fellowship to heed the call and pursue the Lord with faithful persistence. However, there was one person the Holy Spirit seemed to highlight week after week more than anyone else: my brother-in-law, Rob.

I'm quite sure that I interceded for Rob more than I did for anyone else in our church, often meeting with him one-on-one, praying with him, encouraging him, counseling him, and, at times, even confronting him as the Lord would lead. I had known and loved him for most of my life, as he married my sister and came into our family when I was 15. Rob loved the Lord dearly but, like most of us, he struggled with letting go of the world and faithfully keeping to the path of discipleship. In the final year of my pastorate, the Lord led Rob through a season of tremendous difficulty and personal hardship. In the midst of it all, he chose to surrender to the Lord in a way I had not seen before. As a result, I watched him pursue the Lord with his whole being. I ached for him as I watched him endure some incredibly painful trials. Yet at the same time, I rejoiced to see his humble submission towards His Creator in such a measure that I've rarely seen in others. Then on Thanksgiving Day in 2020 in front of the whole family, Rob openly thanked the Lord for the crushing and the stripping that had taken place in his life, even going so far as asking that it never come to an end. What a remarkable prayer, especially given the measure of the cross I watched him bear! But in that painful and broken place, Rob had become one with Jesus, and it was beautiful to witness.

I assumed that Rob and I would continue to have a long-lasting friendship and that I would be part of his journey into deeper readiness for many years to come, even if it were from afar. But the day after Thanksgiving—not even a full week since I had preached my final sermon in that little fellowship—the Lord unexpectedly took Rob home. In His great wisdom, He had determined that Rob's journey had come to an end. His race was over, and he is now home with the One he most loves. Interestingly enough, Rob was a cross-country coach to many kids, including my own. He was known for telling his runners, "It doesn't matter how you start, it's how you finish." At the end of his life's journey, Rob was all in for the Lord—totally surrendered. He finished well!

My friend, we're not guaranteed tomorrow. If you want to be prepared to meet the Lord face to face, you must go beyond mental assent. Simply giving an intellectual nod to the idea of being made ready will never yield the results that God is after. You must go spirit to Spirit with Him, seeking Him above all else. Your past is irrelevant. It simply has brought you to this point. It's how you finish that is of greatest importance. You are now being presented with an opportunity. You can allow the Lord to awaken His call to readiness within you, knowing that it will require you to learn how to speak the language of the Spirit of God, or you can simply maintain the status quo and continue to feed the beast known as your unregenerate soul. Only one of these will elicit, "Well done," from the Master.

How about you? Will you finish well?

CHAPTER 4

THE FRUIT THAT HE DESIRES

> Hear another parable. There was a master of a house who planted a vineyard and put a fence around it and dug a winepress in it and built a tower and leased it to tenants and went into another country.
>
> Matthew 21:33

In Matthew 21:33-46, Jesus tells us a parable about a vineyard planted by a wealthy landowner who leased his property to tenant farmers. These tenants were tasked with the responsibility of faithfully stewarding his land and bringing forth a great harvest. But somewhere along the line, the hired hands became consumed with themselves and chose to put their own interests above those of the true owner. When sufficient time had passed, the owner sent servants to collect the harvest he expected of them. But the hired hands beat some of the servants and killed others in a desperate attempt to protect their own agenda. So, the owner sent more servants, who were treated in the same way. Finally, he sent his own son to confront the rebellious tenants. However, this time, they plotted to kill the son—the rightful heir to the vineyard—so that their plot to overthrow the master could be realized in full, and they could appropriate his land as their own. And they did exactly that.

In this scripture's historical context, Jesus is addressing the nation of Israel in an effort to expose how the very religious system they had built was directly opposed to the Father's purpose. His rebuke was a forewarning of Israel's imminent judgment and was not the first time God had used this type of imagery concerning

His chosen people. Hundreds of years earlier, Isaiah had received a similar word from the Lord. In Isaiah 5:1-7, the prophet likens both Israel and Judah to a wild vine that yields only sour grapes rather than a cultivated vine yielding desirable fruit. This parable is a commentary concerning their hard-heartedness toward the Lord and their disregard for His desire to produce a harvest. The remainder of Isaiah 5 details their pending judgment, which would be fulfilled in the years that followed. And just as it had been in Isaiah's time, the nation of Israel once again was being held accountable for failing to produce the harvest that pleases Him. In a stunning statement, Jesus delivered earth-shattering news to the religious leaders. Although His words were likely not received in any measure by His hard-hearted hearers, He declared to God's chosen people,

> Therefore I tell you, the kingdom of God will be taken away from you and given to a people producing its fruits,
>
> Matthew 21:43

We could conclude our examination of this passage here and feel a sense of relief that such a heavy word isn't directed at us. We might even rejoice in the fact that as modern-day followers of Jesus Christ, we are the very ones to whom He has offered the Kingdom. But if we interpret these verses through this grid alone, not only would this be an incredibly short and irrelevant chapter in a book on readiness, but we would be guilty of simply harvesting information in our souls without heeding what the Spirit is saying to us. And the Lord is practically shouting for us to take notice of a principle in this parable!

The Father desires fruit, and the fruit He is after isn't grown on trees, vines, or bushes. It is spiritual in nature and only grows in His uniquely created vessels designed exclusively for the production of this unique fruit. And unlike most pots we're familiar with, these vessels have a say in the matter. They can choose to cooperate with God in yielding His fruit, or they can refuse and offer Him nothing in return. You and I are His vessels, and we will one day stand before Him and give an account as to whether we yielded the fruit He desires. This was true of Israel as a corporate vessel, and this parable is a testament to the fact that God is quite serious about His harvest. The corporate vessel is comprised of individuals who, in cooperation with the Spirit of God, must be intentional in the process of fruit development. We should be able to see this when looking at Israel. Fruitfulness is not a forgone conclusion.

Most of us don't think in terms of what God gets out of our relationship with Him. We've been taught that His grace gives without asking anything in return, but such relationships—whether in the natural or the spirit—are one-sided, unstable, and unsustainable. The scriptural truth is that God is looking for a return on His investment in us (Matthew 25:14-30).

He wants fruit. And He is expecting it.

The Bible is pregnant with exhortations to cooperate with Him to that end, and we will examine some specific examples. Yet, because we are self-centered creatures by virtue of the fall, it's far too easy for us to become preoccupied with the issue of what we get out of this relationship. Forgiveness, eternal life, blessings, healings, gifts, and more, are all expressions of God's love toward us; however, He never intended for this to be a one-way street. In a mature love relationship, both sides give just as gladly and wholeheartedly as each one receives. In the same way that a farmer looks for fruit from the ground he works, so is the Lord looking for and anticipating a fruitful harvest from us.

Fruitfulness, then, is another way of communicating God's eternal purpose for humanity. We were created to be a vineyard carrying the specific purpose of providing Him with the fruit He longs for. And He will lavish His grace and His goodness upon us whether or not we successfully produce that fruit because it's His nature to do so. Yet there will come a time where He will demand an accounting. We mustn't live under the delusion that all He cares about is our happiness and well-being. There is more to the story, and it is imperative that we gain an understanding regarding the following key questions:

1. What, specifically, is the fruit that the Lord wants to produce in me?
2. What is my responsibility in this process?
3. How is that fruit produced in me?

In addressing these questions, there are some fundamental principles of sowing and reaping to consider. My father is a farmer, and my mother is an avid gardener. In watching them both over the years, I have gleaned some practical wisdom when it comes to working the ground. As I highlight these five principles of sowing and reaping, please keep in mind that these are earthly types and shadows of spiritual truths. Hopefully, they will help us to recognize the fruit that the Lord longs to produce in us, as well as the necessary process for its successful cultivation.

PRINCIPLE #1: THE HARVEST ALWAYS BEGINS AS A SEED

Regardless of what you're growing, how it's grown, or the size of the yield you're anticipating, all plants—and therefore all fruit—begin as a seed. Seeds are not the final product; they merely contain the potential for the final product. (There's that word "potential" again!) But a great deal must happen so that the life within the seed can move from the realm of possibility into full manifestation. When you and I received the finished work of salvation and committed our lives to Jesus, something very real took place within us. In this divine transaction, the Holy Spirit moved into our spirit, and He came to stay, leaving us forever altered. However, when He came in, He came in seed form, or spiritual potential, rather than in full manifested maturity.

Salvation was not the end of His work in us, it was merely the beginning.

I know I'm being repetitive, but I cannot stress this enough. There is no telling how many people have passed through the veil separating this temporal life from the next one wrongly believing that simply praying a prayer of salvation is all that the Lord required of them. God help us in our blindness! The Lord wants fruit, not just a plot of ground with ungerminated seeds in it! Yet much of the body of Christ is actively peddling a message claiming that the great harvest coming at the end of the age (Matthew 13:39) is a massive throng of people entering into a salvation experience with Jesus. I sincerely hope for revival in my lifetime leading many to find Jesus. Far too many have died and gone to hell over the millennia, and the Father's heart aches over each lost soul. Yet whether or not we see that come to pass is a separate issue from the promised end-time harvest.

Salvation is the sowing of the seed. Harvest is the maturity of the life within us.

A day is surely coming when, "the plowman shall overtake the reaper and the treader of grapes him who sows the seed (Amos 9:13)," meaning that the Lord will do a quick work of transformation in those who allow it by cooperating with Him in the process of maturity. But God has never been satisfied with a mere "salvation experience" alone. I know that phrasing it that way is potentially offensive to some. I don't mean to downplay the magnitude of salvation in any way—it is quite the remarkable gift! But in comparison to what He's offered us, simply knowing Christ as Savior is a small thing indeed! The great push in the New Testament is towards discipleship, not salvation.

In Matthew 13:1-9, Jesus shares the parable of a farmer who sowed good seed pretty much anywhere and everywhere. Some fell along beaten down pathways and were quickly devoured by the birds. Other seed fell among rocky soil and produced plants with shallow roots that eventually withered under the heat of the sun.

Still other seed fell among the weeds which eventually choked the life out of the seedlings that sprang up from the ground. But some of the seed fell on good soil and produced a harvest.

While we know this parable has to do with our receiving the Word at salvation, nowhere does Jesus teach that what was sown into our hearts in that moment of salvation is the end product that He desires. God doesn't go about sowing bunches of fully ripened grapes into us any more than a farmer plants whole ears of corn. No! He sows potential in the form of seed. And the seed He uses must endure a readiness or maturation process just as a kernel of wheat must fall to the ground and die in order to bring forth the desired fruit (John 12:24).

I am deeply concerned that, as the body of Christ, we seem to put far more attention on sowing seed and comparatively little emphasis on being made ready. It's equally disturbing that, through a false understanding of grace, many of us have wrongly concluded that the harvest comes instantaneously at the moment of salvation. In doing so, we empower immature converts to wrongly believe that what they have experienced in the Lord—His seed being planted within them—is all that God desires and all that He requires. Such thinking can cause us to lower our expectations concerning what it means to have the new life of His Spirit. If I read of promises in scripture to those who have been born again, yet I do not experience them in my own life, I may all too easily respond in one of two detrimental ways. The first is to dilute my expectations as to what it means to have new life and walk victoriously in Christ, thus robbing the gospel of its full power. The second is to think that because I'm not presently experiencing abundant life, I must be the root of the problem so I just need to try harder to manifest that life. Neither of these self-reliant, self-focused approaches is what God is after. The Creator of the seed and the Architect of the seed principle will never circumvent the very process He put into motion. **A seed must always endure a maturation process, and**

that is precisely what is needed for us to enter into the fullness of what God has in store.

PRINCIPLE #2: THE FRUIT OF THE HARVEST IS DETERMINED BY THE SEED THAT IS SOWN.

The fact that we're specifically referred to as a "vineyard" is by no means coincidental. Like my mother, I enjoy gardening, but I'm nowhere near as skilled a gardener as she was. In fact, I'm quite horrible at it. When I plant my garden each spring, my goal is to fill it with as many varieties of vegetables as I feel ambitious enough to grow, while using every square foot of space available. I "over sow" because of my dreadful track record of killing more plants than I nurture through to the harvest. I overcompensate by planting way more than I need in hopes that at least some of my plants will actually produce something edible by the end of the season. In doing so, I am simply demonstrating that I am content with harvesting a minimal return of non-specific vegetables. However, when someone plants a vineyard, he's after one very specific kind of fruit. Peaches don't grow in vineyards. Grapes do. Likewise, the Father intends for us to produce a very specific kind of fruit. In Genesis 1, we're told that the fruit trees God created brought forth fruit, "each according to its kind," (Genesis 1:12 NKJV). That word "kind" is important to Him. When He speaks of the vineyard, He's not saying to us, "Good luck! I hope you come up with some type of edible fruit I can enjoy." No! He's looking for something quite specific.

In all my years of watching my father farm, I never once saw him harvest peanuts from cotton seed. If a yield of peanuts was what he wanted, then he planted peanut seed. What is sown into the ground determines the nature of the harvest. The Holy Spirit points us to a very specific harvest in Galatians 5:22-23. In that passage, Paul tells us, "...the fruit of the Spirit is love, joy, peace, patience, kindness, goodness, faithfulness, gentleness, self-control."

Remember, God is not random with His wording. When He uses the fruit analogy here, He has not forgotten that He's pointing to a harvest of fruit in Matthew 21 and in Isaiah 5.

He is looking for the fruit of the Spirit to be produced in us.

When we view Paul's teaching on fruit through the lens of the Spirit, we ought to be able to see that he isn't simply pointing to random attributes that God wants to see expressed through His people. He is, rather, describing the nature of a specific person. Each of the attributes mentioned in Galatians 5 are found in one man—the Son of Man. Paul is describing an "other than" kind of life than what had previously been seen on earth—a completely different kind of person than Adam and his offspring. This new kind of man is none other than the Lord, Himself. I've heard this passage referred to as the "nine different fruits" of the Holy Spirit, but that is not what is being said. There aren't individual "varieties" of spiritual fruit. The use of the word fruit is singular in nature. "The fruit of the Spirit is…" not "the fruits of the Spirit are…." There is one fruit, and it is the life and nature of the Lord Jesus. Galatians 5 simply describes what His life looks like. Essentially, Paul is simply saying that the fruit—or the evidence—of the Holy Spirit within us **is the life of Christ**.

Let's look back at Matthew 13 in greater detail. In the Parable of the Sower, Jesus tells us in verse 19 what the seed is, but like most everything pertaining to the things of God, we need Him to open our eyes in order to gain understanding. He explains that the seed is the "word of the kingdom." This phrase has been interpreted in different ways. Some have suggested that Jesus is referring to the written word, meaning the scriptures. Yet at the time He told this story, the full counsel of scripture wasn't even complete. It would take another 70 years for the rest of scripture to be written, and the Bible wouldn't be canonized for another 300 years beyond that.

Besides, Jesus was quite emphatic when He clearly articulated that life isn't found in the scriptures, but in the One of whom the scriptures testify (John 5:39).

Some believe "the word of the kingdom" refers to the message of the gospel. There is certainly a measure of truth in this perspective, though something much deeper that is being spoken of than just a message. According to 1 Peter 1:23, we have been "born again, not of perishable seed but of imperishable, through the living and abiding Word of God." And the living and abiding Word of God that Peter is speaking of is the very One being testified of in John 1:1—"In the beginning was the Word, and the Word was with God, and the Word was God." This verse isn't referring to something written down or even spoken of, but rather to the One of whom the Father has been testifying since the beginning of Creation—Christ, the Eternal One. The message always has been… is… and always will be Jesus, the Son of God. As Paul writes in Ephesians 1, the entirety of the eternal plan and purpose of God was "set forth in Christ," (v. 9), and that plan and purpose is "to unite all things in Him," (v.10). He intends to fill His people with His very life, and this is explicitly said in Ephesians 1:23 when He refers to the church as His "body." There is no doubt, then, that the seed of Matthew 13 is actually the Seed (with a capital S) –Christ, Himself.

God's intention is to conform us to the image of the Son (Romans 8:29) so that He might be "the firstborn among many brothers." It's vitally important that we understand the Father's ultimate desire. He loves His Son so much that He wants to replicate His life wherever He can. Christ, the Seed, fell to the ground and died (John 12:24) at the cross, and being raised from the dead, He now sows Himself into the hearts of those who allow Him entry. And that Seed is meant to come into a place of full maturity bearing the fruit of His nature, and readiness is the process of maturation. Just as no natural fruit is picked before it is fully mature, thus fully ripened, we are meant to come into a full maturity whereby Christ's life and nature is expressed in our daily lives. In our interaction with others, we are meant to exude the aroma of His life. There is literally an exchange of life being offered to us: His life for ours. Maturity, then, is simply, "He must increase, I must decrease," (John 3:30). Remember this: One day you will stand before God's throne and give Him an account of the presence of this fruit in your life. We'll be judged according to these criteria:

"Was the life of My Son produced in you?"

"When others looked at you, did they see Him, or did they simply see you?"

A reliance upon works, good intentions and rebuttals based on doctrinal understanding will be of little value to us as He probes the vineyard, looking for fruit.

It is foolish for us to trust in our own capacity to reproduce Christ in our inward man. That should go without saying, yet far too many have bought into a deception that they must "try harder" in order to live a godly life. I spent many years trying to live for the Lord, as opposed to living in the Lord, and like a hamster on a wheel, all of my efforts got me nowhere. Trusting in our own efforts at self-improvement—not only in an attempt to conquer sin but also to produce the kind of character God desires—is absolutely a fruitless endeavor (pun intended). Even when there's an outward appearance of success, and there oftentimes is as the flesh is quite good at producing counterfeit fruit, we must recognize that man is absolutely incapable of producing the fruit of the Spirit. It is literally called "the fruit **of the Spirit**" for heaven's sake, not the fruit of our best efforts!

As fallen humanity steeped in flesh, we are quite incapable of manufacturing any of the characteristics of His divine life. We may fool others, and even ourselves at times, but man-made fruit is nothing like the real things which can only be produced by the Spirit. Take His love, for instance. Far too often, we confuse human compassion for the love of God. But we're dead wrong as the two are nothing alike. Human compassion has no power to save us from sin and death, but God's love offers us eternal life (Romans 6:23). Human compassion would not lead someone to lay his life down for an unrighteous man, but God's love did just that (Romans 5:7-8)! Human compassion is often more associated with producing a positive feeling in others than acting in their best interests, thus it is quite incapable of confronting others in their sin in a way that could lead them into repentance. Man's concept of love doesn't even come close to God's.

I was spending time in the Lord's presence one morning, meditating on His goodness when He spoke to me very clearly:

> "Real love wraps a towel around its waist and readily gets down on its hands and knees, serving the Father first and foremost by obeying Him, and likewise, serving those He loves. And it does so at the most inconvenient of times, without the slightest objection."

It was quite beautiful. And then He dropped the hammer:

"You know nothing of this kind of love."

I was shocked to hear the Lord say this to me, and then conviction hit me like a brick bat. I recalled several instances when I had offered my human concept of love as it was convenient to me or when it served some hidden agenda. I thought of other times when I had obeyed the Lord in doing what He had asked, only to do so with a deep seated (and presumably hidden) objection over being inconvenienced. I then remembered other times when I had served others willingly, only to turn bitter because I wasn't recognized for my sacrifice. While He didn't need me to validate it, I quickly acknowledged the truth of what He had spoken to me.

I then repented for trying to emulate Him apart from a complete reliance upon Him, and I then expressed my earnest desire for Him to cultivate His love within me!

As a stark contrast to my own confession of human compassion, please consider both Moses and Paul. Scripture has given these two men in whom the love of God was manifest in full measure as both cried out to the Lord asking to be eternally cut off from Him in order that their brothers and sisters might come into right relationship with God (Exodus 32:32, Romans 9:3). What an incredibly selfless thing to ask for! Please know these were not mere religious words, hastily or half-heartily spoken. Something of the selfless love of God had taken hold of their hearts to such a degree that they were willing to eternally lay down their lives on behalf of others. In this way, the nature of Jesus Himself came forth from within these two men, just as He had testified in John 15:13: "Greater love has no one than this, than to lay down one's life for his friends," (NKJV).

The same is true of each of the attributes mentioned in Galatians 5. We must see the importance of this! Until we recognize that the counterfeit fruit produced through our own fleshly efforts is glaringly inadequate and obviously lacking when compared to the true fruit of His nature, we'll never learn to submit to Him. He doesn't want the counterfeit. He means to live through us! He wants another kind of life to be expressed through us than Adam's kind of life (1 Corinthians 15:45). It is an impossible task by all accounts, yet we serve the God of the impossible! And, until we acknowledge that only He can produce within us the fruit He requires, we will only get in His way by relying on our own efforts. To journey with the Lord into readiness is to enter into the Sabbath rest promised in Hebrews 3, ceasing from our labors and learning to lean on the One we love: Jesus Christ, the Author and Finisher of our faith.

We must understand that Jesus is the true Vine, and His Father is the Vinedresser, which is made abundantly clear in John 15. Furthermore, we are merely branches (John 15:5). Branches and farmers alike are absolutely incapable of making fruit. I learned that as a farmer's son. My dad was at the mercy of many factors beyond his control; therefore he was unable to make a bountiful harvest come forth through effort alone. He simply learned to take care of his responsibilities and then trust the Lord for the outcome. The same is true of a branch, which is not the vine. It's just a branch. The branch is a conduit of the life of the vine, meant to support the fruit that the vine produces. The vine will go on living if the branch is separated from it, but the branch cannot. The life is in the vine, and it is the vine that produces the fruit.

The same is true of us. We are simply meant to be conduits of His life. As Paul put it, we are "jars of clay," containing treasure (2 Corinthians 4:7). What is the treasure? It is Christ! And the all-surpassing power that is capable of producing fruit is His very life and not us. Our function is simply to "abide in Him," (John 15:5). Abiding is not a doctrinal position; it is a relationship. We must choose to be tethered to Him in a life of utter dependency, following where He leads, looking to Him at all times. As we do, He will absolutely produce the fruit that the Vinedresser desires. He's quite good at it!

PRINCIPLE #3: THE SEED MUST NOT REMAIN A SEED. IF IT DOES, THERE WILL BE NO HARVEST.

The seed must not remain a seed. If it does, the harvest has failed. I am a true southerner, and one of my favorite foods is fried okra. I remember one spring when I planted two 20-foot rows of okra in my garden, only to discover a few weeks later that none of it germinated. Imagine my disappointment! All that work of tilling the ground and planting the seed and no fried okra to show for it! When a seed is sown, anything less than a bountiful harvest is unacceptable. There is much that must happen to that seed after planting. It must endure a necessary process of maturity. We see that process in the natural as a seedling begins to emerge and eventually grows bigger and taller, developing leaves necessary for photosynthesis and flowers that eventually give way to fruit. At the same time, there is much going on in the development of the plant that is not seen. Beneath the surface of the ground, the root system, which is needed to provide adequate food, water, and oxygen to the plant, is developing and growing along with the growth taking place above ground. If there is a deficiency in the care of the plant at any point between planting and harvest, the fruitfulness of the plant could be compromised.

We have already sufficiently addressed the fact that salvation is not the harvest, but if we fail to translate the nature of plant development to the nature of God's harvest within us, we can all too easily get discouraged along the way. A Seed (Christ) has been planted within us. Much has to happen to that Seed before we see the fullness of Christ's life produced. It must germinate. It must grow. It must be nurtured. It must be fed and watered (John 6:53), meaning we must be firmly rooted in the Lord (Isaiah 37:31). Our hearts must continually be cultivated so that we don't grow hardened towards the Vinedresser (Hebrews 3:8). We must constantly reach for the true light, which is Christ (John 1:9), abiding in fellowship with Him. All of this points to an ongoing, intentional cooperation with the Lord with the harvest in mind. At any point in the readiness process, if a breakdown occurs, the harvest could be impacted. The good news is, the Vinedresser is great at getting things back on track for fruitfulness if and when we show ourselves to be unfaithful along the way. But that will require repentance and a willingness to once again become intentional towards yielding a harvest. Passivity pertaining to our relationship with God, is akin to neglect in a garden. It will absolutely stymie the development of the plant. In the case of my okra, the ground, which was mostly clay soil, seized up from a lack of adequate moisture. Had I been attentive, I could have helped alleviate the problem by applying mulch or watering regularly. My passivity cost me.

PRINCIPLE #4: IT TAKES TIME FOR THE SEED TO MATURE.

In our 21st century "everything at our fingertips" mindset, this can be a difficult concept to align with. Perhaps one of the reasons why we tend to gravitate towards a salvation only message is that it requires very little from us on the back end. A quick prayer of faith and a little ongoing maintenance in the form of regular church attendance, daily (or at least weekly) prayer times, and an occasional glance at the scriptures are enough to satisfy the Lord's requirements, or so we think. But if we truly want to bear fruit, much will be required of us (Luke 12:48). There are no shortcuts in the development of a plant, nor are there any shortcuts with the Lord. Patience, after all, is one of the attributes of His life. It's easy to forget that even the man, Jesus of Nazareth, had to endure 30 years of life on earth, fully aware of His mission, yet restrained from walking in it. Throughout those three decades, He fully submitted to His Father's process of readiness before stepping into the fulfillment of His missional assignment. There was no rush to get ahead of the Holy Spirit, and He had no desire to enter public ministry before the Father's appointed time.

My encouragement for you is not to look for quick results. Don't think you can pray harder or fast more often to speed up God's timetable. He's not in a hurry. As I noted earlier, the plowman will one day overtake the reaper, and I believe that day may be sooner at hand than we realize. Even so, God will not be rushed, nor does He need our guidance concerning what "areas of our lives" should be addressed. The Father is the Vinedresser, and He has eons of experience and an infinite supply of expertise. To point out to Him the issues we would prefer Him to be working on even as He is pruning us in a different area is not only futile but counterproductive. It would be far better to get on His page and submit to His pruning schedule. He knows the number of your days, and He has a strategy for producing the life of His Son in you. He's more than capable of doing above and beyond all that you could ask for, so you can trust Him as a loving and perfect Vinedresser.

PRINCIPLE #5—THERE IS ALWAYS A MULTIPLICATION OF THE SEED AT HARVEST.

This is perhaps the most glorious of the five principles, and although I mentioned this before, it bears repeating: The Father so loves His Son that He desires to multiply His life wherever He is allowed to. His desire was to conform all humanity to Christ, but sadly, most are unwilling. Even worse, far too many of us within the church have resisted His attempts to bring forth the harvest. But the Vinedresser will work with what He is given, and in many, Christ will be multiplied! This does not mean that we become Him. He alone is God, and nothing will ever change that! We will simply become filled with His life to an unprecedented measure. That is quite the statement, but it is absolutely true! Even what was seen in the apostles following Pentecost was a drop in the bucket compared to what will be witnessed in the bride of Christ. She will radiate with the goodness of God so much that John described her as being "clothed with the sun," (Revelation 12:1). When the rest of creation looks upon her, they will see the radiant Son of God. His love, His joy, His peace… all will radiate from her as continual expression of His nature as His divine nature is multiplied in the many! What a beautiful ending to the first chapter in the story of humanity… and a great segue into eternity!

Before concluding this chapter, I want to draw a vital distinction between fruit and works. Too often, I've heard fruitfulness used synonymously with being used by the Lord in proclaiming the gospel, evangelizing the lost, or walking out some other type of ministry such as healing the sick, giving a word of prophesy, or teaching a Bible study. But as we've seen, fruitfulness has nothing to do with activity but is instead directly related to the life that emanates from us. Winning the lost, ministering to the poor, casting out demons, healing the sick, and preaching the gospel are all good things. But they are not fruit in and of themselves. They are good works. And while God has created us with specific good works in mind, which He's prepared for us to walk in (Ephesians 2:10), it is possible to do works and never truly know the Lord (Matthew 7:22-23). We have conflated these two concepts, as have the "many" whom Jesus mentions in Matthew 7:22. If we fail to understand the difference, we can easily be led into a false sense of accomplishment and security, wrongly believing we are walking in our created purpose, yet producing nothing of the Lord's nature and even worse, not even knowing Him.

There is a trap in thinking that God's primary concern is activity, but such an emphasis simply demonstrates our tendency to put the cart before the horse. Yes, He's prepared good works for us to walk in, and yes, the fruit of His nature will be manifested through those good works. But the fruit must be present, or else—even in what we deem to be good works—we'll simply be manifesting our self-nature. When we put an undue emphasis on works, we end up putting pressure on one another to busy ourselves for the Lord before there has been any measure of real maturity within us. I'm afraid this is exactly what we've done over the years. As a result, so many of us are manifesting our own flesh in the name of ministry, thinking that the Lord is quite pleased. But the manifestation of Adam's life through us is unacceptable to Him, regardless of whether it comes forth in the name of Christian ministry or in the form of blatant sin. If we will just recognize the simplicity of the message and remain faithful to pursue the Lord relationally, He will take care of the good works, which will flow out of the presence of His life. Learning first to "abide in Him" will result not only in true fruitfulness, but also guarantees that we will walk in the works He's prepared for us ahead of time. Remember, faithfulness—i.e. obedience—is a virtue of His life.

Matthew 25 does, in fact, point to a final judgment that specifically refers to outward works; however, we need discernment in handling this scripture. As I already stated, God has prepared good works for His people to walk in. But the purpose of the work is not the work itself. The purpose of the work is something greater—the testimony of the Son. Jesus said as much on two separate occasions recorded in the book of John. The first is in chapter 5 when he said,

> But the testimony I have is greater than that of John. For the works that the Father has given me to accomplish, the very works that I am doing, bear witness about me.
>
> John 5:36

He reiterates this in chapter 10 by saying, "The works that I do in my Father's name bear witness about me…" (John 10:25). The purpose of any "good work" is to testify of the person of the Lord Jesus. For example, when Jesus raised Lazarus from the dead, that tremendous display of power testified that His life is greater even than death itself.

In a similar manner, the Father has prepared good works for you and me to walk in. The purpose of those works is the same as those given to the Son—to testify of Christ's life within us. When we become a conduit of His life, allowing His Spirit to lead us in a work in an act of obedience and submission to His will, He can be seen by others in the work. When that happens, the work testifies of Christ in the human vessel that is "doing" the work. For example, if I am led by the Lord to share His love with a stranger in public, as I walk in obedience to Him, His life can be seen in that very simple act. But, if I put the cart before the horse and try to walk in a good work apart from His leading and His empowering grace (Zechariah 4:7), there is no testimony of Christ in the work. In such instances, it just becomes a seemingly "good idea" that originated from me, and nothing of the Lord will be witnessed by others. Always ask these two important questions: who is leading us, and who is the source of our "ministry"? If the answer to both is not the Lord, then the work bears no testimony of Him.

True fruitfulness, which is bearing the character and nature of the Son, is an inward reality that cannot be counterfeited through behavior manipulation. Having said that, as Christ is formed in the inner man, there will undoubtedly be an outward expression of His life. This is by God's design. Jesus said, "No one after lighting a lamp puts it in a cellar or under a basket, but on a stand, so that those who enter may see the light," (Luke 11:33). As He conforms us to the image of His Son, He would display that life in a public way for all to see so that the Son may be glorified. The works referred to in Matthew 25:35-40 are mentioned with this flow of the Spirit in mind, and they are evidence of fruitfulness and NOT the fruit themselves.

CHAPTER 5

THE WATCHTOWER

> Let me sing for my beloved, my love song concerning his vineyard:
>
> My beloved had a vineyard on a very fertile hill.
>
> He dug it and cleared it of stones and planted it with choice vines;
>
> He built a watchtower in the midst of it, and hewed out a wine vat in it.
>
> Isaiah 5:1-2

The two descriptions of the Father's vineyard found in scripture—one in Isaiah 5 and the other in Matthew 21—both specifically refer to a tower in its midst. As with every aspect of scripture, this repetition is neither trivial nor coincidental. Clearly, the Lord has something He wants to say to us about this key component of the vineyard. When the Holy Spirit began speaking to me from these passages, I heard Him tell me quite distinctly to pay close attention to the tower, explaining that it would be a "key to understanding" the pathway to fruitfulness—or bridal readiness.

A watchtower, an integral feature of vineyards in ancient Israel, served two primary purposes. First, the tower served as a living quarters for tenant farmers and their families. The harvest required dedication from those responsible for its oversight. Therefore, their families not only contributed to the labor, but they sacrificed the comfort of their own homes in order to provide a 24/7 watch over the vineyard. The second purpose of this two-story structure was that its top floor served as a vantage point from which the tenants could stand guard over the property. Both of these functions provided significant clarity regarding what the Holy Spirit was speaking to me as well as a deeper revelation of the readiness process.

THE LIVING QUARTERS

A vineyard tenant's top priority was the production of grapes for the owner. As a hired steward, everything else in his life became secondary, which is fitting since fruitfulness, in the truest sense of the word, is the very thing for which he would one day be judged by the owner. In the same way, as disciples of Christ, our highest priority should be yielding the fruit of His life back to Him. This is a profound statement and one that we all too easily could gloss over, and I will repeat it so that you might feel the weight of it:

As disciples of Jesus, our highest priority should be yielding to the Father the fruit that He desires from us: Christ's life within us!

Few of us would deny the truth of this statement, but as with many truths in scripture, it's easy to give mental assent to it without offering evidence that we truly believe it in our day to day walk. The Lord has no interest in religious sentiment. He's looking for those who mean what they say and say what they mean. If you question whether that's true, just ask any of the Pharisees who were so vehemently confronted by Jesus Himself time and time again, simply for preaching a message they refused to follow. It's worth examining, then, whether we've truly made bearing the likeness of the Son our highest priority.

I would ask you to prayerfully consider the following questions, and as you do, remember that the Father has charged you with the great responsibility of bearing the likeness of the Son. You will one day stand before Him, giving account for these questions. So, as you consider them, please know now is not the time for pat, religious answers. This is an occasion to let the Holy Spirit pierce your heart and bring clarity.

- Do you truly believe that the Father's intention is to conform you to the image of His Son?
- Do you truly believe that He can and will do just that, if you allow Him to?
- Do you understand that, of all the blessings you have been promised in Christ, the best by far is being filled with His life?
- Do you diligently seek that greater infilling of His Spirit, contending for the subjugation of your own flesh to the will and purpose of God?
- Are you learning in all things—whether good times or bad, prosperity or lack, sickness or health—to seek the person above all else?

Anything less than a wholehearted "yes" to those questions simply reveals that we've not yet come into the fullness of the revelation of Christ within us. As with all invitations of the Lord, a "no" answer is not a sign of hopelessness but an opportunity for repentance. It simply means that we've loved our own lives more than we've valued Him. He will gladly and readily give you the revelation necessary for the diligent pursuit of Him above all else. All you have to do is ask with a sincere heart.

Just as there was a reckoning for the tenants in the vineyard, we will be held accountable for the measure of Christ that is formed within us. It will be the very basis for the judgment of the righteous. The Father has made a significant investment in us, and He is anticipating an acceptable return. The investment I'm speaking of has nothing to do with money or talents or giftedness or anything in the natural for that matter. He has sown the life of His Son within us, and if we stand before Him having failed to arrive at any measure of maturity, it will be the equivalent of having buried His precious investment in the ground. We will not be judged according to the number of churches we planted or the Bible studies we led or the number of souls we brought into the Kingdom. We will, however, be held accountable for the measure—or lack—of Christ within us.

Please remember, I'm not against works. The Lord has created specific works with each of us in mind, and those works are opportunities for His life to be manifested through us. However, His ultimate purpose for humanity goes far beyond any outward thing. His eternal purpose is Christ's life being fully established in His people, and it's to that end that He diligently works within us. Consider Paul's exhortation:

> ...for those who love God all things work together for good, for those who are called according to His purpose. For those whom He foreknew He also predestined to be conformed to the image of His Son, in order that He might be the firstborn among many brothers.
>
> Romans 8:28-29

In "all things," God is working to conform us. This speaks of transformation. In "all things" God would transform us...but to what? To the image of His Son, according to His purpose, which He keeps in view at all times concerning us. This goes far beyond outward activity, but if all we focus on are external matters, we'll all too easily miss the gravity of what Paul is expressing here. Works will flow out of the transformation of our inner man, but we must keep the primary thing as the primary thing.

It is for fruitfulness that Christ is laboring, and we must be single-heartedly tenacious toward that end.

As a teenager working on my father's farm, I understood firsthand that a farmer doesn't clock in and out of work every day. He doesn't show up at 9:00 am and leave at 5:00 pm. Much of the time, he isn't able to put unfinished work aside for another day, and his work week is rarely confined to Monday through Friday.

He understands there is a window of opportunity to carry out his responsibilities, and whether it's time to plant, fertilize, water his crops, or deal with pests, he must diligently approach each in a timely manner with the harvest in mind. A failure to do so could prove to be disastrous. He is, furthermore, not in control of the weather and must learn to work within the boundaries of the circumstances that come his way. The old adage, "Make hay while the sun is shining," is very much part of the life of a farmer.

The Lord, having chosen the farming analogy quite intentionally, is communicating something important. Like farmers in the natural, we should have a sense of urgency and recognize that we are given opportunities which, if missed, can negatively impact His harvest within us. We are not in control of our circumstances just as a farmer can't control the weather. Yet we must learn to cooperate with the Lord within the boundaries of our circumstances with the harvest in mind. Consider Israel in the wilderness once again. Each day was an opportunity for them to learn how to trust God in a deeper measure while cultivating a lifestyle of obedience to His command. Yet trial after trial exposed an unwillingness to yield, and their hearts became hardened towards Him, leading nearly every one of them to fall into unbelief. Rather than steadfastly progressing towards the land of promise, each missed opportunity to learn submission only served to delay—and eventually disqualify—them from inheriting their God-given dwelling place. Israel is a picture for us! Our daily choices will determine whether or not we'll reach our Promised Land.

Such a statement will undoubtedly be rejected by those who either believe that God's sovereignty doesn't allow for our free will choices or that His grace trumps them. But if either of those are true, why did the apostles press the issue of readiness so heavily? I fear we adopt our pet doctrines based on what best suits our choices, worshipping all too often at the altar of convenience while denying the need for sacrifice and personal responsibility. It is all too common for many within the church to presume upon God's kindness while failing to recognize that He honors our choices. We must choose to abide in Him if we wish to bear the fruit of His nature, and that is a choice that must be made daily. It will not happen if we take a passive approach to our relationship with Him. Yet a flippant *que sera sera* "whatever will be, will be" approach to the harvest only guarantees that there will be no harvest in us.

Dietrich Bonhoeffer observed, "Cheap grace is grace without discipleship, grace without the cross, grace without Jesus Christ, living and incarnate."[14] As believers, our goal is Christ living manifestly within us, but this will never happen without the cross. Please know that when I mention the cross here, I am not speaking specifically of the cross of Christ. We've become quite comfortable with the idea of our Savior hanging on His cross, yet He tells us in no uncertain terms, "Whoever does not bear his own cross and come after me cannot be my disciple," (Luke 14:27). Jesus dies on His cross. Who do you think is meant to die on yours? Remember, our spiritual marriage to Jesus will entail a death to our old self—the very death that the Apostle Paul spoke of in Galatians 2:20. He writes, "I have been crucified with Christ. It is no longer I who live, but Christ who lives in me." Paul could say that because of how he allowed the Holy Spirit to deal with his self-life and shift Paul's desire towards the Lord and away from the gratification of the flesh. It's His desire to do that with you and me, but we must cooperate with Him in the process.

The church in our day is run amok with cheap grace. The discipleship required to bring forth the manifest life of Christ within the believer is now shunned as "legalism" or a "works mentality." Yet apart from an absolute commitment to the person of Jesus Christ leading us to willingly forsake the cares and pleasures of this world, we cannot lay claim to the reward of bridal intimacy with Him. Such a self-indulgent, "I'll-have-my-cake-and-eat-it-too" approach to our relationship with God is utterly contrary to the gospel for

---

14 Bonhoeffer, Dietrich. (1966) The Cost of Discipleship. New York: Macmillan.

which our spiritual fathers laid down their lives, and it will yield only the sour, wild grapes of Isaiah 5. Such bitter, counterfeit fruit is reflective of the self-life and a stubborn resistance to God's will.

Please don't misunderstand. I am not saying we simply need to work harder to produce something for the Lord. That is the exact opposite of my point. What is required of us is a Hebrews 4:11 commitment: "Let us therefore strive to enter that rest." Ceasing from our own efforts is what makes way for the coming of the Lord within us. You and I can't be Christ; that is an impossibility! So, stop trying! You weren't meant to rule your own life; you've been bought with a price (1 Corinthians 6:20). Stop using His vessel for your own pleasure—even that word "pleasure" refers to some twisted desire you have to produce something for God on your own merits! You now belong to Him, and He wants to inhabit you to such degree that He is able to live His life through you, and that's exactly what He'll do as we learn to rest in Him. Ceasing from effort, however, is not a natural function of the unregenerate soul. When our self-life assumes the throne of our inner being—which God designed for Himself—it becomes a deity in its own eyes, thus seeing no need to relinquish control. This is precisely what happened as a result of the fall, meaning we're all in the same boat, dealing with a soul that suffers from a god complex! Lest you think I'm judging the soul too harshly, remember Paul's words in Romans 8.

> The mind set on the flesh is hostile toward God; for it does not subject itself to the law of God, for it is not even able to do so, and those who are in the flesh cannot please God,
>
> Romans 8:7-8 NASB

We must see this:

The mind of the self-life is incapable of submission. It is not to be taken lightly!

The believer, then, is at war against his own unrenewed soul. Someone recently suggested to me that a believer's soul is "neutral." Neutral?! Where in the world do we get such notions when scripture is so clear? The "carnal mind," as it's called in the King James translation, is 100% hostile toward God and His agenda. The Greek word translated as "carnal" is *sarx*, which means of mere human origin or empowerment[15]. The carnal mind, then, is the mind that remains under the power of self. It has not yet come into a place of submission to the life of Christ. It is the seat of power for the unregenerate soul which is openly hostile to God. It is anything but neutral and must be conquered by the Lord. By contrast, the mind of Christ is fully yielded to the will of the Father to such a degree that He was fully emptied of himself and became obedient to the point of death (Philippians 2:5-8). We are either walking in the mind of Christ or the carnal mind of man. There is no third option. This explains the present carnality in the body of Christ. In our ignorance, we have persisted in seeking input from our carnal minds, as well as our unrenewed emotions, all the while wondering why we're not experiencing the fruitfulness of abundant life that Jesus promised.

As we allow the Lord to conquer us, He will bring renewal to our souls. Bear in mind that His conquest hinges on our choices. If we desire to remain in control, He will not override our decision. If we faithfully choose submission, however, He will prevail. What is needed on our parts, then, is the zeal of the Lord to arise within us helping us to cooperate with Him as He targets the treasonous dictator known as our flesh. We must be realistic as to the nature of the battle, understanding that it will require great vigilance and devotion.

Passivity and apathy have become the hallmark, not only of the "greasy grace" church, but also of those who suggest that God's sovereignty means that He always gets the results He desires. He

---

15 Strong, J. (1890). Strong's exhaustive concordance of the Bible. Abingdon Press.

does not. We have no comprehension of how much it breaks His heart to watch the unsaved choosing to spend eternity apart from Him. Likewise, we have no idea how much it grieves Him when believers persist in producing the wild grapes of self-governance as opposed to the true fruit of Christ's life. Yet, His respect of our free will remains steadfast, no matter how much He hurts. We are free to choose to be committed to the harvest and learn to abide in the Vine, or we can opt instead to believe that everything is going to work out in the end and give ourselves to the pursuit of worldly pleasures. But make no mistake: His harvest will come forth in those who pursue Him in fullness and who love not their own lives, even to death (Revelation 12:11).

Regardless of who you are, where you've been, what you've done, or what you believe, there is a direct invitation for you from the Lord to be made ready for the return of the King. But you must want Him more than you've ever wanted anyone or anything else, and then you must choose to make His inward preparation your utmost priority. It is not a natural desire that propels us into a whole-hearted pursuit of Him, but rather one that is born of the Spirit, through the revealing, or uncovering, of the person of Jesus Christ to our hearts. The Holy Spirit longs to do this for you. Simply ask Him to. But as you do, know that it absolutely will mean the forsaking of everything else (Philippians 3:7-9)! Anything other than our full commitment to Him will not move us down the path of readiness.

THE WATCHTOWER

Our tendency is to watch faithfully and carefully over whatever is precious to us. The fact that there was a watchtower in the vineyard—though perhaps a bit odd to us in our modern context of agriculture—is God's way of highlighting just how important the harvest is to Him. The nature of His Son is most precious to the Father, and His coming forth in maturity within earthen vessels is worthy of being safeguarded. Keep in mind, though, that to the degree that Christ's nature is treasured by the Father, it is equally threatening to—and hated by—Satan. The enemy is terrified of Christ's life coming into a place of dominance in His disciples, and he will do everything in his power to stop it from doing so. He is directly opposed to readiness in the body of Christ, and his warfare against us is entirely focused on the issue of fruitfulness. Of course he is! Why else would we be in so much confusion about this issue which is so basic to Christianity as the early church fathers understood it? Satan has obfuscated the truth by undermining the very foundations of our faith through doubt, confusion, false doctrines, self-indulgence, passivity, and a host of other weapons.

Christ becoming our life will not happen without a fierce battle. There is great conflict over the issue of the harvest, and just as we must be intentional to abide in Him, so must we also be prepared to engage in spiritual combat in order to secure what He has promised! Christ is our Canaan. And just as the Israelites were required to take up their weapons and fight to receive God's gift of the Promised Land in the natural, so, too, must we engage in spiritual warfare to come fully into our spiritual land of promise—the spiritual, eternal dwelling place known as "abiding in Christ."

In biblical times, there were two primary enemies of the vineyard: human thieves and small animals such as foxes, jackals, and badgers. Both had the ability to devastate the harvest. We'll explore the symbolism of each of these over the next few pages using a traditional interpretation which I know the Lord will use to speak to us. However, I will prepare you in advance by saying that the Lord blew my traditional interpretation right out of the water as He opened up the Word in a way that I've never seen it before! Once we've examined the more conventional understanding of these symbols, we'll explore them again in the following chapter. Let me go ahead and warn you now for what lies ahead: brace yourself!

A DEADLY ENEMY

The natural harvest of a vineyard is grapes. And grapes, especially in Israel during the days of the New Testament, were prized for the wine that they produced. Notice that the tower is not the only structure in the vineyard. There is also a winepress. Ultimately, vineyard owners desired wine. Water was not as readily available in that part of the world, and many of the water sources were contaminated. Water, then, was often unsafe for drinking.

Wine, on the other hand, was quite plentiful. While it was fermented, it didn't have nearly the alcohol content that our modern-day wines have. This is because the juices from the grape were allowed to ferment naturally without added sugar and yeast as we do today, which results in a more potent finished product. However, there was enough fermentation to provide for its preservation and long-term storage. Given the shortage of reliable water, wine became the beverage of choice. There's even a report from 1800 B.C. suggesting that there was more wine in ancient Israel than water. Not only was it valued as a drink, but it also was used as medicine, a disinfectant for wounds, a cleaning solution for homes, and as dye for fabric. It should come as no surprise, then, that grapes were a highly prized commodity and therefore a target for thieves.

In the Luke 12 passage we examined in the introduction, Jesus likened His return to a thief coming in the night, warning his followers to be ready. Once again, God chose His words carefully. Thieves don't announce their arrival ahead of time. They come when they are least likely to be seen, and such will be the case with the Lord. His coming will happen during a time when most of the world is soundly sleeping, including, quite sadly, much of His church. In the Parable of the 10 Virgins, the bridegroom was delayed, and all 10 had fallen asleep. But each was awakened to the cries announcing His arrival (Matthew 25:1-6).

My friend, in our day, far too much of the church of Jesus Christ is dead asleep when we all should be standing in the tower with our eyes wide open, earnestly anticipating His return. But there is a cry arising from the true prophetic voices of our day, much as the warning that emanated from a wild-haired man wearing camel skin who lived in the Judean wilderness calling the people of God to prepare the way for the coming of the King (John 3:1-12). And while it's easy to shrug off the foolishness of the Lord's chosen vessel, the consequences of dismissing the voice of the Lord will be nothing short of devastating.

But this isn't Jesus' only mention of thieves. In John 10:10, Jesus tells us, "The thief does not come except to steal, and to kill, and to destroy. I have come that they may have life, and that they may have it more abundantly." The traditional interpretation of this passage is that the thief is Satan, and it is certainly true that the "accuser of the brethren" is just that—a thief (Isaiah 14:13)! He is also a murderer (John 8:44) and a destroyer (Revelation 9:11). In the context of the Parable of the Vineyard, however, it's important to note that his stealing, killing, and destroying is not random, but focused. His goal is not simply to wreak havoc and frustrate Christians randomly, merely keeping them from well-deserved promotions or arbitrarily causing them to have flat tires at inconvenient times. Rather, it is to stop Christ from coming forth in God's people and to do so at any cost.

I'm concerned that we have a short-sighted and self-centered view of who Satan is and what he is after. He is a thief who would steal the harvest, kill the life of the Seed within us, and destroy the branches of the Vine so they cannot produce the fruit that the owner of the vineyard desires. His aim isn't simply to make us miserable and ruin our day because we claim to love Jesus and sing loudly with arms lifted high when the music starts in church. His mission is to disrupt the multiplication of the Seed, and he knows each of us was created to be a vineyard unto the Most High God.

Think about it. Christ already crushed Satan's head once, and because He did, our enemy's fate is sealed. Satan knows there's a bride coming, within whom the Seed of Christ will increase to such a place of maturity that she will look more like the One whom she loves than she does fallen Adam. The life of Christ will be multiplied within the many—a corporate bridal company—thus paving the way for the return of the King! When He comes, Satan will be bound for a thousand years and eventually cast into eternal judgment. Knowing this eventuality, He is strategic in nature, wanting to delay the harvest and cling to every last possible second he can. He is terrified of God getting His end-time vessel and will stop at nothing to delay it just one more generation by keeping the bride of Christ from being made ready. He will, therefore, relentlessly concentrate his strategic resources on those believers who are intentionally and intently focused on the path to maturity. Temptation, threats, fear, intimidation, bitterness, unforgiveness, false doctrine, religious thinking, passivity, confusion, and more will be hurled against the saints who are pressing into readiness. And if we're not watchful, the enemy will catch us quite unprepared.

Please know that I am not suggesting we become fixated on the devil. But at the same time, I am not OK with our remaining so naïve that we're ignorant of our very real and dangerous adversary, who, if left unchallenged, will utterly thwart God's eternal plan for our lives.

Our maturity and readiness in the Lord is directly related to our willingness to stand in the day of battle and relentlessly contend for His eternal purpose. Warfare is one of the primary tools God uses to grow us into full maturity. David wrote in Psalm 144:1, "Blessed be the Lord my Rock, who trains my hands for war, and my fingers for battle." As we mature in the Lord, we discover that the frequency and intensity of our spiritual battles only increase rather than decrease. There is an exponential element to this. The more we fight, the more we grow. The more we grow, the greater threat we become to the enemy. The greater the threat, the more targeted his attack.

Many of the battles we face are allowed by God for the purpose of showing us that He's quite capable of changing our circumstances. In our younger years, Heather and I were involved with Youth With A Mission. Upon returning to Hungary from an outreach in Bosnia, we experienced a miraculous provision of the Lord in a most unexpected way. I was driving our group of nine in a rental van which had been involved in an accident the week before. The radiator was severely damaged, and given the limited resources in Bosnia, all we could get was a quick patch job. When we set out, we were very much concerned about how it would hold up on the 300+ mile drive to Budapest. Nevertheless, we launched out in faith, believing that the Lord would get us safely to our destination.

About halfway through our journey, I anxiously watched the needle on the temperature gauge steadily move into and then beyond the "red zone." I immediately pulled over and shut the engine off right on the shoulder of the highway. We were stranded with no idea where the next service station was, no money, and a deadline for our arrival, and none of us were mechanically inclined. As I sat behind the steering wheel feeling overwhelmed and helpless, a voice from the back of the van suggested, "Let's pray and ask the Lord to heal our van!" Being the great man of faith that I am (sarcasm intended), I mumbled under my breath, "You guys pray. I'm going to look for a mechanic!" But then the Holy Spirit quickly convicted me of my unbelief, and I joined in with the rest of our team. After a few minutes of fervent intercession, someone suggested I try starting the engine to see if the Lord had answered our prayers. It took some convincing, but I finally turned the ignition switch, and the engine started up again. All nine of us watched as the needle climbed steadily back toward the red zone. I was just about to turn it back off so that we could figure out how to get help. But as I reached for the key, the passionate prayers from the back of the van kicked into high gear. I then watched in amazement as the needle crossed briefly into the red just before immediately dropping back into normal range where it stayed for the rest of our trip.

Did Satan have anything to do with the accident or the overheating? I'm convinced he did, since our whole purpose for being in Bosnia was to minister for the Lord. Yet at the same time, we were in a spiritual battle, and I had been hit with such intense doubt and faithlessness that I couldn't discern what the Lord was wanting to do in the midst of the fight. Thankfully, the rest of the team had my back. As they pressed into the Lord, He dramatically changed the circumstances and proved to each of us that He is trustworthy. In this particular battle, the circumstances miraculously shifted right before our eyes. But that is not always the case.

Many years later, Heather and I experienced an attack unlike any I had ever known. For weeks, the enemy came at us relentlessly in the night, disrupting our sleep in a most debilitating way. Night after night, we tossed and turned, averaging only two or three hours of broken sleep a night, and some nights no sleep at all. I had experienced occasional bouts of insomnia in the past, but this hit us both and persisted for some time, despite our prayers to the Lord and our rebukes of the enemy. A friend alerted me that this was a spiritual attack of a different nature than we had previously experienced, and that in the midst of it, the Lord wanted to teach us a new kind of warfare. Clueless about what this meant, I pressed into the Lord for a change in circumstances, believing that of course His priority was our being able to sleep. But as the circumstances stayed the same, fatigue gave way to stress, and stress turned into fear. Eventually despair set in. This was not the victory the Lord had in mind.

Our battle raged on for three months. Night after night we tossed and turned, while day after day we contended and believed for sleep. I couldn't see what I couldn't see, namely that God was not primarily interested in changing my circumstances. Eventually that debilitating season ended, and our sleep was restored. However, a few months later, the warfare returned. This pattern continued for over a year. (Did I mention that I'm a slow learner?) Eventually, I clued into what the Lord was doing and realized that the spiritual ground He wanted me to take had nothing to do with my circumstances and everything to do with a work of maturity He wanted to do within me. It wasn't about sleep. It was about readiness. But as I persistently fought for my own will, I was actually resisting His! On top of that, I had succumbed to fear, despair, and doubt in a most crippling way. Instead of standing firm on the day of battle, I had taken a serious beating. However, once the breakthrough came and we came onto God's eternal ground—that is, once we aligned with His will and purpose—we began to experience true victory. That came not as a quick change to our situation, but a bending of our will to His and a deepening of our trust in Him as a good Father.

On the heels of this revelation, I came to see many previous battles in a much different light. Far too often in my journey with the Lord, I fought for a change in circumstances rather than asking my Father to define the objective. How many painful blows had I absorbed needlessly—discouragement, despair and condemnation—all because I had wrongly assumed that God and I were fighting for the same outcome. Undoubtedly, we were not. I now know that when warfare hits, my responsibility is to go before the Lord and ask Him to show me what His specific purpose is in allowing the battle and how He would have me stand and fight in the midst of it. He has also shown me that if I'll contend for "higher ground"—His eternal purpose, both for me, my family and others—He will take care of the circumstances in His way and in His timing. But please understand: God's heart was not simply to put us through the torture of missing out on precious sleep.

His plan was to allow us to experience a measure of suffering so that—with eternity in view—He could gain unconquered territory in our souls.

In the process, He was doing exactly what He promises to do in Romans 8:29. He was conforming us to the image of His Son, who spent His life on earth as a suffering servant without even a whimper of complaint. Although this higher ground warfare is rarely preached in our churches or written about in Christian literature, it is a key to moving forward in the readiness process. If we wish to see a bride made ready for the Lord, and moreover, if we wish to be a bride made ready, we must learn to contend for the life of Christ to come forth in His people above all other secondary issues. His bride will be one that is not content simply to contend for her own needs, but rather, she will take up the sword to fight for the will of her Beloved above all else. As she does, He will faithfully "supply every need of [hers] according to his riches in glory in Christ Jesus," (Philippians 4:19).

Please know, the Lord is not indifferent toward your circumstances. He cares for you in the midst of the battle, and none of your suffering is lost on Him. Yet He willingly allows you to experience pain temporarily in order to gain the inward, eternal ground of Christ, even if the circumstances persist unto death. In comparison to eternity, decades of pain in the temporal realm will seem as "light, momentary afflictions," (2 Corinthians 4:17). Yet in the moment, He is always merciful to provide all you need. But the question is this: What truly constitutes a need? Our greatest need always is for spiritual transformation, and because of this, our warfare against the enemy must be fought on spiritual ground, not just in the realm of temporal "things." The church has, for the most part, missed the boat on this issue. Even when the Lord intends to change your circumstances, His primary goal is always the maturity of your inward man. How can I make such a statement? Because Romans 8:28-29 tells us so:

> And we know that for those who love God, **all things work together for good**, for those who are called **according to His purpose**. For those whom He foreknew He also predes-

> tined to be conformed to the image of His Son, in order that He might be the firstborn among many brothers.

In all things, the Father's intention is to conform you inwardly to the image of the Son! Don't let short-sightedness or a desire for instant gratification cause you to fixate on what's happening in the natural realm. God sees far beyond today into eternity, and the fruit He is producing in you is everlasting. The day is coming when today's suffering and painfully desperate circumstances will be irrelevant in eternity!

As the Lord warned, you must be wise as a serpent (Matthew 10:16), understanding that you have a very real enemy who wants to steal God's harvest in you. However, resist becoming fixated on Satan, which will lead you onto dangerous spiritual ground. Remember, the Lord is our very source of life, and we must be vigilant to remain in Him. As we fix our eyes on Him, He will make us aware of the presence of our enemy and how to resist him. Ours is simply to follow the lead of the Lord of hosts in the day of battle. When He leads, fight for the nature of Christ to be formed in you first and foremost. Understand that while God may allow Satan to strike you in the natural, perhaps even physically, his weapons are spiritual in nature. Fight him on that ground, standing firm in the power and peace of the Lord Jesus Christ, resisting the enemy's attempts to lead you into confusion, fear, despair, hopelessness, or bitterness.

As we secure the eternal ground of inward conformity to Christ, He very often will shift the battle into addressing secondary or circumstantial issues. At times, He'll simply alter our circumstances once they have been used by Him to produce the fruit He intended. At other times, He may alert us to begin to address the enemy directly, believing for a change in our circumstances. If He does, pray confidently toward that end. I am not making a doctrine out of refusing to address temporal things in prayer. That is not at all the point! I'm simply pointing out that our highest priority should always be to align with God's highest priority. At the same time, He is not obligated to change anything, so hold all things loosely before Him!

BEAUTIFUL BUT DECEPTIVELY DANGEROUS

Another primary enemy of vineyards is the fox. While thieves would invade as the fruit was ripening, foxes would primarily devour the tender shoots of the vine as they began to sprout and grow, killing the branches and destroying the harvest.

In Song of Solomon 2:15, the attendants of the bride urge her to, "Catch us the foxes, the little foxes that ruin the vineyard, for our vineyards are in blossom." The "vineyards in blossom" refers to the budding intimacy taking place between Solomon who is a type of Christ and the Shulamite woman who is a type of the Lord's bride. Her attendants' exhortation is to decisively deal with the little nuisances whose presence is disruptive to true intimacy. Anyone who has been married for any length of time can recognize that very often conflicts over trivial matters can prove to be the greatest barrier to the union that God desires between a husband and wife. In the context of our bridal intimacy with Jesus, this verse warns us not to take lightly the little distractions and temptations. While they may seem benign in our own eyes, they are guaranteed to diminish the harvest.

It's worth noting that foxes are not visibly threatening animals. They're actually quite small and particularly skittish. They don't evoke immediate fear when you encounter them like a wolf or a lion would. Rather, their beauty can be extremely striking, giving them an allure not often associated with predators. If you had no prior knowledge of foxes, you'd likely fail to recognize them as enemies. But looks, at least as far as foxes are concerned, are definitely deceiving. They are potentially dangerous animals, particularly for vineyards.

A few years ago, the Lord gave Heather a dream about a fox. She and two of our friends—a married couple—were in an enclosed garden tending to the plants when a fox unexpectedly walked up to them. All three immediately agreed to trap the fox before it did any damage and were quickly able to do so. However, as they approached the trap, Heather commented on how incredibly handsome it was, and our friends chimed in as well, praising the fox for its beauty. Its coat shimmered with dazzling, vibrant colors, and the features on its face were sharp and elegant. They all were so captivated by the fox's beauty that, instead of disposing of it, they agreed to keep it as a pet. Heather woke up in a start, recognizing that this was a warning from the Holy Spirit—both for us and for our friends. The traditional scriptural interpretation of foxes is that they represent little "pet sins," which we often tend to excuse, overlook, or tolerate. Yet these "minor" transgressions may be at the very heart of what is robbing us of an intimate relationship with Jesus.

This is an accurate interpretation of Heather's dream regarding what was going on in our friends' lives at the time. If left unaddressed, sins that we consider minor can become real problems in our journey in the Lord. This is why it's vitally important that when we invite Christ to be the Lord of our lives, we don't give Him limited access to His "temple," but instead invite Him to clean out the whole "house." Many of us were wrongly taught that God's grace means that sin is not that big of deal to Him. Paul was accused of teaching this false belief and adamantly refuted it in Romans 6: "What should we say then? Are we to continue in sin that grace may abound?" (v. 1). In other words, should we just adopt the position that sin isn't a big deal to God, since grace abounds more than whatever sin we engage in? He then answers his own question in verse 2: "God forbid!" (KJV) Why was Paul's response so impassioned?

Sin—no matter how big or small it may be, based on our self-manufactured, sliding scale of holiness—separates us relationally from God, and we were not made to be separated from Him. Remember, His very purpose in creating us was so that we could be joined to Him in intimate friendship. However, sin of all stripes and colors hinders relationship. This is true of husbands and wives. It's true of parents and children. It's true of friendships. And it is absolutely true regarding our union with God in Christ, not because He's offended by our sin, or that He's unforgiving when we fail. Rather, it's because light has no fellowship with darkness (2 Corinthians 6:14), and God, who is light (1 John 1:5) will not abide sin. (Please bear in mind, I am not suggesting that sin causes us to lose our salvation. This would mean that sin is more powerful than God's grace, and that most assuredly is not the case! However—whether we realize it or not—sin always disrupts the flow of intimacy with Him.)

Sin also opens a door to the demonic. And just as this was true in the garden at Adam's fall, it also is true of you and me today. Our disobedience gives Satan a measure of influence over us, and the more we yield to him, the more influence he gains over us. Paul said it this way: "Don't you know that if you offer yourselves to someone as obedient slaves, you are slaves of that one you obey?" (Romans 6:16 HCSB). This is why the more we yield in a particular area of sin, the more power that sin has over us. Even sins that some might consider "innocent" can end up being demanding taskmasters over us. God didn't design us to be slaves to His enemy. He formed us to be bondservants to His Son, so the "little foxes" of our sin must be caught and dealt with as the threats that they are. Only the Lord can do so, but we must allow Him to. And while confession and repentance are surely necessary in granting Him access, if there are sin patterns that we can't seem to be freed from, then deliverance is needed. The good news is that we have a deliverer who is fully capable of evicting the demonic from our lives.

Please know that if there are any areas of your life in which you are enslaved to the demonic, they must be dealt with in order for you to continue your journey into readiness. That does not mean you need to go on an introspective "demon hunt." The Lord is fully aware of any open doors within you, and His full and loving intention is to set you free. But He will not do so without your cooperation. This involves allowing Him to sever all attachments to your "pet sins." You must be willing to walk away… forever! As you make that choice, ask the Lord to arise as deliverer to break the enemy's hold over you. You may not initially need someone versed in deliverance ministry to walk with you through this process, but if you find yourself stuck at some point and unable to move forward, ask the Lord for help! He either will be that for you directly, or He will be that for you through someone else. God is 100% committed to the good work He began in you, and He will be faithful to finish it.

Another traditional interpretation of the foxes is that they refer to the cares of this world, which compete with the Lord for our attention and affection. Hosea 2 makes it clear: the Lord will not share us with "other lovers," no matter how innocent they may seem to us. Instead, He woos us into a passionate and loyal desire for Him and Him alone. One of the enemy's strategies is to seduce our hearts with temporal pleasures and earthly cares. And when our hearts become entwined with the pleasures of this world, we cannot live with His eternal purpose as our ultimate destination. Scripture is clear. We cannot serve two masters. Should we attempt to live in this dichotomy, we will end up loving one and hating the other, or become devoted to the one and despise the other (Matthew 6:24).

Like the beauty of the fox, there certainly is an appeal to the world's enticements, and on the surface, many of them don't seem to be inherently bad. After all, we won't find any Bible verses warning us against watching TV, but therein lies the danger. If we're not careful, we can become addicted to it, prioritizing our time and efforts into pursuing our favorite shows, sporting events, or movies. Not only will these distractions pull on our hearts to steer us away from intimacy with the Lord, but they easily and quickly can become temptations for us to compromise and fall into outright sin as we allow ourselves to be subtly influenced by what we watch. They are not called "programs" without reason!

Please don't hear this as a rebuke on TV. I enjoy watching sports, some movies, and a few TV shows from time to time. Thankfully, the Lord has given me a great deal of freedom in this area, as I used to be quite addicted to entertainment. My love for it not only led me to waste vast amounts of time, but it also eventually led me into compromise and exacerbated a struggle that I had with lust. Again, as I have responded to His invitation to make Him my primary pursuit, He not only set me free from lust and an addiction to entertainment, but today I spend much less time in front of a TV and more time with Him. My encouragement to you is to hold all things loosely before Him. If He says, "No more," in any area of our lives—whether it's entertainment, a pursuit of money, a hobby, or even working too much, then our answer must be an immediate, "Yes Sir!" When He begins to strip something from our lives, the degree to which we complain, resist, and even rationalize why it couldn't be the Lord's will, is the degree to which that thing is bound up within our hearts.

Bear in mind, Jesus never asked us to withdraw from the world. In fact, in His most intimate, recorded prayer to the Father, He specifically requested, "I do not ask that You take them out of the world, but that You keep them from the evil one," (John 17:15). He intends for us to wisely navigate the responsibilities, pressures, pleasures, temptations, and all other things associated with living in this world, not necessarily avoiding them completely, but to meet them head on with hearts that are entirely His. We get ourselves into a ditch when we think that because we're Christians, we must altogether avoid anything worldly. But for as long as we're in this world, that would be impossible, so don't quit your day job! At the same time, this doesn't mean that the pursuit of worldly things is in our best interest. Above all else, we must ask Him for wisdom and then allow Him to direct our steps and arrange—or rearrange—our schedules. Earthly things should never eclipse our relationship with the God of all things, nor can we allow them to distract or consume us to the degree that we're no longer abiding in Him. If we don't remain watchful and catch these "foxes," they easily will do just that.

As we now clearly see, the watchtower is neither trivial, nor decorative. Placed within the Father's vineyard with great intention and much thought on our behalf, this highly significant structure is full of purpose. Its existence speaks of our need for vigilance and perseverance in being made ready for His highest purpose.

Yet we've only begun to scratch the surface of its full meaning…

CHAPTER 6

THIEVES AND FOXES AND WOLVES, OH MY!

> It is the glory of God to conceal a matter, but the glory of kings is to search out a matter.
>
> Proverbs 25:2

Now that we've explored thieves and foxes from a traditional interpretation, let's consider a significantly different perspective that the Lord gave to me concerning these enemies of the harvest. Please understand that what I'm about to share will be readily received by some, a significant challenge for many, and an outright offense to others. I want to share two vital points with you before moving forward:

First, the Lord Himself is prompting me to share the content of this chapter, and I must obey Him. The day is surely coming when I will be required to give an account regarding my obedience to Him in this life, and to be honest with you, I have a much greater fear of disobeying Him than I do of upsetting you. My experience has been that when we come to the Lord entrenched in our own dogma, we only prove ourselves to be unteachable. All I ask is that you allow the Holy Spirit to reveal Christ to you, the Living Word, so that He can instruct you as He desires.

Secondly, my heartfelt desire is to be used by the Lord to help make His bride ready for His return. However, if she's clinging to filthy graveclothes instead of putting on her wedding gown, then simply ignoring her attire will not be helpful. And although it's not easy to be corrected, when it's the Lord who brings correction, it is life-giving. I share this as one who has become quite familiar with the Lord's woodshed, and I would encourage you to let Him correct you as needed.

A DIFFERENT KIND OF THIEF

In our discussion of thieves in the previous chapter, I referred to John 10:10: "The thief does not come except to steal, and to kill, and to destroy. I have come that they may have life, and that they may have it more abundantly." Although I'm confident you and I are in total agreement that Satan is a thief, a murderer, and a destroyer, in the context of this verse, Jesus was not speaking directly about the devil. Now, having said that, let me be very clear: I have no interest whatsoever in defending Satan, and I wholeheartedly believe that he is behind every attempt at thievery, murder, and destruction that has been carried out in this world. Yet at the same time, it is incredibly beneficial to view scripture within the proper context. There is something which the Holy Spirit longs to show us in John 10, which many of us may have not yet had eyes to see.

Let's look at the larger context of John 10, and as we do, we need to keep in mind that the Bible wasn't written with the divisions of chapter and verse. These numeric additions weren't included until about 1500 years later, long after John was available to comment on the accuracy of these textual divisions. The break between John 9 and 10 is one instance where the well-meaning people responsible for this decision did us absolutely no favor. Why? Because all of chapter 9 and the first half of chapter 10 refer to the same event! At the conclusion of chapter 9, Jesus is in the middle of an intense confrontation with the Pharisees concerning an incident detailed in the earlier part of the chapter. The first half of chapter 10 is a continuation of that conversation.

At the beginning of chapter 9, Jesus encounters a man who had been born blind. When His disciples questioned the Lord regarding the cause of his blindness, Jesus tells them that the man had been born blind so that "the works of God might be displayed in him," (v. 3). Jesus then spits on the ground, and after making mud from His saliva, He "anointed the man's eyes with the mud and said to him, 'Go wash in the pool of Siloam,' (which means 'Sent.') So he went and washed and came back seeing," (v. 7).

There is great significance in this story! The Lord touched a blind man, who had never seen anything, in a highly unconventional way and then sent him to a pool called "Sent" to wash the mud from his eyes. As the blind man obeyed the Lord's command, He received sight. This caused no small uproar among the onlookers who witnessed the miracle. Many began questioning what they had seen with their own eyes as unbelief set in, some even insisting that the man who claimed to have been healed was not the blind man they all knew.

So the "experts" were brought in. You know who I'm talking about! The Pharisees—self-appointed shepherds of Israel who delighted in forcing others to do what they were incapable of—the ones that Jesus mercifully and openly challenged as being "blind guides," (Matthew 23:16)! And because it was a Sabbath, they were in an especially foul and judgmental mood. In an attempt to get to the bottom of the day's events, they pulled the now seeing man aside and questioned him relentlessly, only to finally acknowledge that a genuine miracle had indeed taken place.

Addled that Jesus was behind the miracle, the Pharisees quickly resorted to a tried-and-true tactic. "OK, sure," they reasoned among themselves, "maybe a miracle happened. But this guy performed it on Sunday! There's no way that God was involved! Obviously, He used demonic powers!" These "white-washed tombs" (Matthew 23:27) then harassed the once blind man who, by this point, saw far more clearly than they did! And while they did their best to convince him to renounce Jesus, he held his ground and boldly testified of the Son of God. This "sent one" was beginning to see what the blind leaders of Israel could not.

Afterward, Jesus sought the man with new found vision, and when He found him, He revealed Himself to be the Messiah. And because the man born blind was receiving more than just physical sight, he recognized the One who stood before him as the Son of

God and worshipped Him. When the religious leaders, who always seemed to be lurking in the shadows, witnessed the newfound relationship between Jesus and this "sent one," they made no effort to hide their anger and resentment toward Him. Seizing the moment (as He has a knack for doing!), the Lord addressed their spiritual blindness:

> For judgement I came into this world, that those who do not see may see, and those who see may become blind. Some of the Pharisees near Him heard these things and said to Him, "Are we also blind" Jesus said to them, "If you were blind, you would have no guilt, but now that you say, 'We see,' your guilt remains."
>
> John 9:40-41

Then, just as the story is starting to get really interesting, chapter 9 ends! But the conversation continues in John 10:1.

> Truly, truly, I say to you, he who does not enter the sheepfold by the door but climbs in by another way, that man is a thief and a robber. But he who enters by the door is the shepherd of the sheep.

At this point, it's important to note that the Holy Spirit is drawing a distinction between His "sent ones," to whom He gives sight and who carry the true testimony of Christ, and those self-appointed leaders incapable of truly seeing. This is chapter 9's primary premise and provides the context for what follows in chapter 10. In verse 1, the Lord explicitly states, "…he who does not enter the sheepfold by the door but climbs in by another way, that man is a thief and a robber." Jesus isn't speaking of spiritual thieves but human ones. Israel's religious leaders were presumptuous, unseeing men, but God had a different form of leadership in view. He would counter these self-proclaimed "experts" with those whose eyes He would open and send out with the authority of heaven, which foreshadowed what took place at Pentecost when uneducated and ordinary men stepped into the sheepfold as the true leadership of His house. Their qualifications would have nothing to do with Israel's religious system and everything to do with Jesus' touch which caused them to see as they had never seen before—and then His commissioning of them to go forth bearing His testimony.

In verse 8, Jesus declares, "All who came before me are thieves and robbers..." referring to all who would presume to step into a place of spiritual leadership that He did not appoint. In verse 10, He reveals that the true motivation of these thieves is, "to steal and kill and destroy." It's this same group of people with the same motivation whom He addresses in the Parable of the Vineyard in Matthew 21—a religious leadership who, in their lust for recognition, power, and control, would conspire to kill the very Son of God. Jesus is not simply calling out a spiritual thief in this verse. He is openly challenging the physical hosts used by Satan to carry out an evil agenda—an agenda that is targeted against the life of the Son coming forth in a final and glorious harvest!

As the heir of all things (Psalm 2:7-8), the Son of God is a threat to the self-centered desires and self-seeking motivations of rebellious leadership who may have knowledge of the scriptures and a smidgen of outward piety but no true intimacy with Him. From God's perspective, the issue never has been about appearances. He sees past the religious façade of illegitimate leadership and knows the secret motivations of the heart (Hebrews 4:12). He is not fooled. The Son's arrival on the scene forces hidden agendas out into the open, demanding a choice from us all, especially those who lay claim to a position of leadership in His house.

It's His way or the highway, and there are no exceptions.

Those thieves had a decision to make: repent, get on board with Him, and come to know the God of mercy or rebelliously stand against Him in open hostility and incur His wrath. While this may seem too harsh for our current culture of false grace, this is precisely why there is a warning of steeper judgement for those in the Lord's priesthood (James 3:1).

This is the very same imagery used by the prophet Jeremiah when he stood in the House of the Lord crying out,

> Has this house, which is called by my name, become a den of robbers in your eyes? Behold, I myself have seen it, declares the Lord.
>
> Jeremiah 7:11

This is the scripture Jesus quoted in Matthew 21:13 as He cleansed the temple with a whip of cords. His judgment against those who profited from the worship of God was touching on a wider, systemic problem throughout Israel. Most of their religious leadership had turned the priesthood into a self-serving institution. As arrogant, self-righteous men, they made much of themselves and cast judgments upon the very people they claimed to serve. They lusted after power and notoriety, believing that their training and education had positioned them as experts in the ways of God. Concerning themselves only with external appearances, inside they were full of rot (Matthew 23:27), and in a day when Israel desperately needed true shepherds, they were the blind leading the blind (Matthew 15:14). Completely resistant to the harvest God desired to reap within His covenant people, the religious leadership killed the very Seed that will one day produce a full harvest. It is no accident that the Parable of the Vineyard, in which the Lord announces His judgment on this false leadership, is given to us in the same chapter (Matthew 21) that includes the cleansing of the temple and the cursing of the fig tree, both of which point to a failed, illegitimate leadership and a dead religious system.

It should go without saying that these thieves were not the "sent ones" God desired to serve as His priests. His true sent ones not only know they are called, but they also understand the purpose of their call and remain faithful to the One that called them to the very end. Jesus wasn't condemning the thieves of Israel in this passage. His fierce opposition was rooted in kindness and mercy as He appealed to them to humble themselves and repent before it was too late. Yet, because of His great love even for thieves and robbers, the Lord was never afraid to confront those who were steeped in religious pride—something He continues to do today.

OF FOXES AND WOLVES

Now let's consider the foxes once again. Again, we've traditionally interpreted these vine-spoiling critters to be the so-called "minor" sins or the cares of the world that would hinder our intimacy with the Lord. Now to be clear, I'm not advocating for indulging in either of these. (If there is a doubt, please re-read the previous chapter.) However, scripturally speaking, there is evidence that something else may be on God's mind in using the fox analogy. In the previous chapter, I shared that the Hebrew word used in Song of Solomon 2:15 is *shual*, which can refer to both foxes and jackals.[16] This word is only used seven times in the Old Testament—two of which are found in this passage. Here it is used symbolically with no concrete interpretation. However, Ezekiel also used this Hebrew word symbolically, along with a crystal-clear explanation, and it is his interpretation that warrants our attention:

> Son of man, prophesy against the **prophets of Israel who prophesy**, and say to **those who prophesy out of their own heart**, 'Hear the word of the LORD!'
>
> Thus says the Lord GOD: 'Woe to the foolish prophets, who **follow their own spirit and have seen nothing**! O Israel, your **prophets are like foxes** in the deserts. You have not gone up into the gaps to build a wall for the house of Israel to stand in battle on the day of the LORD. They have envisioned futility and false divination, saying, 'Thus says

16 Strong, J. (1890). Strong's exhaustive concordance of the Bible. Abingdon Press.

> the LORD! But **the LORD has not sent them**; yet they hope that the word may be confirmed. Have you not seen a futile vision, and have you not spoken false divination? You say, "The LORD says," but I have not spoken.
>
> Therefore, thus says the Lord GOD: 'Because you have spoken nonsense and envisioned lies, therefore **I am indeed against you**,' says the Lord GOD. 'My hand will be against the prophets who envision futility and who divine lies; they shall not be in the assembly of My people, nor be written in the record of the house of Israel, nor shall they enter into the land of Israel. Then you shall know that I am the Lord GOD.
>
> Because, indeed, because they have seduced My people, saying, 'Peace!' when there is no peace—and one builds a wall, and they plaster it with untempered mortar—say to those who plaster it with untempered mortar, that it will fall.
>
> Ezekiel 13:2-11 NKJV

In this passage, the foxes (or "jackals" as some translations interpret it) do not represent "little sins" or "cares of the world," but rather the false prophets who were not sent by the Lord and who were prophesying words of peace while living in a time of warfare (v. 6). They were the blind attempting to lead the blind, speaking out of their own souls and not by leading of the Holy Spirit (v. 3). Their message was popular and tickled the ears of the hearers as they promised good times, prosperity, happiness, and all that man's soul desires, yet it was a message in direct opposition to the Word of the Lord, Who was very much against them:

> Because you have uttered falsehood and seen lying visions, therefore behold, I am against you, declares the Lord God. My hand will be against the prophets who see false visions and who give lying divinations. They shall not be in the council of my people, nor be enrolled in the register of the

> house of Israel, nor shall they enter the land of Israel. And you shall know that I am the Lord, your God,
>
> vv. 8-9

In Judges 15:4, the Hebrew word *shual* was used again in a context highly worth noting. Samson, who had married a Philistine woman, went to be with his wife (in the marital sense), only to discover that her father had given her away to another man. In a fit of jealous rage, Samson caught 300 foxes, paired them by twos, and tied their tails together with a burning torch between each pair. He then set the foxes loose in the Philistines' wheat fields, utterly destroying their harvest. Foxes, in this instance, were used by the Lord in His judgment of Israel's enemy, but what's most important is the symbolism of foxes devastating the harvest!

Let's move on to the New Testament, which was written in Greek, not Hebrew. In Acts 20, when Paul is addressing the overseers of the Ephesian church, he warns them by saying, "I know that after my departure fierce wolves will come in among you, not sparing the flock," (Acts 20:29). The Greek word *lukos* is translated either as "wolf" or "jackal,"[17] and while there is the possibility of variance in the exact definition, the imagery is consistent. Just as the "foxes" in Jeremiah's day were false prophets, so too were the "wolves" of Paul's day false shepherds who were scheming to lead the flock astray.

Again, the imagery that the Holy Spirit uses in scripture is not random, and we must approach these passages with discernment. He consistently equates false prophets and false shepherds to foxes and wolves who, if left unchecked, will destroy the harvest. When the people of God are beholden to leaders that are neither appointed nor recognized by heaven, the harvest cannot come forth! False leadership is an incredibly serious affront to the Vinedresser, whose great purpose for humanity is tied up in fruitfulness.

---

17 Strong, J. (1890). Strong's exhaustive concordance of the Bible. Abingdon Press.

I understand that much of the Israel of scripture, particularly the Israel that the prophets knew, lived before the full manifestation of Christ, but it doesn't change God's eternal purpose and the harvest He has always kept in view concerning humanity. Obviously, those who lived before Jesus walked the earth were living during a different dispensation than the one we are presently under. But regardless of the dispensation, our response to Him must be the same: a humble heart, submission to God, and a willingness to be stripped of self. The pillars of the faith—such as Joseph, David, Daniel and others—did not see the full manifestation of Christ within a people while living on this earth. Yet these men chased after the Lord's heart and yielded a harvest of first fruits that was pleasing to the Vinedresser.

Israel was given to us as a type and shadow of the church in the present dispensation. When we see this, we will understand that false leadership has always been a pressing and contentious issue. It was true of Korah and Dathan in the wilderness who rebelled against Moses, God's anointed leader. They were incapable of leading the Israelites into Canaan because God didn't choose them. It was true of Jezebel and Ahab along with a host of wicked kings who repeatedly turned a nation away from the Lord. They could not shepherd Israel rightly before God because they didn't know Him themselves. It was true of the false prophets in the days of Jeremiah and Ezekiel. They had no way of speaking the word of the Lord because they didn't have ears to hear Him in the first place. It was true of the Pharisees and Sadducees who had come onto the scene in Jesus' day. They should have led the way into receiving Messiah as King over Israel, but they could not recognize Him, even as He stood before them. It was true of the Judaizers of Paul's day, who were clinging to a dark and dead religious system instead of running to the light that is life (John 1:4). In so doing, they incited many to turn away from the Living God.

And we must see that false leadership is a cancer in the body of Christ in our day, as well. Satan has been intentional about infiltrating God's people through whatever open doorways he can find, and he will have a harlot church that will join with the Antichrist in the last days (Revelation 17).

OH MY!

Paul understood that false leadership will persist until the Lord returns, hence the warning in Acts 20—a warning that we would be well served in heeding. Satan's goal in propping up false leadership is the destruction of the harvest. He's terrified of Christ coming to a place of mature expression in believers, and he'll do anything to stop it. I would urge you to take an honest assessment of the present-day church. In nearly 2,000 years of Christianity, we have not only failed to progress from the foundation laid by the apostles in the short years following Pentecost, but we have actually regressed, quite substantially. We could have many impassioned and thought-provoking discussions as to why this has happened, tossing about many theories and contrived explanations. But given the scriptures we've just examined, perhaps we've ignored the very principle that now smacks us in the face:

We've been listening to the wrong leadership.

Right leadership is critical! This is precisely the point of 1 and 2 Samuel, 1 and 2 Chronicles, and 1 and 2 Kings. I fully believe each individual is personally responsible for the choices he makes, but false leadership can drive the well-intended right off a cliff. Instead of following Moses and Joshua into Canaan, we've let Korah and Dathan capture our hearts… and it's little wonder why we continue to delay the coming forth of His bride!

While it's easy to see when others are being led astray, short of a direct revelation from the Lord, it's impossible for me to see the deception in my own life. That's precisely why it's called "deception." We have wrongly believed that we can discern between truth and falsehood by relying upon our own ability to reason, even though Paul clearly teaches that such understanding only comes from the Holy Spirit (1 Corinthians 2:14). Outside of a dependence upon the Lord, we are incapable of true discernment (1 Corinthians 12:10). Our utter reliance upon Him—not just in word but in all things—is the only way we can genuinely avoid deception and recognize the "wolves" that have gained entrance to the sheepfold. This requires humility and a teachable spirit. We've become far too trusting of those claiming to have the call of God on their lives, and we've failed to heed the warnings of John who urges,

> Beloved, do not believe every spirit, but test the spirits, whether they are of God; because many false prophets have gone out into the world,
>
> 1 John 4:1

As a result, anyone capable of giving lip service to Jesus and especially anyone who does so with charisma is readily and foolishly embraced without consulting the One on whose behalf they claim to speak.

Deception comes in various forms, ranging from perverted gospels that have fallen far from the good news proclaimed by the apostles to inconspicuous deviations from the true message and subtle manipulations of scripture serving to divert our focus from the person of the Lord Jesus Christ. Please know that my intention isn't to expose every fallacy that has come down the pike, nor is it to suggest that I somehow have a corner on the market of truth. I do not. I am simply calling the church to return to the right foundation. Nothing other than the unconditional, uncompromising preaching of the person of Jesus Christ and His desire to manifest His life within His people ought to be acceptable to those who claim to know and love Him. And I don't mean just using the correct words. The "foxes" and "thieves" who've gained access to His House often espouse correct doctrinal truths, only to emphasize secondary things, such as your gifts, your ministry, your miracle, your healing, your destiny, your blessing... But know this:

The focus of our faith must never be on the benefits of knowing Jesus: Our eyes must be fully fixed on the Lord Himself.

Likewise, we must never base the message of the kingdom on wealth, success, or easy living. It is imperative that we recognize these temporal things as potentially being deadly idols that all too easily and quickly will capture our hearts and lead us astray from our first love. If only we would return to the simplicity of intimacy with Jesus Christ then the secondary things of this life would be added to us just as He promised (Matthew 6:33). It's imperative that we keep all things in their proper perspective. We must find contentment in knowing that Christ Himself is our eternal reward and not simply a means to gaining some other "blessing" or external reward! He will forever be the object of the bride's affection and eternal devotion.

Sadly, much of what is emanating from the present leadership of the contemporary church is little more than flesh-centered, self-help teaching dressed up in Christian verbiage. The true gospel is nothing if not supernatural. As Christ-followers, we are not called to teach man-made tenets, doctrines, or principles for others to put into practice through their own efforts, strength, and wisdom. That is the essence of religion, and Paul railed against a religious mindset with everything in him (Galatians 1:9-10, Philippians 1:15-17, 1 Corinthians 11:4-5, Galatians 2:11-14). In so doing, he provoked the intense ire and backlash of the pharisaical thieves and foxes of his day.

Instead, we believe in Christ and Him crucified (1 Corinthians 2:2), which goes far beyond His death on the cross. His was a crucified life—a total submission to the will of His Father in every possible way, even when it meant His literal death. We testify—

both in words and in deed—of the fact that He is risen and that He lives in us! We uphold the truth that we are being conformed into His image, meaning His crucified life is growing into a place of prominence within us, impacting our outward behavior. We recognize that, while Jesus had His physical cross, we are meant to bear our own (Luke 9:23), upon which we are being delivered from the self-life by the crucifixion of our flesh. We stand against soulish, self-centered Christianity and embrace the supernatural reality of what has taken place within us: We have exchanged our lives for His! This is what it looks like to be a disciple of Jesus Christ.

Deception is a nasty foe, especially once we've given it a foothold. The most convincing lies, by nature, are subtle and alluring. We need a litmus test on the journey of readiness, and indeed, we do have one: Christ and His crucified life! If the message we have embraced...

- Points to Jesus in all things—not just in words—but truly modeling a love for, obedience to, trust in, and reliance upon Him at the expense of our own gifts, ability, or twisted concept of spirituality...
- Testifies of His eternal life surrounding His eternal purpose, versus a pursuit of the pleasures of a temporal life and an obsession with external circumstances...
- Upholds the denial of self and a "not my will, but yours be done" (Luke 22:42) posture before Him in all things...
- Promotes the crucified life in the believer rather than a life of self-indulgence ...

...then we have the right message. However, anything other than that—anything—is a false gospel.

Meanwhile, the current state of the American church is chaos. We are...

- Embracing a false gospel that has been conflated with the American dream, twisting the words of our Beloved and the writings of the apostles into a get-rich-quick scheme and a "live-your-best-life-now" self-help tool.
- Preaching biblically unsound and dangerous end time eschatology that encourages a belief that things are simply going to get progressively better or that the church will be raptured out before the return of the Lord, thus nullifying the exhortation of Jesus to be made ready for His coming.
- Perverting and obsessing over the gift of prophecy—which is intended to be the testimony of Jesus Christ (Revelation 19:10)—and instead making it the testimony of "me, me, me," always demanding to hear more about "my destiny, my ministry, my prosperity, and my breakthrough.
- Fixating on the miraculous, wrongly believing that signs and wonders will turn an unbelieving world back to God, forgetting the biblical precedents in both the wilderness of Sinai and Israel in the 1st century A.D., proving that such signs will never convince an unbelieving world.
- Slopping man's twisted perspective of grace around casually, forgetting that all of God's attributes are held in perfect tension, including mercy and judgement, kindness and severity, forgiveness and holiness, and grace and discipline.
- Bending over backwards to affirm one another about how good we are and, in doing so, abandoning the foundational, biblical understanding of the total depravity of humanity and our dire need for the "other than" life of Christ to emerge within us.
- Gravitating toward universalism and the unbiblical notion that there are only the "saved" and "not-yet-saved" thereby forsaking the story of the rich man and Lazarus through

which the Lord is shouting a warning to our hearts (Luke 16:19-31).

- Peddling a lifeless and meaningless religious philosophy while going through the motions and giving mental assent to "the teachings of Jesus," without putting any actual faith in Him, thus relegating Him in our own thinking to the realm of dead philosophers and enlightened thinkers.
- Promoting a divisive, humanistic "social justice gospel" that is rooted more in the writings of Karl Marx than in the truth of scripture, thus becoming an extension of American politics while marring the lines between holiness and sin.

We spend millions of dollars annually buying admission to Christian conferences, books written by our favorite mega-church millionaires, music CDs recorded by the latest and greatest "worship bands," t-shirts sporting clever Christian sayings, and "sermon downloads" purporting to "equip the body." As if luring victims into a trap, we offer free doughnuts and styrofoam cups of coffee to accommodate anyone willing to endure our watered down, yet polished, version of the "good news." We conflate worship with entertainment, often dazzling audiences with a clever mix of technology and talent, all in the name of offering "the sacrifice of praise." And who cares if the lyrics to the songs being sung are scripturally sound? We think that the pastor or guest speaker should be "relevant" at all costs, using various forms of media, sprinkling his messages with colorful humor, and repeating memorable catch-phrases to solidify the three points of his sermon, which had better be tied up neatly in 45 minutes, tops! We dangle these carrots in front of the faces of self-proclaimed disciples of Jesus Christ, wrongly believing that if we impress them with our man-made add-ons to the gospel, they'll keep coming back and perhaps one day move on to maturity in the Lord… or at the very least toss a few bucks into the overflowing offering plates as they're passed through the congregations. Then we shake our heads in amazement and wonder how the church has become so immature, so confused, and so worldly.

We are wallowing in confusion, hype, and soulish manipulation and utterly confused as to what, or who, is our message! It is no wonder we are a laughingstock to the world—we are largely promoting the wrong man! While we should be pointing others to Jesus Christ, we are, instead, simply operating out of the unredeemed soul of fallen man.

Dear friend, none of it is working, and I'm concerned that we're actually further away from the Canaan of eternal purpose now than were our church fathers on the day of Pentecost! So many of us in the body of Christ are following the wrong leadership, and the prophesied end-time harvest is being unnecessarily delayed.

If you are...

- Serious about being made ready for the Lord's return...
- Tired of aimlessly wandering around in the wilderness of American Christianity...
- Feel as though you're always busy but never drawing any closer to manifesting His life in your day-to-day living...

Then I urge you: don't walk, run!

Run out of the religious system of the institutionalized church and find a body of believers where the leadership is consistently preaching Christ. If you can't find a gathering like this, then ask the Lord to lead you into a relational fellowship where you can be encouraged in your pursuit of Him. There are voices crying out in the wilderness, compelling the masses to leave the wasteland of religion and come fully into Christ. You may have to search to find them, but they do indeed exist, and they are faithfully pointing the way to Canaan for those who have ears to hear.

Sadly, far too many God-appointed leaders have abandoned their first love. I resolutely believe in the grace of God and His mercy toward all who have breath in their lungs, and I am convinced that—first and foremost—He is calling these individuals back to Him in right relationship. Yet, the system that has been built within the contemporary church doesn't accommodate or reward those who preach the crucified life and the preeminence of Christ. There is a forcible amount of worldly pressure on church leaders to play the game, put rear ends in seats, and ensure there's enough money in the coffers, and if they don't conform, they are ridiculed, scorned, and cast aside. This is because holding fast to the gospel that Paul preached is neither a popular nor a lucrative endeavor. The stone whom the builders rejected and who has become the foundation of the church is not sought after and admired by the masses (Matthew 21:42). Just as the apostles experienced in their day, to truly proclaim Him will result in an onslaught from the religious establishment. God's leadership mantle is not for the weak, the fainthearted, or the easily swayed.

We also have wolves in the sheepfold—the very ones Paul warned us about—and we must be especially aware of these false leaders in this hour. Many are seeking selfish gain, while others are plants of the enemy, intentionally assigned to create confusion in the Lord's house. In either case, these men and women are not in right relationship with God and have no business leading His flock. Please know that I have no desire to incite a witch hunt; that would be the wrong response. I'm simply warning the body of Christ in whatever way He calls me. We must be aware of these jackals, and while the Holy Spirit will expose some of them, many will remain as a test for the hearts of His people. We must ask for discernment in the midst of the battle!

We're coming into a time in which we once again will need the authority and the wisdom of true apostleship, and I sincerely believe the Lord is already raising up "sent ones" who will walk in that role with great authority. These are mostly obscure, unknown believers who haven't sought to build their own kingdoms. Operating under the Lord's cover of hiddenness, they are enduring the process of being tried and proven, and in this refining fire, they're learning to follow the Lamb wherever He leads. At His appointed time, the Lord will provide these men and women with the right platform in front of the right people. However, just as it was with John the Baptizer, this likely will come about in a most unexpected way, on an unexpected stage, at an unanticipated time. Although much of the church will despise them, the Lord will use His sent ones in a mighty way to prepare His bride for her wedding day. Their arrival on the scene will signify the end of man's kingdom as well as his plans for the church, which will provoke the wrath of the false leadership.

My friend, it's crucial that you hear my heart in this. I'm addressing this issue, first, because of the Holy Spirit's direction, and I refuse to make any apologies for my obedience to Him. But I also have a deep burden for the bride of Jesus Christ to become all who He intends for her to be. Far too often, when the Lord confronts His people, it is perceived as criticism or negativity instead of iron sharpening iron (Proverbs 27:17). We have become quite thin-skinned and unable to hear the loving rebuke and correction of the Lord which He offers from a place of undying love. Love never rejoices in iniquity (1 Corinthians 13:4); it confronts it. If you'll allow Him to, He will confront the deception in your own heart. I say that not as someone unfamiliar with His discipline, but as one who is learning to enjoy His correction as well as His sharp rebukes. His words may sting at first, but they are words of eternal life (John 6:68). When He confronts, He is not against you. Quite the contrary, He is zealous for you, and it's in that zeal that He longs to cleanse His temple.

I understand this may seem harsh and difficult to hear, but we must not—we cannot—be too squeamish to heed the Lord's reproof. Many in our day would reject the idea that labels such as "thieves" or "wolves" could possibly apply to any of us who are living under the new covenant. Yet He is the same yesterday, today, and forever (Hebrews 13:8), and His word stands for eternity (Isaiah 40:8). I assure you that the Lord is not pleased with a leadership who has been charged with preparing a bride, yet seems to be stuck wandering in circles in the wilderness. As for those who would seduce her affections away from an undivided devotion to Him, promoting their own agenda in the house of God, I assure you, His anger is kindled against them! We've wrongly promoted the concept that "God's always in a good mood," without understanding His nature as a protector. Paul declared the false leadership of his day to be "enemies of the cross of Christ," (Philippians 3:18) directly under the influence of the Holy Spirit.

I urge you to submit my words to the Lord and ask Him to reveal whatever it is that He wants you to see. Then let your response be one of loving obedience in whatever it is that He's calling you to do. But make no mistake: If the present leadership were capable of preparing the bride of Christ, we would have already wrapped this thing up, living in the millennial reign of Christ on the earth. We would have hastened the Lord's return. We cannot afford to be dishonest with ourselves. It's high time we ditch our own strategies and adopt Heaven's plan to make ready the people of God. God, give us leaders who will preach Christ and Christ alone!

CHAPTER 7

COME OUT OF HER, MY PEOPLE

> Therefore let us go to him outside the camp and bear the reproach he endured. For here we have no lasting city, but we seek the city that is to come.
>
> Hebrews 13:13-14

If foxes and thieves in the vineyard were our only issue, it would be enough to warrant an urgent call to repentance; however, the situation within the church is actually far worse. The enemies of the cross have been allowed free reign for too long and now are not only welcomed and embraced within the fold but vehemently defended by the very sheep who are being led astray. This is precisely what happens when wolves are allowed to shape the culture of the flock. The leaven of deception that has been kneaded into messages and declared from pulpits around the western church has now worked its way through the entire lump (Galatians 5:9). God's eternal purpose has been mostly forsaken and replaced with the whims of man. Called to be the body of Christ to the world, the church has failed. Think of it! A body is meant to carry out the desires of the head. If my arm no longer heeds the instructions of my mind and is therefore not surrendered to my will, I have a serious problem. That is precisely where we stand as a people—no longer tethered to the will of the Master.

The word "church" is somewhat of a vague concept and over the centuries has evolved into a variety of meanings depending on who is using the term and the context within which it is used. The Greek word *ekklesia*—from which our modern English word "church" is derived—literally means an "assembly or congregation of called out ones."[18] While an entire chapter could be devoted to the etymology of the English word and how it deviates from the original Greek, that would require much more detail than necessary for the purpose of this book. I simply want to call us back to the scriptural meaning and the resulting implications. To do so, however, I'd like us to first consider the nature of types and shadows since understanding them can help us gain insight into the assembly God is looking for.

TYPES AND SHADOWS

Paul revealed to Timothy that God, "... dwells in unapproachable light, whom no one has ever seen or can see," (1 Timothy 6:16). The apostle is not merely referencing physical sight here, as the Greek word *horao* is often translated as "perceive, as with spiritual perception.[19]" He is saying that God is not fully knowable to man. Certainly sin had a bearing on our ability to comprehend Him, but Paul is hitting on a much deeper truth. God, in His transcendence, is an "other than" being, and therefore, quite impossible for us to relate to, as we're simply too limited in our ability to grasp His nature! It's akin to light that's far too brilliant for the naked eye to perceive, which is precisely how the apostle describes it. Although it would be easy to gloss over this verse, it presents us with a bit of a profound dilemma, as God's greatest desire is to be in relationship with us. How can the unapproachable God enter into union with a creature that can't even approach His very nature?

In His love for us, God's Son, who is "the exact representation of [the Father's] nature," (Hebrews 1:3 NASB) openly invites us, "Come to Me, all who are weary and burdened, and I will give you rest," (Matthew 11:28). How can this be? What happened between "unapproachable light" and "Come to Me?" The answer ought to be clear: the incarnation of Christ! When Jesus lived on earth as one of us, humanity was allowed to see and relate to what

18 Strong, J. (1890). Strong's exhaustive concordance of the Bible. Abingdon Press.

19 Strong, J. (1890). Strong's exhaustive concordance of the Bible. Abingdon Press.

previously had been obscured from our vision: the nature of the Ancient of Days. In the person of Jesus Christ, we have come to behold what had previously been incomprehensible—God's very life! Because He wrapped Himself in flesh, and then showed us His true character in real life situations, we can say along with John the beloved, "We have seen His glory, glory as of the only Son from the Father, full of grace and truth," (John 1:14). Was John referring to some mystical golden cloud that surrounded Jesus 24/7? No! He was speaking of the glorious life of God that emanated from the Man, Jesus of Nazareth, through a myriad of ways depending on how the Father was leading in the moment (John 5:19).

Up until the arrival of the Son, the nature of God had been somewhat of a mystery, as no man had ever seen Him (John 1:18). One of the beautiful mysteries of the Incarnation of Christ (and there are many!) is that for the first time, mankind gained at least some small semblance of understanding as to the nature of the Father, whom He represented perfectly (John 14:9). Even in an earthly body, God was and is still pure light. But in Jesus that light now has an "external form" (pay attention to this term!) that is discernible to you and me. Holiness now has a name—Jesus Christ the Son of God—who obeyed His Father in all things and at all times, even unto death. Love is no longer a squishy sentiment; it has substance to it thanks to the way Jesus the Man openly and freely gave Himself selflessly to undeserving sinners on Calvary's hill. Peace is personified in the person who stilled the storm with an authority unlike any other and was able to do so as an extension of the inward calm that had Him sound asleep just moments before. Truth walked among us, confronting the foolish and crooked systems of man, easily dismantling the false arguments of even the most well-learned and articulate scholars. Jesus Christ is the full embodiment of the eternal Godhead, and all that God is was revealed in the God-Man.

It was forever the Father's intent to show Himself through the Son. The Incarnation was not merely a contingency plan resulting from the fall. The Father, who is Spirit (John 4:24), always desired that His only begotten Son would represent Him to His people (Hebrews 1:3). This is the only way for humanity to enter into intimate relationship with the God of unapproachable light. Not only that, but the Son also embodies the full plan of God for humanity and is, therefore, the blueprint of His eternal purpose. Jesus Christ is the *huios* Son and the Temple of the Living God (John 2:19), and He is the means by which you and I can realize God's purpose for our existence. Everything that has been spoken of in the Bible revolves around and points to the Son! Jesus wasn't kidding around when He told the religious leaders of Israel that the scriptures testify of Him (John 5:39). In all things, and at all times, the Father is pointing to His beloved Son.

It's way too easy for us to think of the old covenant as pertaining to the Father and the new covenant as highlighting the Son. That type of thinking merely reveals our immaturity. Even the Law,[20] if viewed rightly, speaks of Christ. Paul says as much in his letter to the Galatians: "the Law has become our tutor and our disciplinarian to guide us to Christ, so that we may be justified…" (Galatians 3:24 AMP). Within the Mosaic covenant, there were external forms that were meant to reveal some things about the nature of God: the commandments, the Tabernacle, the Ark of the Covenant, the priesthood, the sacrificial system and the festivals. Each of these communicated spiritual realities that exist in Christ. The Amplified Bible puts it this way:

> Therefore let no one judge you in regard to food and drink or in regard to the observance of a festival or a new moon or a Sabbath day. Such things are only a shadow of what is to

20 "The Law" is used here synonymously with the old covenant, as Paul does in his letter to the Galatians, and not simply in reference to the commandments, the civil laws and/or the ceremonial laws under that Covenant

> come, and they have only symbolic value; but **the substance [the reality of what is foreshadowed] belongs to Christ,**
>
> Colossians 2:16-17

Each of these external forms merely served as copies and shadows of heavenly truths (Hebrews 8:5), all of which are summed up in the one perfect Man—Christ Jesus. The Father's intent for the old covenant, then, was to foreshadow the Son. It was merely a lens through which Christ was meant to come into view.

There were those living under the dispensation of the old covenant who rightly discerned the purpose of the Law: men like Moses, Samuel, David and others, each of whom saw beyond the external forms to the person that was being proclaimed. Though they never laid physical eyes on the Man, Christ Jesus, they saw Him with spiritual eyes. This does not mean they had visions or dreams or spiritual encounters, though they well could have. It does mean, however, that through this covenant, these men saw the coming of the Seed that was promised to Adam in the garden (Genesis 3:15) and again to Abraham on Mt. Moriah (Genesis 22:18). They saw His nature in the very system God had provided as a dim representation of the life of the Son. They responded to Him in faith, recognizing that the very God who dwells in unapproachable light longs to fellowship with His creation, and they gave themselves to the pursuit of Him. They recognized that these external forms were not ends in themselves, but rather glimpses of Messiah, through whom God would transform the inner man.

Others who failed to discern the spiritual nature of the covenant and the relational nature of the God who had established it only saw a set of rules, traditions, practices, forms of worship, and holy days that were to be observed. They had no vision for anything beyond! They bastardized God's law, turning it into a dead, religious system while becoming fixated on doing what was required. They could not see that the God of Creation was giving them a dim preview of His nature through this very system in a desperate desire for relationship with them. They cared little for matters of the heart or their own inward bankruptcy and focused exclusively on behavior modification through pietistic exercise. They exchanged the type and shadow of heavenly things, which was meant to lead them into greater dependence upon Him, for a man-centered system obsessed with propping up the self-life. This is why, when Jesus arrived on the scene, He openly rebuked their ilk declaring,

> You have heard that it was said to those of old, 'You shall not murder'... but I say to you that everyone who is angry with his brother will be liable to judgement,
>
> Matthew 5:21-22

Then regarding lust, He openly challenged them with these words:

> You have heard it said, 'You shall not commit adultery.' But I say to you that everyone who looks at a woman with lustful intent has already committed adultery with her in his heart,
>
> Matthew 5:27-28

He was not imposing a harsher measure of law, but rather pointing to the absurdity of their thinking. They could never deal with the heart of their problem, which was all inward. Only God could... **only He could**... and He would only be allowed to if they sought His help!

God is never satisfied with external appearances. He is focused on the thoughts and intents of the heart (1 Samuel 16:7). He wants to fully possess our inner man and fill us with the life of His Son. He has been communicating this truth to humanity through external forms since the very beginning, and our great struggle is to see beyond the form into the heart of God with spiritual eyes.

As the *ekklesia* of God, the church is an assembly of "called out ones." Called to come out of the very sin and death of "our old lives" (Romans 6:6), we are on a journey similar to our spiritual ancestors, the Israelites. They were called to leave Egypt behind, but as we already know, their journey didn't end when they crossed the Egyptian border and headed into the wilderness of Sinai. It was merely beginning. They were not simply "called out ones," but they were called to the land of Canaan, where God would provide for them a home. In the same manner, the church is ultimately called to a spiritual Land of Promise—God's eternal purpose—which only exists in Christ! That is a spiritual and relational destination, not an external one.

It was in the wilderness that Israel was put to the test (Deuteronomy 8:2), and in that same wilderness, He gave them the external forms of the old covenant. This was not accidental. The wilderness was meant to prepare them for their inheritance of Canaan (Leviticus 20:24), which would be theirs once they learned to obey Him. Bear in mind, these external forms were meant to reveal His nature to their hearts. There were never meant to become dead symbols of religion or works carried out in the strength of their own efforts. They were road signs along the way, pointing to very One who would secure their inheritance. In the same way, our present wilderness experience is meant to prepare us for the Promised Land on our horizon. Yet the danger for us in the present dispensation of the new covenant is precisely the same as it was for Israel. We still tend to gravitate towards external forms rather than locking our spiritual gaze on the inheritance we have in Him in the distance!

A FALSE SYSTEM

Failing to recognize the spiritual nature of this covenant, we've once again fixed our gaze on natural things, appropriating the blessings that are ours in Christ almost exclusively to the temporal realm. What a colossal mistake! It is true that God has promised to meet all of our needs in Christ Jesus (Philippians 4:19), and very often He showers His affection on us in the form of "good gifts" (James 1:17), many of which come to us in the physical realm. But

God is Spirit (John 4:24), and the blessings that are ours in Him are largely spiritual in nature, existing in the "heavenly realms," (Ephesians 1:3 AMP). In fact, David put it this way: "The Lord is the portion of my inheritance, my cup [He is all I need]..." (Psalm 16:5 AMP). What is meant to be a covenant that offers us the Lamb of God as our eternal reward has been twisted into a system of temporal gain and financial prosperity. Like Esau, we have laid down our birthright, which is a relationship with Jesus, for something that immediately satisfies our fleshly appetites (Genesis 25:27-34). We forget that Paul, in the same letter guaranteeing us that God would meet all of our needs, said he'd learned that the secret to living in true prosperity is to be content in all things—a contentment that remained whether he was hungry or well fed, experiencing excess or need (Philippians 4:11-12). This contentment had nothing to do with circumstances or temporal things.

In a similar way, we've exchanged the supernatural mystery of the good news, "which is Christ in you, the hope of glory" (Colossians 1:27), for a set of rules and traditions that have become ends in themselves. Far too often, we teach the scriptures as principles to be acted out in our lives rather than a testimony of the living Christ, and we view His "teachings" as philosophies to be embraced in our day-to-day living rather than heeding His call to lay our very lives down before Him (Matthew 16:24-26). Rather than training the flock how to rest in the strength of the "last Adam" who is "a life-giving Spirit" (1 Corinthians 15:45). we're fostering a reliance upon "the man of dust" (v. 47), and we're sowing death in the form of dead works.

We've also confused our thoughts for His, as well as our ways, forgetting that both His thoughts and His ways are much, much higher than ours. In our confusion, we've wrongly assumed that our plans for our lives are exactly what He wanted all along, embracing the lie that He's for "our best life now." In our pursuit of what seems right to us (Proverbs 14:12), we stand on scriptures that "promise us" our desires, contend with an enemy we believe is simply out to rob us of temporal blessings, and fast for our "breakthrough," all the while failing to yield our will to His and forgetting the biblical truth that we don't even know "what to pray for as we ought," (Romans 8:26). We make our own plans and assume that God will be there help us attain them if and when we need Him, meanwhile Paul reminds us that only those "who are allowing themselves to be led by the Spirit of God are sons of God," (Romans 8:14 AMP).

Perhaps most sadly, we've settled for the outward appearance of spirituality while neglecting the transformation God desires to bring about within us. Our contemporary reinterpretation of grace offers the impression that it's a spiritual "get out of jail free" card that can be played easily and often. We dismiss the need for true repentance, wrongly thinking that God is blind to our unconfessed sin. Holiness has become a dirty word, and those who preach it are labeled "legalists." We no longer see victory over sin as being attainable, despite the admonition of the apostles (Romans 6:12-14, 1 Corinthians 15:34, 1 John 3:6-7), and therefore, we slip into compromise and apathy. We go to church faithfully, put money in the offering plates, sing loudly and passionately when the music starts, and pray often in public, yet inwardly, if we're being honest, we are no more conformed to the image of the Son today than we were five, ten, fifteen or more years ago. We reason that it's OK that we still struggle with lust, still occasionally drink to excess, and still talk to our spouses like they're garbage, because, "Hey… nobody's perfect!" What really matters, or so we've deluded ourselves into thinking, is the devotional we post on social media every day, the pro-life bumper sticker on our car or the loud "Amen!" we've been known to offer when the preacher stirs our emotions on Sundays. We're attracted to the outward, to the horrific neglect of the inward, often measuring the fruitfulness of other ministries through outward signs such as the crowds they attract, the reach of their influence, the charisma of their leader, the quality of "worship music" they produce, or their proliferation of signs and wonders.

But throughout the western church, there is a severe shortage of true disciples.

Does that sound too harsh? Do you honestly believe the church has grown in maturity since the Day of Pentecost? After receiving the Holy Spirit as the Seed of Christ within them, this small gathering in the upper room, went forth in a dramatic and powerful way to shake the world, not because of the signs and wonders that followed them, but because of the life that had taken hold of their hearts. Though they were mostly common, uneducated men, it was evident that they had "been with Jesus," (Acts 4:13). Their greatest concern was making a people ready for the Lord's return, and in the process, they offered their own lives as a drink offering to Him. Holiness, in their view and the Father's, was non-negotiable and not something they approached legalistically. It was, rather, a natural outflow of Christ in them. God's love possessed them—both love for Him and love for those whom He loved—leading them to take on the very nature of the Lamb. Fear was purged from their midst and replaced by the faith of the Son of God as they readily and boldly marched to their deaths for His sake. They understood that what was taking place within them was not a result of man's efforts but a work of the Holy Spirit. Moreover, they lived what they preached, and they preached with their lives! There was no "do as I say, not as I do" mindset among them, but rather, their message was aligned with Paul's declaration: "Imitate me, as I imitate Christ" (1 Corinthians 11:1). Bear in mind, all of this transpired at the birth of the church. Christianity was an infant! And while they were not perfect by any means, His disciples grew in the very readiness message they proclaimed—even when the churches they planted faltered and fell into the deception of false teaching—all because they had met God in the person of Jesus Christ.

A comparison of the church in its infancy with our version of Christianity today leaves much to be desired. We bear little resemblance to our spiritual fathers. We are compromised in our understanding of holiness, confused regarding what is sin and what is not, and clueless as to how to address it. God's love has been conflated with human compassion, and in the process, has been reduced to sentimental goo. Confrontation is perceived as "unchristian" even though the first message given after Pentecost—which was most assuredly received as love by those with "ears to hear"—addressed the crowd as murderers of the living God, compelling them to "Get out while you can; get out of this sick and stupid culture!" (Acts 2:40 The Message). Faith—true faith that doesn't just grasp blindly at a desired outcome but trusts in the person of Christ—is in short supply. Instead, we've chosen to pursue safety and comfort over radical obedience to the voice of the Lord, diligently building our own little kingdoms rather than forsaking all to know Him. We no longer believe that God will do what He has promised to do, which is to conform us to the image of the Son (Romans 8:29). Instead, we're either believing Him for outward things or believing that He needs our help in causing Christ to be formed within us.

Many will resist this cry for course correction as too difficult a message, or perhaps just a threat to the lives they have worked so hard to fashion for themselves, and therefore will reject it. I understand both. It's painful to experience the rain of God's loving judgment as He washes away the false constructs we've pridefully built on the wrong foundation. Our fear of letting go of all that we hold precious may provoke us into a posture of defensiveness. But something much worse than a few rain clouds are headed our way, and we must have the Lord's wisdom to weather the global storm that is fast approaching. Our early church fathers loved not their lives even to the point of death. Yet the contemporary church has become so enamored with all that this transient life offers us that they have created pet doctrines that mischaracterize the gospel as a tool for enriching our personal lives. They preached and lived and labored and wrote with eternity in mind. We, on the other hand, remain bound by the confines of worldliness. Something is amiss, is it not?

Years ago, while pastoring a small church and leading the "worship team," the Lord confronted me about what I had mistakenly referred to as "worship." Having pointed out my hypocrisy for singing songs that I didn't truly mean, He told me to pull music out of our services for a "season of recalibration." One of the songs we frequently sung contained these lyrics: "You are my daily bread, your very word, spoken to me." Later on, the Lord spoke to me again saying, "You sang this song for all those years, but you didn't really mean it. You rarely spent time eating of Me as the Bread of Heaven." In love, He confronted my lack of intimacy with Him and exposed the fact that I equated singing songs about intimacy with intimacy itself. I claimed to come to Him daily just to hear His voice every time I sang this song, yet what was going on behind the scenes was a completely different story. Like a Pharisee, I was boasting of something in a very public way that was not true of me behind closed doors. I was deeply convicted. I repented and began pursuing daily, intimate communion with Him, which has incredibly impacted my inner man.

Please listen... God is not against music, just as He is not against any of the outward forms He has given us. He didn't restrict our church fellowship from praise songs because He is anti-praise. He was lovingly showing us that while the outward form was intended to lead us into a deeper, spiritual reality of Christ's life within, we were simply camping out on the ground of the outward form thinking that His life was in it. But it was not, nor will it ever be. Life is in the person and never the outward forms meant to reveal Him.

We now have a culture that is fixated on outward forms. The institution of the church is madly in love with its messaging, its worship format, its programming, its way of doing ministry, and the idea of reaping material blessings for maintaining the outward forms. But there is a severe lack of Christ in His own body! Like Israel who went before us, we have a become a false system.

OUTSIDE THE CAMP

This is not meant as criticism. Like a doctor seeking an accurate diagnosis for a cancer patient under his care, I am simply trying to have an honest conversation about our present condition. Without facing the truth of our disease, we have no hope of seeking the Lord as our cure and obeying Him as He seeks to deal with the root cause. As the body of Christ and the betrothed of the Lord (2 Corinthians 11:2), we have a choice to make: remain in our current state of confusion, wandering in circles in the wilderness, or make the difficult but necessary journey to Canaan, forsaking all that the wilderness offers.

Paul railed against the outward forms because he well knew there was no life in them. Going so far as to call those who pushed circumcision—the very entrance into the covenant that God had established with Israel—"those who mutilate the flesh" (Philippians 3:2), he urged believers not to be beholden to outward experiences alone but to press into Christ in the inner man where He offers Himself as a life-giving Spirit. The book of Hebrews is dedicated to calling Israel out of a reliance on external types and shadows and onto the ground of the Spirit. In Hebrews 13:9, the writer emphasizes the fact that God's grace is what strengthens our hearts not the adherence to outward forms, which in their case had to do with following dietary laws and "strange teachings."

He goes on to say that, as followers of Christ Jesus, we can eat of something that those who cling to outward forms have no right to partake—Christ, our spiritual food (Luke 6:53). He then drops the hammer, pointing out that the Lord was symbolically crucified "outside the camp," which was a place of rejection, thus leading to the dramatic conclusion: "Therefore, let us go to Him outside the camp and bear the reproach He endured" (Hebrews 13:13). If you truly want Christ—the substance of all that God has been speaking since the beginning of time—you must leave the outward forms behind. In so doing, you will be despised by those who refuse to join you. Just as Israel was in Paul's day, far too many of us are living in the camp of the present religious system and just as fixated on outward things.

Dear friend, please know that I am not telling you to leave your church fellowship. That's neither my heart, nor my place. Only the Lord can do that. What I am saying is that we had best heed the edification of the writer of Hebrews. There is a system we are not meant to be a part of, and its are tentacles are wrapped around the souls of God's people. It clings to outward forms and is in direct conflict with the inward reality of Christ as life. It offers cheap substitutes in place of the joy of true intimacy with Him, much as a drug dealer offers an artificial and short-lived high. But in our attempt to eke satisfaction out of fleshly forms of godliness, we, like Esau, are trading in our eternal inheritance.

Is it so hard to believe that we could follow in the footsteps of Israel and once again turn the things of God into another false system? Do we not see the edification of the scriptures to avoid going the same direction? Do we not understand that we're just as prone to the same foolish religious tendencies as they were? Do we honestly believe that God came to establish another mere system? He absolutely did not. Peter, John, James, and Paul did not "attend church." They were the church. They were called out ones, the *eklessia* of God, who carried more life within them than we've ever witnessed in our modern day "church services." They didn't plan outreaches or program ministries or put on conferences or dance around during concerts led by professional musicians. They didn't sell books or CDs, and they weren't clamoring for notoriety. They were just ordinary men who had been with Jesus… in their hearts. And He kissed them with His presence, which utterly transformed them from within. And through these men who had none of the trappings of modern-day Christianity, God turned the world upside down (Acts 17:6)!

Last year, as I was driving to Atlanta to visit friends, I heard what I call the "audible, internal voice of the Lord." It was inaudible, but there was such a clear impression of the Lord in my spirit that I knew it was Him, and He said to me with great clarity, "My people have hitched themselves to a dead horse called "the church," and it's high time they come out from her!" I immediately thought of Revelation 18:4."Come out of [Babylon], my people, lest you take part in her sins..." The sad reality of the end time church seen in Revelation 18 is that it is fully immersed in a Babylonian culture. Notice that the call isn't, "avoid going into Babylon," but rather a mandate: "Come out!" We must see that the false church system is just another extension of Babylon's reach into the souls of humanity, and as believers, we must have nothing to do with her.

The Lord actually brought to my mind the song, "Goodbye Yellow Brick Road," using it to show me that the present church system is an "Oz," glittering with false promises of maturity and discipleship when what is truly needed is the simplicity of journeying through life in communion with the Lord Jesus in our inner man. Upon hearing this, I did not stop attending a fellowship, nor do I believe this is what the Lord was saying to me. If He tells you to, by all means, do it! I recognized that the false system has ties to my soul. That is to say, I still very much loved my outward forms. But in the wake of that conversation, I am learning to lean into Him more than I ever have in the past, making a very intentional effort to seek true fellowship with Him on a daily basis. I want Him to correct, instruct, rebuke, encourage, and lead me as He desires to. As I've allowed Him to strip the outward things, I have come to know an intimacy I had not previously known possible, and I have experienced more of His life within me than at any other point in my past! The system didn't do that for me, He did!

Here is the truth: the false religious system can never make us ready for Him. It is not designed to. In fact, the danger of the system is that it lulls us to sleep by providing a false sense of security. Only Christ in the inner man can truly dress us in the readiness that He will require of us on our wedding day. Adherence to doctrines, rules, rituals, practices, or external forms of worship never will.

Do you truly desire for the Spirit of God to prepare you as His bride? If so, you must get off the hamster wheel of the false system and come outside the camp to Christ.

CHAPTER 8

A NEW WINESKIN

> Neither is new wine put into old wineskins. If it is, the skins burst and the wine is spilled and the skins are destroyed. But new wine is put into fresh wineskins, and so both are preserved.
>
> Matthew 9:17

We're going to have to make some changes if we want to stop wandering around in circles in the wilderness. Simply upholding status quo Christianity has failed to prepare a corporate bride in nearly 2,000 years of church history. Why not at least consider a new approach? With that said, let's now turn our attention to a necessary paradigm shift that must take place within us, so that we can move on to readiness. This shift is the equivalent of a new wineskin. The new wine that the Lord is offering us is simply incompatible with the wineskins of the past. Just as the disciples were required to leave behind the old wineskin of Judaism to come into a deeper expression of Christ within, so too must we leave behind our old, immature beliefs, concepts, and practices. How? By allowing the Holy Spirit to shift our focus off of ourselves and onto Him.

A TWO-WAY STREET

I was born again when I was just a kid. To be quite honest, I'm not even sure of the date. I must have been somewhere between 11 and 14 years old. I had been to so many church services, conferences, and youth retreats that warned of the horrors of hell that I was terrified at the thought of being confined there for all eternity! So, every chance I got, I responded to an altar call, pledging my life to Jesus afresh and anew just in case I had backslidden since my previous "salvation experience." I remember one particular summer, I "got saved" on at least four different occasions, and each time I vowed that "this one" would somehow be different than the last. I grew so frustrated during this season that one day after school I quietly whispered, "I'm tired of all the guilt and confusion, Lord. Either come in now and make a difference or leave me alone, because I'm not going to keep on praying this prayer every few weeks for the rest of my life!" Perhaps that was not the best way of phrasing it, but it had the effect of driving a much-needed stake into the ground. I didn't question anymore. I just accepted the truth that, whether I felt it or not, He answered my prayer. Regardless, in my very limited understanding of the nature of my relationship with Him, my primary motivation for pledging my life to Him was self-preservation. I simply did not want to go to hell.

Whether hell was a factor in your original response to Jesus or not, it really doesn't matter. For each of us, we came to the Lord at salvation based on what He has done or has promised to do for us. Think of it. He saves us from hell. He forgives us of our sins. He washes the guilt and condemnation away with His blood. He offers us eternal life. He grants us access to the Father. These are very real and powerful benefits of being in covenant with Him and likely had much to do with drawing us into an initial courtship with Him. But whatever the reason, the basis for our attraction to Jesus was how the relationship would benefit us. Thus, our motivation, at least in the beginning, was somewhat self-serving.

Please don't misunderstand me. I am in no way implying that we are necessarily in the wrong for this. It just simply is what it is. In our fallenness, we are egocentric creatures who are always looking to benefit ourselves. And because God so desires relationship with fallen humanity, He's quite confident enough to break into our self-centered little worlds, offering us free gifts to initiate a relationship with us. He is a God of tremendous love and mercy.

He sows where He knows He will not reap a return, and He freely gives to those He knows will never give back. That is His breathtakingly generous nature, and nothing will ever change it. We were not wrong in accepting His gifts. But He never intended for blessings and gifts to remain the point of focus, and He certainly never wanted this covenant relationship that we've entered into to be a one-way street.

One-sided relationships either fail or remain shallow and relatively lifeless, and He did not die on the cross to initiate a shallow, lifeless friendship with us. Quite the opposite, He's looking to go as deep as we will allow Him, and as we do, He stands to gain in the process. While it may seem far-fetched to think that we could offer something to the God of creation, multiple parables speak to this truth. The Parable of the Vineyard in Matthew 21 (which we've been focused on), the Parable of the Sower in Matthew 13, and the Parable of the Talents in Matthew 25 all paint a picture of a God who has invested in us and is expecting a return on that investment. He has planted the Seed of His Son within us, and like any good farmer, He's desiring that Seed to fully develop and bear mature fruit. He stands to gain, and thus also stands to lose, something very precious to Him. And if you're going to yield the return He's looking for, it's almost certainly going to require a necessary change of mindset.

Now let me be clear: As soon as I hint at the idea that God wants something from us, some of us will immediately fall into the trap of thinking "service." That is not at all what I'm talking about. There is absolutely nothing any of us could ever do for the Lord. He has no need. He's completely self-sufficient, and thus, doesn't ask us to do anything for Him. Make no mistake, I'm not denying the truth that He has prepared good works for us to walk in. That is absolutely the case, as we've already made clear! Yet, paradoxically, God doesn't need us to walk in those good works. In love, however, He has invited us into the joy of co-laboring with Him. There is a profound difference between laboring for and with. A misunderstanding of this will lead us into putting the cart before the horse in a most costly way.

A tendency towards doing was vividly displayed in the moments immediately following the fall. Having eaten of the fruit that was off limits to them, Adam and Eve's eyes were opened, and they saw what they had previously been unable to see—their own nakedness. And what was the immediate reaction to their newly discovered predicament? Do something! Make it go away! Fix the problem! And in that moment, religion was born. Yet the fact remained that only God could cover their guilt, which He did through a blood sacrifice—a type and shadow of the Lamb of God.

This demonstrates fallen man's tendencies to try to work his way out of a spiritual bind through his own efforts. We see it clearly in a host of false religions, each adhering to a system of outward works as a means of ascension. Yet this thinking is potentially just as prevalent within the church. A slight deviation from the scriptural truth of co-laboring with God as He both empowers us and leads us can result in a twisting of His invitation into a self-help mechanism.

Intimate love has always been and will always be the basis for our relationship with God. Everything else, including the works He's prepared for us, flows out of that intimacy. Such is the case for any marriage in the natural, or at least it should be. Staying busy doing things for God, or even for your spouse for that matter, is no substitute for the true union God has created us for. Far too many forsake the invitation to intimacy with Jesus for a life of busyness for Him. Remember, our entire purpose is tied up in knowing Him. Works will flow out of that love relationship, but the foundation must always be intimacy.

Clearly, God's concern isn't merely securing us as able-bodied workers. That is not the return He's looking for. He nonetheless stands to gain in His relationship with you. When we were born again, we entered into a covenant with God that is meant to grow into something far beyond an experience of salvific love, which is the love we experienced for Jesus at salvation. It is meant to grow into a mature love, and it will if we'll cooperate with Him in the journey. Mature love beckons us to come off the ground of "what I stand to gain in this relationship" and onto the ground of "what the Lord desires."

Now, let's be clear about some things. God is God, and He doesn't just have love for us; He is love! Man, in his fallen state, is utterly incapable of truly loving anything beyond himself. As a result, this relationship will always be imbalanced since God is the true source of all good things (James 1:17). Love comes from Him, not us (1 John 4:7). Yet His desire is to conform us to the image of the Son. He wants Christ within us in full measure, and He would transform us within so that we begin to take on His nature. This transformation is meant to happen at such a deep level that we come into a place of loving Him with the same love with which He loves us. That is precisely what He stands to gain in us—a heart that will love Him as He has loved us.

MATURE LOVE

Over the years, I have had the joy of counseling several newly engaged couples, and I've advised them each in much the same way:

"When you first begin this journey, the love that you have for one another is an immature expression of love. That's not to demean it in any way or question your love for one another. But having walked this path over the last 25 years, I can tell you there's a much deeper, more mature expression of love down the road. The kind of love I'm speaking of is only forged in the fires of adversity. It is not a feeling or an emotion but a commitment that is borne out over time through personal sacrifice. Your attraction to one another today is largely centered around how the other person makes you feel, or on what they do for you. But over the next several years of your life, that attraction will become less prominent. And if you will allow the Lord to have your marriage, it will give way to a self-less, mature love, which is a much stronger bond than what you presently have. This love will develop through financial difficulties, relational hardships, temptations, health struggles, sleepless nights with sick babies, loss, and other hardships. That's not to paint a negative picture of marriage, and it's certainly not to say there won't be beautiful, fun, and exciting times along the way. There will! But don't go into this covenant with rose-colored glasses and don't be caught off guard by the difficulties that most assuredly will come your way. You must be prepared. They are designed by the Lord to mature your love for one another. How you respond to these situations will determine the strength of your commitment to each other. The nature of this journey requires you to move from a place of being primarily concerned with what the other person does for you to a desire to become something for them. It is the death of self—the cross—that is being offered to you."

I've seen this play out in my own marriage, and I'm confident that it's no different in our eternal relationship with the Lamb of God. Our bridal preparedness for Him requires that we traverse the same pathway to mature love as the Shulamite woman in the Song of Solomon. In this beautiful book—which is given as a type of the bridal intimacy the Lord longs for in His people—she made three key statements which highlight this progression:

1. The first is in chapter 2 where she said of her husband, "**My beloved is mine, and I am his; he grazes among the lilies**," (Song of Solomon 2:16). By this point in their relationship, the couple has weathered the uncertainty of their initial attraction for one another, and their love has been consummated. In her declaration, the bride is expressing her delight in the fact that her bride-groom, for whom she has been longing, is no longer withheld from her. He is now hers. This is a type of salvific love. When we receive Jesus as Savior, He becomes ours, and we rejoice in that fact that He has given Himself to us! As the source of eternal blessings and

promises, there is genuine excitement in knowing that He is ours for all eternity. But there remains a deeper love.

2. In subsequent chapters, Solomon and the Shulamite endure a tumultuous season of separation and trial, which is inevitable in our journey with the Lord. As the honeymoon phase of our post-salvation relationship ends, the trials begin in earnest. They are meant to. The Shulamite emerges on the other side of her trials reunited with her husband and with a deeper appreciation for him. Her emphasis has shifted, as she says of him, "**I am my beloved's, and my beloved is mine; he grazes among the lilies**," (Song of Solomon 6:3). The testing resulted in a measure of maturity, and she's no longer primarily concerned that He is hers, but rather delights in knowing she has become more fully His. This subtle but real distinction concerning her posture towards her bridegroom must become true of us as well. The trials are meant to expose our weaknesses and reveal the One we've put our hope in, who is not bound by any limitations. If we come through them rightly, we gain a knowledge of and appreciation for Him we could not otherwise possess.

3. There remains an even deeper expression of maturity, which is shown in chapter 7 as the bride declares, "**I am my beloved's, and his desire is for me**," (Song of Solomon 7:10). In this place of fully expressed mature love, she is consumed with being Solomon's to the point that she no longer has any selfish claim of possession over him. Her only concern is his desire and how she might satisfy him. Self-centeredness has been rooted out of her, and her greatest desire is to be worthy of Him. This is precisely what a bride "made ready" looks like. She's weathered the trials and the storms of life. She's been battle tested. In the process, her flesh has been crucified, and she's come to know the Lover of her soul in a very deep and powerful way. She's moved well beyond the realm of self-centered love and into an expression of mature love for Jesus. His desire is her only concern.

In chapter 8, we can see that mature love has been "awakened" (v. 4) within the woman as she emerges from the trials of the wilderness wholly leaning on her beloved. Her leaning reveals her total dependence upon Him. There is no longer an independent spirit within her only a willingness to fully submit and trust in her beloved. Her desire is for the person not for the way he makes her feel or the things he does for her. This is the full expression of mature love, and it's this deepest form of love that Christ will produce in His bride.

For that to happen within us, we must first embrace the fact that He longs to move us beyond a Song of Solomon 2:16 love. If we don't—and we're largely not being taught of this reality in the false system—we will not rightly discern the very trials and hardships meant to move us onto the ground of Song of Solomon 7:10 love. Our Beloved has done a great work in us, and He's lavished some beautiful gifts upon us. But there is still much selfishness and soulishness within us, and the soul must be conquered if we are to move beyond an obsession with "my needs, my pain, my desires, my expectations, my disappointments, and my blessings." We are predominantly under the control of the flesh, and the cross is needed to set us free. If we'll give him our "yes" and "amen" as He beckons us onto the ground of maturity, He'll deal with our flesh and transform us into the bride He has created us to be. In the process, we'll discover a mature love—His love—springing up within us, for Him.

This progression of maturity is also evident in the picture of sonship. By nature, a child is quite consumed with himself. As an infant, he is always demanding attention, oblivious to the concerns of others around him. When he's hungry, he cries, regardless of whether or not mom and dad are able to feed him in that instant. The same is true of most everything else in his little world. When he's tired, he cries. When he's wet, he cries. When he poops, he cries. And we certainly don't fault the child for this; we just accept it as part of the journey towards adulthood. As he progresses towards maturity, eventually learning to submit to instruction and discipline, he puts away childish things, becoming less consumed with self and more aware of the needs of others. Like the bride, he is meant to mature in love.

LEARNING TO YIELD

When I was about 11 years old, I had one of my first encounters with the gift of prophecy. I didn't particularly care for my pastor at the time because he was extremely long-winded, and as a growing boy, I resented the fact that he made me wait an unreasonably long time for our Sunday ritual of hitting the buffet at Pizza Inn. Incidentally, this is a prime illustration of selfish immaturity! I resented him even more when he outlasted the buffet's 1:30 pm cutoff time, which seemed to me to happen more than it should have. But on this particular Sunday, he decided that rather than preaching, he would give prophetic words to every person in attendance. *Every One In Attendance.* I was not at all pleased with this decision and was already preparing myself for a Wendy's cheeseburger instead of all-you-can-eat pizza when I realized we were sitting on the front row and were the first family summoned. He briefly prophesied over my parents before grabbing me with both hands by the ears, and in great theatrical fashion, he began to weep. At first, I thought he was just faking it, but soon the Lord hit me too, and I began to tremble and sob from a deep place within. He didn't say much, and to be honest, he didn't really need to. The presence of God was tangible. After a brief word that I don't even remember, be began this simple phrase, "Yield to me, my son! Yield to me!" Each time, the intensity of the Lord's presence strengthened. These words cut into my heart like a dagger, and little 11-year-old me was ripped to pieces. Without the natural understanding, which would come many years later when the Holy Spirit would connect the dots for me, I knew in my spirit that the Lord was marking me for a lifelong journey into true yieldedness before Him.

Looking back, I now view that word in its simplicity as perhaps the most defining prophetic word anyone has ever spoken over me. I have since been on a pilgrimage of discovering what it means to truly yield to Him. I still have much ground to cover and am grateful for the Lord's patience towards me. I'm confident, however, that our readiness process requires an ever-increasing yieldedness of the inner man towards Him. And incidentally, we can appear quite spiritual to others (and even ourselves!) outwardly speaking while remaining inwardly unyielded to Him. I'm living proof of that, having been in a place of active, full-time ministry for a number of years, yet remaining quite stubborn and unteachable in many ways. Good deeds and religious zeal are not the end game in this. If they were, the Pharisees would be married to the Lord. It is a tender heart totally submitted to Him through and through that He desires. This truth runs perpendicular to much of what is emanating from the false system, which would seek to lead us into outward busyness. We need an overhaul in our thinking to truly walk in cooperation with the Holy Spirit and for us to allow Him to bring our love into a place of maturity. That will require intentionality on our part.

We must learn to approach our relationship with Jesus with His desires in mind. My journey of readiness began in earnest a few years back when I began coming before Him in times of prayer asking how I could be a blessing to Him. As simplistic as this may seem, the Lord has absolutely honored my request, and He has begun to usher me into a deeper expression of love for Him.

Until we begin the transition away from self-focus, we'll never be able to fully lean into Him with the intentionality required for full readiness. Because He's after the death of the self-life, a failure to shift the focus off of us and onto Him will lead us to resist the cross and shun His attempts to prepare us for eternity. But once we make that shift, we become teachable, and readiness becomes our priority. In this way, we will be compelled to cooperate with His loving correction and discipline, both of which are necessary for the full expression of mature love.

WAX ON, WAX OFF

Please don't view the message of readiness as another self-help message. If we see it that way, we simply expose the truth that we're more confident in our own ability to produce the fruit He desires than we are capable of trusting Him to bring it about. It's critical that we understand God's role as both the Vinedresser and the Vine. We are merely branches. At the same time, passivity will get us nowhere! We must choose submission to Him in order for Him to produce the fruit He longs for within us. In so choosing, we acknowledge that we belong to Him and are not our own. Such yieldedness requires obedience, leading us to put our choice into action. This is anything but a passive endeavor!

Both a self-help and a passive approach to maturity are ultimately self-centered and fail to recognize the authority and power that God alone possesses. He is not only capable of producing a bumper crop of the sweetest fruit in the universe, He knows just how to release its fragrance in a dark and dying world. Like the natural fruit of the vine, the fruit of the Spirit is at its best in the crushing of flesh. You and I were made not simply to be harvested but to be thrown into God's winepress where the flesh will be trampled underfoot in order that the essence of Christ may come forth in greater measure! We'll talk more about the role of hardship, but for now, know that as we transition away from self-centeredness and into an awareness of His desires, we present ourselves to Him as the wineskin needed to contain this new wine!

Far too many of us are still the main characters in our own gospel story. Sure, we acknowledge Jesus to be the one responsible for our salvation, but we've allowed ourselves to be duped into thinking we can graduate from Christ and move on to bigger and better things. This is why every message I preached for three years at our little fellowship in South Georgia focused on the person of the Lord. The Holy Spirit had convicted me that there is absolutely nothing and no one in any way bigger or better than Him. He is the Alpha and the Omega (Revelation 1:8, 22:13). All things begin and end with Him. There is no higher revelation, no deeper mystery, and no greater blessing. This was not a popular decision, as some suspected me of teaching remedial Christianity, but my motivation was not to win a popularity contest. If it were, then I would have been unfit to be entrusted with His sheep. The fact that we think of Jesus merely as a doorway into a vast and marvelous kingdom that is somehow separate and distinct from Him not only betrays our ignorance but also indicates our self-centeredness. Too often we're seeking to be titillated by the benefits of knowing Him, yet content to sacrifice true intimacy with Him. All that God has promised—whether eternal life or blessings or miracles or healing—"in Christ, they are all answered 'yes,'" (1 Corinthians 1:20 AMP). Did you catch that? Our "yes" is in Christ, and there is no "yes" apart from Him. We receive the blessings and benefits of knowing Him as we come to know Him. If we grow weary of pursuing Him, it only reveals that we've drifted back into a self-centered mindset. Christ is the center of the universe. We are not. We exist for His purposes not for our own.

I'm reminded of the original *Karate Kid*, which will always rank among my all-time favorite movies. If you've seen it, you'll remember that when Mr. Miyagi began teaching karate to the main character of the movie, 17-year-old Daniel Russo, he had a very unorthodox methodology. From Daniel's perspective, he should have been practicing his punching or kicking techniques, but rather than giving him formal karate lessons—which is what Daniel was expecting—Mr. Miyagi required him to do several days of hard labor around his house. Hour after hour, Daniel begrudgingly endured the grind of waxing cars, sanding wood floors and painting both a wooden fence and an entire house! You may know the story well enough to remember that each of these chores were designed to create and reinforce Daniel's muscle memory. Most notable among these tasks was polishing Mr. Miyagi's collection of vintage cars, accompanied by Mr. Miyagi's persistent exhortation: "Wax on, wax off! Wax on, wax off!"

The physical motion required to perform this task readily translated into defensive karate techniques—a fact that was revealed quite suddenly when Mr. Miyagi launched a flurry of punches and kicks at an angry, unsuspecting Daniel! In that moment, the young student realized that his concept of learning had been fatally flawed. He wanted the safety of a classroom. What he got instead was an immersion into Miyagi's brand of karate.

Like Mr. Miyagi, the Holy Spirit doesn't teach in a classroom setting. He has no interest in imparting theories and concepts that we then can apply to our situation as we see fit, and He is even less concerned about teaching us what we think we ought to know. Instead, He plunges His bride into real-life, hands-on learning experiences intended to move us along our pathway to spiritual maturity. However, if we instead choose to cling to our old paradigms of immature love, we will only get so far in the journey before resisting His efforts to train us. Like Daniel, it's far too easy for us to cling to our preconceived ideas regarding what is best for us when the Spirit implements His training regimen. All too often, the false system only reinforces our ignorance, and if we're not careful, we can become hard-hearted, jaded, and even fall into unbelief in the One who labors tirelessly to accomplish His eternal purpose in us. Meanwhile, He is faithfully and lovingly doing what He has been doing since Adam and Eve's fall in Eden: using life challenges as a way of creating spiritual muscle memory of submission to and dependence upon Him even as He exposes and crucifies the flesh! The paradigm of maturing love is the very grid through which we must see every detail of our lives.

There is a method to the madness of the seeming chaos in our lives. In the midst of it all, God is speaking to us of His intent to grow us into maturity. If we could learn to view everything through the lens of His preparing us for eternal purpose, we would experience an acceleration in our journey into readiness.

This is not just another teaching. It is a much-needed paradigm shift. The old wineskin cannot contain the new wine He would release within His people in this hour. Bridal intimacy and *huios* sonship is for the spiritually mature, and the Lord is looking for vessels willing to leave childishness behind. Are you sensing the Holy Spirit stirring your heart over this issue? Are you ready to respond to His call to inward preparation and move on to maturity? If so, ask the Lord to open your eyes as they have never been opened before so that you increasingly become aware of Him and His desires in such a way that changes your thinking and causes you to be the new wineskin He desires. As He does so, He will fill you with a mature love that will have you leaning on your Beloved.

CHAPTER 9

WATCHING

> Truly, truly, I say to you, the Son can do nothing of his own accord, but only what He sees the Father doing.
>
> John 5:19

Sometimes the Lord breaks in and says things so overtly profound that they rattle the windows of our being. Then there are other times when a simple, humble thought carries a quiet depth that must first be unpacked before we are able to comprehend the magnitude of what He's speaking.

Sensing that He wanted to bring greater revelation to the imagery of the watch tower, I continued pressing into Him, asking for clarity. In my spirit, I heard Him ask me, "What does one do in a watchtower?" My immediate response was so obvious, I had trouble believing that it came from Him, but as I followed His lead, He revealed a deeper truth far beyond what I was expecting.

AN EYE FOR THE GENUINE

A watchtower is made for watching—plain and simple. And the most obvious implication, derived from both the parable and the cultural context, is that we must stand guard against the enemies of the vine, the "thieves and foxes." Not only must we remain vigilant to that end, we also need the wisdom and discernment of the Holy Spirit to aid us in our watchfulness.

We have spiritual enemies to contend with that are quite adept at working under the cover of hiddenness, and as we discovered in our consideration of "foxes and thieves" as false leadership, our spiritual foes often resist us through human vessels. Satan is a deceiver who operates almost exclusively from a place of invisibility. He's far too shrewd to do otherwise. His lies would be completely ineffective if we easily recognized him as their source. The more hidden he is, the more easily we fall into the traps he sets for us. It is imperative then for us to maintain a watchful eye and gain understanding as to how he operates.

However, the primary use of the Lord's watchtower is not for watching the *enemy*.

I work for a retail bank, and in doing so, I've learned some things about the importance of discerning the false. Bank tellers, who are trained to detect counterfeit bills, spend no time studying fake money. Instead, they become experts in legitimate currency. They learn the feel of a genuine paper bill, paying attention to its texture and weight. They learn the way it looks, careful to observe the various shades of ink and the proportions of the graphics depicted on each denomination. Even the smell of authentic paper currency is quite distinct from counterfeit money. I've witnessed a seasoned bank teller spot phony money on multiple occasions—once as she was counting a large stack of twenties. While her fingers only touched the forged bill for a fraction of a second, she immediately sensed that something was off.

This should be true of us in the spiritual realm. To think that our time is better spent sniffing out the false and giving all our attention to the enemy would be a colossal mistake. We are obviously called to stand guard against the devil and to resist him when he comes at us, in whatever way he does so. However, our primary purpose is not in pointing out the enemy and exposing the false any more than a bank teller's primary responsibility is in sniffing out counterfeit money. Is it part of our function as disciples of Christ? Yes. But it's not our main purpose. It is imperative that we remember this: our eternal purpose is in a relationship with the Lord.

If we will spend our time getting to know Him, the false will become glaringly evident to us. At the same time, neglecting the genuine opens the door to all types of counterfeits. This has a become a serious problem in the present church environment which places little emphasis on quality time with Jesus. Being with Him is the greatest use of the time we've been given. We must learn to draw near to Jesus, getting to know Him not solely as the one who won our salvation, but truly coming to know Him as a person. We should become familiar with His voice, learning to distinguish "the sound" of it in comparison to the lies of the enemy and the cackling of our souls. We must diligently ask the Holy Spirit to reveal Christ to our hearts and then pay attention as He answers us. As we engage in an intentional pursuit of Him in the day to day, we not only become more discerning, we also find in the process that we are opening ourselves up to Him, granting Him entrance into His vineyard. And this is by design.

God the Father, as we've already established, is the Vinedresser. He has not only sown the Word into our hearts as Seed, but He's also the one who watches over it, bringing it to fruition (Jeremiah 1:12). Only He can bring it to maturity. He waters it. He feeds it. He provides the proper conditions for growth. He will even weed the vineyard. But you are the steward of the vineyard, and as such, whether you're aware of it or not, you control the access to His vineyard. This is how the Vinedresser designed it through the gift of free will. If you want the Creator to tend the Vine that has been planted within you, you must give Him access in your inner man. As we come before Him in love, we are giving Him the admission He requires. If we fail to do so, though He owns the vineyard and has every right to come in whenever He wants, He will honor our choices, even unto His own heartbreak. Likewise, if we choose not to resist Satan in his attempts to get into the vineyard to attack the branch, the Lord will not override our choice. While the sovereign God is both all-knowing and all-powerful, you have been given the authority to override His will for your life. This means that you are the only one capable of stopping Him from causing the Seed of Christ to become a life-giving Vine within you!

Many of us struggle to recognize the role of personal responsibility in true spiritual maturity. A prime example is the misappropriation of Romans 8:28, which may be among the most frequently quoted Bible verses in the contemporary church:

> And we know that for those who love God all things work together for good, for those who are called according to his purpose.

Some believe that since God is working everything out for our good, little to nothing is required of us in the process. Failing to connect the dots between the missed opportunities God provides us with in our day to day lives to respond to His loving instruction, along with a lack of true spiritual fruit, they believe that in the end, everything will come together for their eternal reward. But the scriptures do not support a passive approach to readiness. Romans 8:28 does assure us that God is working in all things. In other words, He's doing His part, but as One who gives the gift of free will, He expects us to steward that responsibility wisely. "From everyone to whom much has been given, much will be required," (Luke 12:48 NRSV). Furthermore, He's working to bring forth His concept of good, not ours. As I've made clear throughout this book, His "good" is His eternal plan and purpose. What that looks like is revealed in Romans 8:29—conforming us to the image of the Son. The Son "humbled Himself by becoming obedient to the point of death…" (Philippians 2:8). Therefore, our willful obedience to Him is paramount in the fulfillment of God's idea of good! Conversely, our failure to cooperate with Him will hijack His attempts to fulfill His eternal purpose insofar as we are concerned.

Isaiah 5 is clear: even the people of God can and will produce wild, sour grapes if our hearts are not postured rightly before Him. Isaiah 5:24 says, "they have rejected the law of the Lord of hosts, and have despised the word of the Holy One of Israel." We may look at this on the surface and think, "but I love both God's law and His word, so I'm in no danger of producing sour grapes!" But what does it truly mean to reject His law, and what does it look like to despise His word? As to the law, Paul says in Galatians, "...the law has become our tutor and our disciplinarian to guide us to Christ..." (Galatians 3:24 AMP). Likewise, the word speaks directly of Christ, Himself (John 1:1, John 5:39). Thus, to reject God's law is to fail to come to the person, and despising the word is a forsaking of the person. Isaiah's edification has everything to do with the fact that the people of God had abandoned their first love and walked away from Him.

A MATTER OF BELIEF

I am discovering that our journey of being made ready is closely linked to the issue of belief. Do we truly believe in the Lord? The immediate, religious answer is "yes!" But to truly believe in Him is to faithfully and consistently acknowledge the following, not just in word but in action...

- That He absolutely will be faithful to watch over His word concerning both His return and the readying of the bride **and fulfill it**.
- That the Vinedresser is capable of producing the fruit of His Son's life in us.
- That He intends on doing just that, **if we'll cooperate with Him!**

As we learn to cooperate, we open the doors of our hearts, allowing Him entrance to His vineyard. If He's present—that is to say, if we're abiding in Him and He in us—He will produce fruit (John 15:5). Therefore, fruitfulness comes down to whether or not the Vinedresser is granted access to His vineyard. If He isn't, it's because of one of two things: either we simply do not want Him there or unbelief has shut Him out. Quite frankly, many simply do not want the Vinedresser in the vineyard, as was the case in Jesus' parable. Those self-centered tenants had their own agenda involving the pursuit of the things they loved. It would be foolish for us to think that because we've entered into salvation we are somehow different from those tenants, when the truth is, unless we've allowed the Lord to deal with our flesh to such a measure that we now desire His agenda for our lives above our own, we will fight to keep Him out. Fruitfulness happens when we assume a "not my will but yours be done" posture before Him.

As to the issue of belief, we need to clarify something. The Greek mindset, which has heavily influenced western culture, sees belief as a function of the mind. That is not how the Lord sees it! Romans 10:10 plainly tells us that it is "with the heart one believes and is justified." Likewise, Hebrews 3:12 says that it is an "evil, unbelieving heart," that can lead us to fall away from God, much as the Israelites did in the wilderness. In our understanding of Christianity, we've been taught that if we acknowledge a creed or a statement of faith, it's akin to belief, but this does not jive with scripture. Mental assent is a function of the soul and has nothing to do with true, biblical belief. Soulish belief is a western concept that disregards actions and only focuses on words and ideas. Biblical belief is centered in the heart and always points back to actions. Jesus addressed this issue in Luke 6 when He said,

> The good person, out of the good treasure in his heart, produces good, and the evil person, out of his evil treasure, produces evil, for out of the abundance of the heart, his mouth speaks. Why do you call me 'Lord, Lord,' and not do what I tell you?
>
> Luke 6:45-16

There is a story of a famous tightrope walker, Charles Blondin, who was known for showcasing his talents 160 feet above Niagara Falls. "The Great Blondin" devised some highly creative ways to make the 1,100-foot, death defying journey from the United States to Canada and back. He crossed on stilts, riding a bicycle, walking backward and even with a sack over his head. He was even known to somersault his way across, and just for fun, he would often dangle from the tightrope from one hand as part of his act. On one occasion, he appealed to the crowd that had gathered by asking, "Who believes I can cross the falls while pushing a man in this wheelbarrow?" The mob went wild with excitement, as men, women and children alike all shouted, "We believe!" But when asked who would volunteer to make the journey with him, no one made a sound[21]. The truth was that, while the throng gave mental assent to the idea of Blondin carrying someone across the Falls safely, not a single person truly believed in him in the truest sense of the word.

This same dynamic existed in Jesus' day, as the multitudes who came to witness Him heal the sick and raise the dead failed to put their belief in Him. In fact, many of those same people later cried out for Him to be crucified (Matthew 27:22). This should give us pause.

Simply believing that Jesus dies on the cross 2,000 years ago is not akin to believing in Him. Salvation is "by grace… through faith," (Ephesians 2:8). "By grace" means it is a work of God extending Himself towards us in love, doing what only He could do. In keeping with the biblical truth that faith without works is dead (James 2:26), "through faith" means we access this free gift through a belief that we acted upon. Such is faith! For salvation, the action is in turning away from our old life, committing ourselves to Jesus, choosing to love and obey Him and receiving His forgiveness. In a similar manner, everything that God offers us comes "by grace through faith." That includes readiness. Only He can bring

21 Author unknown. "A Lesson In Faith – The Charles Blondin Story" Inspire21, 12 Mar 2019, https://inspire21.com/a-lesson-in-faith-the-charles-blondin-story/

it about, but His free gift is accessed by belief **accompanied by an action.**

Actions will always align with true beliefs, meaning they will betray areas of hypocrisy within us where we've simply given lip service to something without truly believing in it. If we have trouble allowing the Vinedresser into the vineyard even though we desire Him to come in, it is because we are struggling with unbelief in our hearts. If we pitch a fit and evict Him from the vineyard when He begins to prune away the dead limbs of our hearts, there is an issue of unbelief. If we're not responding towards Him with increased desire for fellowship despite our circumstances, we are stuck in unbelief. If we're not seeing fruit come forth, I assure you, there's an underlying thread of unbelief to blame. That is not meant as condemnation, but as an appeal for us to recognize how we've hindered Him so that we can repent and grant Him the access needed to make us fruitful. Our unbelief has caused us to lower our expectations concerning discipleship and what it looks like to be a follower of Jesus. We're quite eager to believe things about Him but truly struggle when it comes to fully entrusting ourselves to Him. Yet our unbelief is perpetuating immaturity in the House of God.

Incidentally, belief is a matter of choice, not feeling. Repenting of unbelief simply involves a conscious decision to believe in Him going forward and choosing to trust that He will do what He's promised to. It's simply a matter of "getting into the wheelbarrow." Your soul will most assuredly resist as you choose belief in Jesus. Your emotions and your sense of logic will cast doubt on your decision to trust Him to do what only He can do, just as they would if you jumped into a wheelbarrow 160 feet above Niagara Falls! But you must learn to fight back, living from a place of faith rather than feelings and thoughts. True faithfulness comes in the face of great doubt emanating from the soul.

Christ is the Vine. Only His life within the branch can bear fruit, and it will do just that if we'll believe Him with our hearts and act on that belief. The Father is the Vinedresser. Only He knows how to care for the branches, pruning and training as He sees fit. He will make us capable of bearing more fruit than you ever thought possible if we'll believe in Him and act accordingly. How do we act on such belief? By seeking and remaining in fellowship with Him. He is meant to be our life, so live as if He is more important than every breath of air you take into your lungs. The only open-ended question asked in the Bible is as follows: "When the Son of Man comes, will He find faith on earth?" (Luke 18:8). He will; the readiness of the bride guarantees it. The great open-ended question before you, however, is will He find it in you?

The Apostle John, in referring to many in Jerusalem who witnessed great and powerful miracles of the Lord first-hand, yet remained in unbelief, quotes the prophet Isaiah:

> "Lord, who has believed what he heard from us, and to whom has the arm of the Lord been revealed?"
>
> Therefore they could not believe. For again Isaiah said, "He has blinded their eyes and hardened their heart, lest they see with their eyes, and understand with their heart, and turn, and I would heal them."
>
> John 12:38-40

There is a close connection between tender-heartedness, scriptural belief and spiritual vision. In fact, the old adage applies: Seeing (in a spiritual sense) is believing. They are one and the same. Likewise, hard-heartedness and unbelief equate to spiritual blindness. This is a key point. Until unbelief has been dealt with, you are incapable of being a watchman.

EYES TO SEE

Watchfulness is necessary for cooperation with the Vinedresser. To behold Him is to believe Him, and to believe Him is to fling the gate of the vineyard wide open and allow Him to do what

He does best. We must learn to fix our spiritual gaze on the Lord. Habakkuk put it this way:

> I will stand at my guard post and station myself on the tower; and I will keep watch to see what He will say to me, and what answer I will give [as His spokesman] when I am reproved,"
>
> Habakkuk 2:1 AMP

Notice the wording of this passage. Watching and listening go hand in hand. In other words, my full attention must be on Him so that I can see what He's doing and hear what He's speaking.

Christ must always be the focus, just as the cloud/pillar of fire was for the Israelites (Exodus 13:21). When the cloud moved, they moved with it. That is a physical picture of a spiritual reality. We are meant to have our spiritual eyes opened, beholding the Lord at all times, so that as He moves, we follow Him, and when He speaks, we obey Him. Does this mean I'm just supposed to think about Jesus all the time? No! It's not with the soul that we behold the Lord but with our spirit. It means He must become our heart's one true desire. It is with the heart that one believes, and belief is akin to seeing. We must have hearts that yearn for Him above all else, and we must learn to act on that desire, pursuing Him in all things! Sadly, even within what we call the church, Christ is not our primary pursuit. We've become enthralled with our forms of worship and our messaging and all of the "stuff" of Christianity. We've lost sight of Him, forsaking the mandate of Habakkuk to become His watchman!

Too often, we've only been taught of the need to seek the Lord for big decisions, such as where we are to live, what job to take, who we are to marry, who to vote for, etc. But He wants to go much deeper, solidifying the truth that we are no longer our own but in every way bought with a price (1 Corinthians 6:20). If we've entrusted ourselves to Him for salvation, He has a legal claim on us. We belong to Him. We are a vineyard, and He is the owner! He would use our circumstances to teach us how to yield all things to Him and live as His bondservants (1 Corinthians 7:22), but our failure to behold Him with spiritual vision has kept Him outside His vineyard and us stuck in self-centered living.

Before moving forward, let me demystify what it means to see in the spirit. I used to have trouble grasping this concept. I've known many people who have had direct, spiritual encounters involving visitations of the Lord, interaction with angels, open visions, dreams, and various other experiences, all of which can be genuine spiritual experiences. I've experienced some of these myself. But while these can certainly be valid, they are not necessary for the kind of seeing in the spirit that the Habakkuk passage is exhorting us to. The Lord is not promising supernatural phenomena for His people, but rather, encouraging us to use the spiritual eyes He's given us.

In John 9:39, Jesus said, "For judgment I came into this world, that those who do not see may see, and those who see may become blind." Spiritual sight, then, is a natural function of believing in Him. As three-part beings, we have three sets of eyes. We have physical eyes, which are obvious and require no explanation. We also have the eyes of our souls, which have to do with our minds and emotions—what we "see" through our intellect or through our feelings. Incidentally, what we "see" with soulish eyes may be vastly different than that which we observe with our physical eyes. Let me give you an example:

Last October, I casually mentioned to Heather that I wanted a specific outdoor grill for our deck. She never said a word to me about it, and I never heard her mention anything to our kids. I certainly never went through the house poking about for hidden presents. Those days are long gone. But one day in early December, she asked if she could take my truck to go Christmas shopping. Upon her return, she phoned ahead and asked me to send my son, Isaac, out to "help her unload." When I offered to help, she instructed me to stay indoors away from the garage and any windows to the driveway. In the natural, I had no proof of what I was getting. I never saw a receipt, and I certainly didn't see my present before Christmas morning. But in my soul, I could "see" that grill, loud and clear. Not only did I have a "feeling" in my gut, but simple logic helped me put two and two together, and I had great clarity in my soul concerning that beautiful Christmas grill! Fortunately for me, I've learned how to act surprised when I open a present that's… well… no surprise.

If we've come into a relationship with the Lord, we also have spiritual sight. If the body is conscious of the natural world, and the soul is conscious of self and others, then the spirit is conscious of God. When He makes His home in us, He gives sight to the blind, causing us to have the ability to see Him with spiritual eyes. Seeing in the spirit, then, is the vision necessary to be aware of Him in any given moment. The scriptural edification to walk according to the spirit is simply an exhortation to follow as He leads. We aren't meant to see Him with physical eyes, though He's capable of showing Himself to us that way. At the same time, we aren't meant to see him through our minds or emotions, though He's quite capable of revealing Himself there as well. We are meant to go deeper into spiritual sight, and it is with those eyes that we can behold Him.

In order for us to exercise spiritual vision, there must be a willful choice to disregard what we see in the natural as well as what we think or believe to be true in our souls, trusting the Spirit of God to speak to us as He desires. Let me illustrate using the story I told you in chapter 5 about when the Lord "healed our van" in Hungary.

As you'll recall, our van had a busted radiator and was prone to overheating. We had no money and could not find a mechanic that was able to fix the problem anyway. As the driver of the van, I literally saw, with my physical eyes, the needle on the temperature gauge move beyond the acceptable range indicating that the van was overheated and unable to move forward. In my emotions, I felt as if we were about to be stranded on the highway in a strange place. As I thought rationally, I reasoned that unless we quickly found a nearby garage, it was going to be a long, cold night in the middle of nowhere. My soulish vision left me believing that we must do something quick to fix the problem! But somewhere in the back of the van, somebody was looking through spiritual vision. They saw the Lord and began to lead us in prayer. I could have seen what they saw, but I was too bound up in natural and soulish sight to truly see in faith. If I had, I could have chosen not to rely on physical sight or soulish vision and trust in something much bigger than either—the Lord. That would have been true spiritual vision. As it was, it is just an exhortation not to follow in my footsteps!

When we yield our natural and soulish vision to Him, choosing instead to see with spiritual eyes, we are assuming our rightful place as watchmen unto the Lord.

WALKING ON WATER

Think of Peter on the Sea of Galilee in Matthew 14:22-33. Jesus had sent the disciples ahead of Him to cross over to Gennesaret while he stayed back and spent time with the Father. As they did, they headed straight into a violent storm that beat their boat relentlessly, stretching the normally 2-hour journey into an all-night affair. Somewhere between 3 and 6 am, the disciples looked up and saw someone walking towards them on the water. Needless to say, they were terrified. Believing it to be a ghost, they cried out in fear. Then the Lord spoke to them. Peter's response was, "Lord if it is you, command me to come to you on the water," (v. 28). Now let's press the pause button and talk about this for a bit.

What did Peter see with his natural senses? A fierce storm. Raging wind. Pounding waves. Water everywhere. The boat going nowhere. And to make a horrible situation even worse, an unidentified figure walking on the water towards the boat! What did he see with his soulish eyes? I quite imagine that this seasoned fisherman, who had spent his life on these very waters, saw little reason for hope and had quite exhausted his expertise in fighting the storm. Perhaps hopelessness. Perhaps fear. Perhaps frustration that Jesus hadn't come with them. Perhaps he was trying to figure out a way to beat this storm and get safely ashore as quickly as possible. We don't know for sure, but one thing we do know: he was not entertaining the idea of getting out of the boat and walking the rest of the way! That wasn't logical. When he saw a ghost-like figure walking on the water, it not only scrambled his brains, it sent his emotions into a state of frenzy. He was terrified and cried out in fear.

But that wasn't the end of the story. Something quickened deep within Peter, and he "saw" that the figure was not a ghost after all, but rather the Lord. He beheld Jesus with spiritual vision and to such degree that he was willing to put his belief in the person into action. Do you see here that Peter had to set aside his reliance upon physical and soulish sight? Do you recognize that he had to choose to perceive the Lord through spiritual vision, and if he hadn't, he would have been locked in the confines of the flesh? He exercised spiritual sight and thus opened the door for the Vinedresser to come in and prune.

As Peter beheld Jesus with spiritual sight, he asked Him to command him to come to Him, eager to obey. Being the Lord's watchman is never a passive endeavor. It will demand a response from us. Even in times when the Lord may restrict outward activity—and there are seasons in which the Lord will do just that—there is still a choice set before us. We can continue to do our own thing, or we can obey the voice of the Lord, following the cloud where He would lead us, whether it be into some activity or a place of quiet reflection. Said another way, seeing in the spirit will always lead us to walking according to the Spirit.

For Peter, obedience meant stepping out onto the waves, which he did. But he made a critical mistake. In his obedience, he did not remain in a place of watching. Everything went well for him as long as he kept his gaze on the Lord. But the moment he stopped watching Jesus with spiritual vision, he resorted back to the realm of the flesh—that is, his natural and soulish senses. The scripture tells us that he saw the wind. In other words, he observed the storm, and in observing the storm, it became his new point of focus. No longer was he walking by faith, consumed with the ability of His God. Instead, he became fixated on his circumstances, not only seeing them with physical eyes, but allowing himself to be dominated by the unbelief, fear, and hopelessness associated with soulish vision. Trapped in the flesh, Peter quickly sank.

In exercising spiritual sight, as opposed to relying upon the fleshly vision he was used to depending on, Peter was acknowledging His need for God. Think about it. Peter had trusted in his own wisdom and strength his entire life. Such is the way of the Adamic life. Scripture describes it this way: "In those days there was no king in Israel. Everyone did what was right in his own eyes," (Judges 17:6). That is a principle. When the King is not enthroned in our hearts, we will simply do what seems right according to our fleshly vision. Perhaps for the first time in his life, on the Sea of Galilee, Peter expressed a willingness to put his life in the hands of Jesus, trusting in His strength and wisdom, not his own. This is precisely why he said to Jesus, "Lord, if it is you, command me to come to you on the water," (Matthew 14:28). He knew that if the Son of God would command him to walk on water, He would make sure that Peter didn't sink. Peter's willingness to watch and obey Jesus, then, was an open door for the King of kings to reveal Himself to Peter's inner man. But when he chose to get back into the fleshly realm, the door to his heart was closed once again to the God of creation. In that moment, Satan is operating once again in Peter, attacking the budding faith emanating from the Vine.

Just is it was with Peter, when we look to the Lord with spiritual eyes, we are acknowledging our dependence upon Him. In so doing, we open the door to the Vinedresser and move ourselves into position to receive the sap from the Vine. Just as walking on water is impossible, you and I been commanded to do the impossible: bear the fruit of His life. But we must keep two things in mind: first, we will be judged according to whether we bear the fruit He desires, and second, He is the God of the impossible! We must get out of a natural, fleshly understanding and see the Lord through the eyes of faith. We must come into a Hebrews 4 rest, ceasing from our own labors, trusting fully in the Spirit of God to do what must be done in us. That place of rest is a relationship of intimacy where we behold Him in adoration. It is not a doctrine but an experiential reality, and as long as we abide there, the door to the vineyard is open to the Lord.

Like Peter, you and I are very much prone to slipping backwards into self-reliance even after experiencing the Lord in a very tangible way. There will inevitably be times along the way where we momentarily take our eyes off Him. When you find yourself having sunk back into the flesh, don't fall into the trap of condemnation. Remember, we are learning to cooperate with Him. Let Him teach you, and when you find yourself trusting in the flesh, simply repent and re-engage with the Lord. Get your eyes back on Him as the true Vinedresser. Notice that Jesus never left Peter's side. When the disciple began to sink, all that was needed was a repentant heart. Hopefully for us, as the Lord brings maturity, those moments will become shorter and less frequent.

Many of us have been taught that the story of Peter applies to seeing God do the impossible in outward ways. I remember when I was instructed how to use the spiritual gift of prophecy for the first time, and the one teaching me harkened back to this story by telling me I needed to "get out of the boat" in order to prophesy. But if we apply this story to outward things alone, we will miss the boat entirely, pun intended. The greatest impossibility in your life is not your need for an outward miracle. It is your need to be made ready as a vessel unto the Lord. Only He can dress you in the required wedding garments for your marriage to the Lamb of God. Only He can produce the fruit of His Son in you. Only He can bring the maturity of the *huios* Son within you. He has every intention of doing so. But it demands watchfulness on your part so that the door to the vineyard remains open to Him at all times.

HE MUST INCREASE, WE MUST DECREASE

The journey of readiness is the journey of the cross. It is the experience of "he must increase, but [we] must decrease," (John 3:30). I used to believe, and wrongly so, that when Paul said that the Spirit helps us in our weakness (Romans 8:26), that I was a mix of strengths and weaknesses, meaning I need the Lord in some areas, but remained quite capable of standing on my own two feet in others. It has taken a great work of humility by the Holy Spirit to show me the truth: I am completely weak in every area. I may not have given in to certain temptations, but that has nothing to do with how strong I am. It is simply an indication of how my weaknesses tend to manifest themselves. Paul is saying quite clearly in Romans 8:26 that we don't even know how to pray. Think about that. The man the Lord called to receive the revelation of the gospel of Jesus Christ openly confesses, "guys, look... I don't even know how to pray."

What a remarkable admission of need for the Holy Spirit. And the Spirit, poised and ready, eagerly takes care of that little detail, leading us to pray exactly as He wills us to, so long as we are watchful of Him, leaving the door to the vineyard open! So, the journey of the disciple lies in embracing the fact that he is weak in every way, yet Christ, who is becoming his life, is more than capable! In all things, no matter how big or how small, He would demonstrate Himself as being more than sufficient. There is no other path to readiness than in the emptying of self, and even that can only be accomplished by Him. As long as the self-life is on the throne of our hearts, we will never be a bride unto Him.

Being a watchman of the Lord is an absolute necessity, and we must learn to take our place in the watchtower at all times, whether good, bad, ugly, or monotonous. He is always there, and He is always needed. Our tendency in our immaturity is to think He's only with us in the good times. Through an Americanized understanding of the gospel, we think that outward blessing is a sign of God's favor, while a lack of external blessing is a sign of His displeasure. We've taken the type and shadow of what was conditionally promised to Israel in Deuteronomy 8—which essentially says remember the Lord and you'll be blessed in external ways—as being equally applicable to the church in an outward way. But types and shadows speak of spiritual realities, and Deuteronomy 8 is directly applicable to a spiritually reality in Christ. That doesn't mean that God never blesses us in external ways. He does! It simply means that His priority under the new covenant is not the outward. As long as we remain in a place of watchfulness, the door is open for Him to enter His vineyard and provide an abundance of blessing. That blessing is primarily internal—His life coming to a place of preeminence within us.

His life in us is all the blessing we have ever or will ever truly need. Again, I'm not saying He will never address outward needs. He will. But if we are locked into a soulish understanding of this promise, we will seek to navigate out of the bad and ugly times by way of our doctrinal formulas. Or worse, we may even question the goodness of God. But if we have the right perspective—that is, if we're seeing the Lord with spiritual eyes—we can rightly discern what He's doing, choosing a place of rest and submission to Him, recognizing that He's come into His vineyard to prune away our flesh,. With that perspective, we can keep the door wide open to Him. I have found, and I'm certain the Apostle Paul would agree, that the greatest times of inward transformation come through bad and ugly times. He said it this way:

> For this light, momentary affliction is preparing for us an eternal weight of glory that is beyond all comparison, as we

> look not to the things that are seen but to things that are unseen.
>
> 2 Corinthians 4:17-18

In the bad and the ugly, we very often don't see the Lord because we haven't learned how to look for Him. We quite like our physical sight, and we're very much enthralled with the eyes of our souls. The self-life is self-serving and will always look to avoid pain. It will try to quickly put an end to times of difficulty and will evoke every thought and emotion it deems necessary in the process. Simply asking the Lord to end the trial does not equate to watching Him with spiritual eyes and may well be an indication that we're merely looking for the Lord with soulish eyes. True spiritual sight will lead us into a place of submission where we say to Him, "not my will, but yours be done" (Luke 22:42). If He's willing, the difficulty will be removed, but I am discovering that, much of the time, He is not willing to do so until I have learned all that He wants to teach me in the storm. His internal work of conforming me to the image of the Son is always more important than my physical or soulish comfort. The Vinedresser prunes, and the shears He uses are quite painful. Our great need in those seasons is to watch Him with spiritual sight in the midst of the pain.

Heather and I have learned a simple but effective question that we often exhort one another with. When one of us is immersed in a trial and doesn't appear to be postured as a watchman before the Lord, the other will ask, "What is the Lord doing in all of this?" It is a simple, but powerful reminder of our need to get our eyes back on Him.

This type of spiritual vision is part of the necessary rewiring God wants to bring about in His church in this critical hour. We are almost certainly standing on the precipice of some of the most difficult times the American church has ever seen. Whether we maintain spiritual vision will mean the difference between a failed harvest and a glorious one for our generation. It could also mean the difference between remaining steadfast to Him or falling away entirely. As the Vinedresser approaches with the intent of doing a deep pruning in our hearts, He's doing so for the purpose of a glorious, eternal inheritance—Christ in you in fullness! Don't harden your heart and become bitter or resentful even when you feel the sting of the Vinedresser's shears. Don't sit in the corner and pout because things aren't going the way you thought they would. Ask Him for eyes to see and ears to hear so that the thief might be shut out of the vineyard and the Vinedresser may be left to prune as He sees fit.

It is in the watchmen that the Lord will bring about His end-time harvest, and as they keep their eyes on the Lord, they will be dressed in a garment of readiness.

CHAPTER 10

WAITING

> But those who wait on the Lord shall renew their strength;
> They shall mount up with wings like eagles,
> They shall run and not be weary,
> They shall walk and not faint.
>
> Isaiah 40:31 NKJV

The watchtower is also a place of stillness. In a military context, watchmen are soldiers commissioned to stand guard over bases, encampments, or other strategic locations likely to be targeted by enemy forces. While military imagery might conjure up visions of heroic exploits carried out in battle, we must be grounded in the reality of the watchman's mission. It is, by nature, a long, arduous, uncomfortable grind, steeped in loneliness and long stretches of outward inactivity. While others sleep or take leave of their assigned posts, watchmen take the path of greatest resistance, maintaining the discipline of waiting. This speaks of the necessary sacrifice and endurance that will absolutely be required of us in the pursuit of readiness. It is not a journey that is primarily concerned with happiness or comfort, and yet in the discipline of waiting, He manifests Himself as joy and peace in our inner being, proving Himself worthy of the sacrifice.

The Bible has much to say on the subject of waiting, and perhaps the most readily recognizable passage is Isaiah 40:31 above. There is a direct correlation between the renewed strength in this verse and the life of Christ coming forth within a readied vessel. In other words, His life is the supernatural strength that is being spoken of here. It is a completely "other than" power—the same power that the Holy Spirit spoke of through the prophet Zechariah: "Not by might, nor by power, but by my Spirit, says the Lord of hosts," (Zechariah 4:6). I make that connection simply because the focus of readiness is exactly that—the coming forth of the Lord as life within us. Thus, a lifestyle of waiting upon Him is integral to the process.

IMPATIENCE—THE VIRTUE OF THE FLESH

We don't particularly like the idea of waiting in our modern western culture. We want all that we think we're entitled to, and we want it yesterday. We have the ability to stream any type of entertainment or sporting event on demand, instantaneously google answers to any question that arises, and have food from our favorite restaurants delivered to our doorstep in less than an hour. An insatiable thirst for convenience has led us, as a people, into a realm of impatience that is staggering. And this mentality has greatly influenced the church. In recent years, many have adopted a false instant-readiness message, believing that all the necessary preparation for meeting Jesus face to face happens the moment we're born again. Others believe maturity comes as a result of quick, easy actions, such as attending church, fasting, or studying the scriptures. The truth is, however, that we are on a lifelong journey with the Lord, and the maturity He desires is an ongoing process requiring our constant attention and cooperation.

With that in mind, what does it mean to wait upon the Lord?

The Cambridge dictionary defines the English word "wait" this way: "to allow time to go by, especially while staying in one place without doing very much, until someone comes, until something that you are expecting happens or until you can do something."[22] Such a definition is not only a bit ambiguous, it also conveys a

22 "wait." Dictionary.Cambridge.org. 2022. https://dictionary.cambridge.org/us/dictionary/english/wait (January 11, 2022).

sense of passively enduring the passage of time, without any sense of purpose in doing so. Merriam Webster gives us something a bit more substantive, defining the word this way: "to remain stationary in readiness or expectation."[23] While the latter is a bit clearer, neither definition touches on the notion of purpose. Not so with the Hebrew concept of waiting! The Hebrew word used in Isaiah 40 is far more complex than either of these English definitions. The root word, *qavah*, means "to bind together or collect, as by twisting (like a rope), to gather, look, patiently tarry or wait for."[24] Certainly, the English concept of waiting is included within the Hebrew concept, but there is a complexity and richness to *qavah* that is omitted from our western concept.

One of the hidden heart motivations behind an impatient attitude is a belief that life should revolve around us and our timelines. When I get impatient with others, which I've certainly been known to do, I am merely put out over the fact that they haven't done what I want, when I want it, in the way that I want it done. When I become consumed with an impatient attitude, I feel I not only have a right but a responsibility to let everyone else know how perturbed I have become. That is the very essence of self-centeredness. The flesh does not like to be inconvenienced. As we've already touched on, the Lord has no interest in giving the self-life what it wants. In fact, He means to do the opposite. He will inconvenience the very life out of our flesh, putting it to death, so that He might increase in us. Remember, He must increase, we must decrease. Those two processes are either happening simultaneously, or they aren't happening at all. Christ cannot increase if we won't allow Him to nail the self-life to the cross. So, the Lord takes aim at our self-centeredness. We can expect, then, that we will not get what we want, when we want it, in the way we want it done.

---

23 "wait." Merriam-Webster.com. 2022. https://www.merriam-webster.com/dictionary/wait (January 11, 2022).

24 Strong, J. (1890). Strong's exhaustive concordance of the Bible. Abingdon Press.

Tragically, many believers just accept impatience as a function of their personality without recognizing that it's actually the manifestation of self-indulged flesh. Rather than making excuses for our irritated flesh, we should begin to recognize why it is irritated. Simply put, God is resisting it. In His love, He is seeing to it that the flesh does not get what it wants. Impatience, then, is not merely a personality issue, it is open hostility towards the Lord! In hearing this, don't fall into the trap of condemnation. When we sin, grace abounds more than our sin (Romans 5:20). Simply confess, repent, and ask the Holy Spirit to help you going forward. But we need a new perspective, which is simply that the hand of the Lord is most assuredly involved when we're not getting our way. Recognizing this will help guard against the temper tantrums we're so prone to throwing. I realize that's easier said than done, but we must become committed to seeing our circumstances through a different grid, contending for it in the place of prayer. Like all of our battles, God will do the work, but we must take arms and fight for it.

One of the areas I've struggled with historically when it comes to prayer is that I've often been quick to pray big, bold prayers for the Lord to do something in an outward way, such as a physical healing or a financial miracle. But I've been quite remiss to stand in faith, believing that God will do something extraordinary in my inner man. My hunch is that this is quite a common problem for most believers. If His priority is internal transformation (and it is!), then we must not shrink back from praying and believing for Him to deal with the Goliath of the flesh-life! We need a new approach to spiritual warfare, rightly discerning that, while we do have a dangerous, external spiritual foe to contend with, perhaps our greatest enemy in the body of Christ is our own flesh. It stands diametrically opposed to the purposes of God in the same way that the Philistine giant did in the Valley of Elah (1 Samuel 17). We must allow the Holy Spirit to stir us up, as He did David, so that we run head long into the battle against our own flesh, contending for its conquest. As He does, impatience will be dealt with.

Understand, however, that as long as we have mortal bodies, we will have the flesh to contend with. It will ultimately be put away in fullness when we step through the veil of eternity, but until that time, we will have to stand against it. Paul's edification for us is to "put no confidence in the flesh…" (Philippians 3:3). In other words, stop giving it free reign. Challenge it. Oppose it. Resist it.

It would be foolish to think of ourselves as "getting better," or "becoming more righteous." That is not at all the nature of this battle. Christ is the righteous One, and our righteousness is one hundred percent a function of our being in Him. The flesh is irredeemable and will be present for the remainder of our lifetime. What should be taking place within us is this: the decrease of the flesh, as to its influence in our day to day living, and the increase of Christ, so that His life is being expressed more clearly. This is a lifelong battle, not a quick, easy fix. It demands patience and perseverance, both of which are attributes of His life, which will become more evident the longer we stand firm in Him.

We should be able to see that maturity is not a quick and easy process. It takes time and a whole lot of learning. God cannot be rushed and won't be convinced to do things according to our timetable. This does not mean that we should become passive in waiting for His process to unfold. We have a tremendous responsibility in the journey. As He resists the flesh, we can either take offense and push back, demanding our own way, or we can joyfully yield to Him and cooperate as He directs us. I am finding, however, that when my perspective changes—that is to say, when I begin to see the Lord's hand in keeping me from getting my own way—I am much more prone to cooperating with Him, but if I simply see my circumstances as random occurrences, I'm more likely to react out of the flesh. Bear in mind that you'll experience a lot of trial and error as you learn to cooperate with Him. Ask the Lord to help you not to get impatient with yourself and guard against condemnation in your failures. He's not after perfection in the way we've come to understand it; He's after yieldedness in His people.

Yielding can be quite a tricky thing, can't it? As I write this, Heather and I are in a season where we're teaching our third child how to drive. Abigail has her learner's permit, and a few days ago, while driving down the highway, I asked her what the difference is between a stop sign and a yield sign. Her answer was, "you have to stop at a stop sign, but at a yield sign, you just have to slow down a little bit." And while that may well be how it's often played out, that is not at all what is meant by yielding. In the context of driving, yielding means you have the right of way unless there is oncoming traffic, in which case they have the right of way. For some of us, oncoming traffic is merely an opportunity to hit the gas pedal and outrun any slow pokes who might keep us from our destination a bit longer than we'd prefer, which is just further confirmation of our need for the cross!

True yielding, in the context of our relationship with the Lord, is akin to the traffic law. Solomon wrote in Proverbs 16:9, "The heart of man plans his way, but the Lord establishes his steps." For the believer, that is meant to be a voluntary redirecting, whereby we yield our plans to God and agree to obey Him in whatever way He speaks to us. In other words, I should recognize that God has the right of way as far as my life is concerned. That doesn't mean I shouldn't make plans until He tells me what to do. I am free to plan my own way when I've not heard the Lord. Yet, in executing my plans, I must hold them loosely, allowing Him to redirect me readily and easily along the way. True yielding is stopping along the way, oftentimes repeatedly, asking the Lord to redirect when necessary. It is never an occasion for stepping on the accelerator and moving full speed ahead with no regard for the will of God!

If we're being honest, that's precisely how most of us have grown accustomed to living. From our perspective, our lives are still very much our own, and we choose to pursue what is important to our own flesh in a way that is comparable to stomping on the gas pedal. Then, when we hit a ditch or break down along the way, we cry out to the Lord to help us start moving forward again.

If the Lord's will never included the road we chose to go down, there's a very high probability that He has no interest in moving us forward again along the same path. We must learn to live in a constant state of yieldedness towards Him.

When we're introduced to the concept of yielding to the Lord, the battle often revolves around submitting the major decisions to Him. But as we mature, we'll find that He would require us to yield more and more in the day-to-day living. Even beyond conscious decisions, we must learn to yield to Him at a heart level in the midst of our circumstances. Remember, He will resist our flesh, meaning we will encounter circumstances in which we are not getting our way. In those times, we must learn to allow Him and not put up a fight. This is the necessary stripping of self that must take place within us so that we can become clothed in Christ (Romans 13:14).

BECOMING ENTWINED WITH HIM

Let's circle back to the concept of *qavah* we discussed earlier. The Hebrew idea of waiting communicates much more than what can be seen on the surface. That is to say, while there is an element of enduring of the passage of time, *qavah* touches on what is taking place in the inner man as we learn to yield to God. Yielding to Him implies waiting on Him. Think of the driving analogy. When I yield to oncoming traffic, I'm waiting on others to exercise their right of way. It's the same with the Holy Spirit. As we wait on Him with the right inward posture, we literally become "entwined with Him" in plan and purpose. In other words, as we say "no" to the desires of our own soul and "yes" to the Lord, we become united with Him in a deeper way, choosing His will above our own.

His thoughts, which are higher than ours, can become our thoughts, and the same with His ways. *Qavah* actually implies tension as the definition includes a "binding" and "twisting." Thus, the Lord binds or restrains our will so that we become twisted or entwined with Him in greater measure. Isn't that a beautiful thought—that you and I can be braided together with the Lord at a heart level?

This is precisely what Jesus exemplified in life and testified of in John 5:19 when he said,

> Truly, truly, I say to you, the Son can do nothing of His own accord, but only what He sees the Father doing. For whatever the Father does, that the Son does likewise.

Bear in mind that when the Lord says "nothing," he means just that. Jesus wasn't speaking of just the major things, such as whether or not to go to the cross, but all things. Even He endured the necessary binding of His own will so that He could become entwined with the will of His Father. He submitted to such a degree that nothing He did was outside of the boundaries His Father had set for Him. Our path of readiness will involve the same binding and twisting. I would also point out here that waiting is closely tied to the watchfulness we discussed in the previous chapter, as evidenced in this particular verse. Not only was Jesus' will restrained, he was braided together with the will of His Father according to what He saw in the Father. The two go hand in hand.

Let me illustrate how this can play out in our lives. A few months back, my oldest daughter Emily, who is pursuing a career as a pilot, fell ill to Covid. She had a very rough time for two weeks, and after the infection left, she experienced a prolonged season of secondary symptoms. She developed inflammation in the lining surrounding her heart resulting in recurring chest pains, dizziness, and shortness of breath. Not only was she sidelined in her pursuit of her career, she was given no definite answers as to the long term impact upon her body. To make a bad situation even worse, her taste and smell had deteriorated to the point where eating was no longer enjoyable. She literally had to hold her nose and force food down her throat so that she could give herself some much needed nourishment. It was a painful season for her not just in the natural but primarily in her soul. If you have children of your own, you'll understand that it was just as painful for Heather and me as it was for our daughter. As a family, we prayed daily for her healing.

In our hearts, we longed for a specific outcome. We were not wrong for desiring her healing; in fact, we were quite in line with the scriptures. Yet we did not see the answer coming in the way we wanted or in our timing. We kept praying, but as we did, we submitted to Him, thus becoming entwined with Him at a heart level. This was not an easy process, and we had to encourage one another daily. But we committed ourselves to a "not my will, but yours be done" posture before the Lord.

As the days went by, she began to wonder if her pursuit of aviation was contrary to the Lord's will for her life, so she laid it on the altar. Days turned into weeks, and weeks turned into months—three and a half, to be exact. Looking back, I am amazed at the faith of my daughter as she held on to the Lord, refusing to let go of Him, even though there were moments of vulnerability where her tears revealed just how difficult the process was. Let me clarify. She was holding on to Him, not to an outcome. Our faith must never be in a desired result. A desired result is incapable of saving us, and it is just as incapable of producing life within us. He, on the other hand, is fully able to do both!

During this process, she completely surrendered her plans, as well as her desire to taste again, to the Lord. Shortly thereafter, a friend of mind asked to pray for Emily's healing. Even though we had been praying for her daily, we were eager for another opportunity to ask the Lord to arise within her circumstances. As he prayed, the Lord supernaturally set her free from a demonic assignment against her and completely healed her body! She was instantly set free of the chest pains and shortness of breath, and within days, taste and smell were fully restored. A few nights later, that same friend had a prophetic word for her. While it was much more detailed than what I'm sharing here, the Lord essentially told Emily that He had taken notice of her waiting upon Him throughout this process. As a result, He announced His intent to surprise her with something very specific for which she has long been praying. In addition, the Lord also confirmed that He was in her pursuit of flying, although how that's going to play out, we have no clue.

This is a perfect illustration of what it truly means to wait upon the Lord. Emily did not passively endure the passage of time, insisting on her own will in the process. Even though her desire for healing was in alignment with scripture, she willingly laid it down before Him and quietly but emphatically said to Him, "not my will, but yours be done." The Lord was gathering her up into His purpose and plan for her life, entwining her at a very deep level with Him. This type of thinking doesn't often fit into our doctrines, but it's precisely what God longs for in each of us. This is not the only season of binding and twisting that she'll face. As she journeys forward in the Lord, she'll find this to become more the norm than a seasonal thing. It is the very process of readiness we must endure if we're to be married to Him in eternity.

God takes note of this kind of waiting. In fact, He's quite attracted to it. It opens the door for the increase of the life of Christ within us. I fully believe that the Lord, in His effort to prepare us for an eternity of obedience to Him, will design circumstances that are well beyond our ability to navigate in order to teach us this principle. We don't like to think of God as sending the storms of life upon us, yet it's right in the scriptures. If you don't believe it, just ask Jonah: "But the Lord hurled a great wind upon the sea," (Jonah 1:4). This was done for Jonah's good and not simply to punish him. Through it, God was gathering Jonah into His purpose in a greater measure. In Jonah's case, he still resisted at a heart level, which is included in scripture as a warning to us. We can suffer consequences and not truly yield to the Lord. Don't make that mistake!

This is also what took place in Genesis 32 as Jacob wrestled with the Lord all night. The scripture tells us this:

> when the Man saw that He did not prevail against Jacob, He touched his hip socket, and Jacob's hip was put out of joint as he wrestled with Him.
>
> Genesis 32:25

Jacob, in the strength of his soul, overcame the Lord's resistance, or His restraint. So, the Lord had to trump up the resistance by dislocating Jacob's hip. What an amazing external picture of the inward reality! God will allow the trial and even send it in order to deal with the soul. If we resist the resistance, we'll miss the purpose of the trial. But God has a way of turning up the heat when necessary.

Please let me be clear. Not every adverse circumstance is directly designed by the Lord. We have a real enemy whose twisted, evil desire is to destroy, and he has limited authority in which to operate. Wickedness comes as a result of his design not the Lord's. Yet even when Satan is responsible, the Lord allows it. While there is a clear distinction between the two, ultimately, the Lord would use both types of circumstances—those He has allowed and those He has designed—to entwine us to His purpose.

DO NOT PRAY FOR RAY!

Our problem in the modern, American church, however, is that we've insulated ourselves from God's maturation process by developing doctrines that suggest He no longer deals with us as He did with Jonah and Jacob. We wrongly think that the new covenant means that He's changed His ways. What garbage! He's the same yesterday, today, and forever (Hebrews 13:8). Jesus said that all the scriptures testify of Him (John 5:39), and in the day He spoke it, that was exclusively the 39 books of the Old Testament. God's nature doesn't change under the new covenant. If He resisted the stubborn will of man in the old covenant, He will resist us under the new covenant. Only now He's resisting us from the inside out! Instead of clinging to our doctrines of outward peace and prosperity even when the trials are upon us, we would be much better off if we learned to wait upon the Lord, allowing him to bind our will and twist our lives together with His plan and purpose.

I was taught in my younger years that we should stand in faith on our interpretation of scriptural promises to compel the Lord to act on our behalf. I no longer believe that to be a biblical concept of faith. The scriptures testify of the Lord, and I must stand on Him in all things. Whatever comes my way, let me be found in Him, and let me be entwined with His will and purpose.

When I was in my early thirties, Heather and I were involved with a group of people zealously praying for revival in the small Arizona town where we lived. A friend of one of these prayer warriors had a serious liver disease and was close to death, so we began to pray for this dear man's healing, pulling out all the scriptures pertaining to healing. One morning, in her private prayer time, Heather began to pray for the man by name, and the Lord stopped her cold and spoke clearly to her spirit, "Do NOT pray for Ray, I am calling him home through this sickness." The Lord's directive was not part of our doctrinal formula, but Heather heard with great clarity and knew it was the Lord. To continue praying according to our doctrines would be direct disobedience to Him.

Sure enough, within the week, this precious saint went home to be with the Lord. Now, this is where it gets difficult for most, but when the Lord speaks, to disobey is sin. Period. No ifs, ands or buts. Had we continued asking the Lord for healing, as much as we might be able to make a scriptural case for it, it would have been sin because the Lord had spoken. Disobedience is rebellion no matter how you slice it. This led me to begin to question how many times I had just assumed to know the will of God without ever asking Him. My failure to wait on Him led me time after time to walk in presumption, assuming that God would come onto my ground rather than understanding that I must come onto His.

Let me be clear. I am not making a doctrinal statement on when and how to pray for healing! God is not only able to heal physically, His desire is to do so. Incidentally, all believers will experience healing eventually. The moment we step into eternity, we will no longer be bound by physical ailments. That is a guarantee! By all means, pray for the sick! But in doing so, be teachable to the Lord at all times. If you witness His healing power, rejoice! If you do not, ask Him if He's trying to tell you something and listen to what He says. When He speaks to your heart, hold fast to His Word and let Him braid you together with Himself.

Our problem all too often isn't that we don't have faith for miracles, it's that we're largely looking for the wrong ones. The greatest display of God on the earth is not the miraculous healing of the sick. It is the transformation of the believer who has allowed the Lord to gather him to Himself. This particular display of power has only been glimpsed in part throughout church history, but the bride will be conformed to His image in a measure of fullness that is unprecedented.

THE QUINTESSENTIAL WAITRESS

There is one final component to the concept of waiting that I've not yet mentioned. Like the Lord when He turned water into wine, we've saved the best for last. We used to call the folks that take your order and serve food in restaurants "waiters" and "waitresses." I'm not sure exactly when, but at some point that was apparently considered politically incorrect, and the language has changed. We now refer to them as "servers." I prefer the old-fashioned terminology, as it provides us with yet another brilliant illustration of what the Lord is after in us.

Waiters exist for the sole purpose of serving customers. Again, I am old fashioned, but today's me-centered culture has this backwards, and too many waiters and waitresses act as if paying customers are an inconvenience to them. Yet how we are served when dining out is part of the overall experience. Even if the food is amazing, the level of service can deter us from eating at a particular restaurant again. If that happens often enough, it will negatively impact the business, so waiters have a tremendous amount of power and responsibility. Their position exists **for the sole purpose of meeting the needs of someone else**.

Imagine eating out only to have a waiter make demands on you about what you should order, how it should be prepared, how long you should have to wait for your meal and what expectations you should have as to the quality of the food when it arrives. How terrible would it be to spend your hard-earned money for the pleasure of having someone else insist that you become entwined with their plan for your next meal? Good waiters are those who do everything within their power to make sure that the opposite is true. They are the ones who bend over backwards to accommodate you because they understand that their role is to provide good service.

On Christmas Eve in 2020, I took my family out to celebrate my birthday. When we walked into the restaurant, we were confronted by a less than friendly greeter who informed us that our party of 6 was too big to accommodate because of their Covid restrictions. We tried to reason with her, stating the obvious that we are family, and we willingly accept the risks associated with eating together on a regular basis. Perhaps we like to live dangerously, but it's what we do! She didn't care. She chose to uphold the letter of the law and seated us at two separate tables. When our waitress came onto the scene, she quickly recognized the absurdity of the situation and took matters into her own hands. We soon found ourselves sitting at one table thanks to her initiative of kindness. Throughout the remainder of our evening, she proved to be the quintessential waitress. She was loaded with personality and made the experience fun, playfully joking with us and complimenting each of us in one way or another. She asked what kind of foods we enjoy and made recommendations that ended up being perfectly suited to our tastes. She threw in an appetizer at no cost as a peace offering for the inconvenience of being seated at separate tables. Throughout the night, she maintained a big, bright, infectious smile and made sure we knew that her goal was to help us have a fantastic experience. Over the course of the evening, we discovered that she was the mother of a small child, and here she was, cheerfully waiting on us, in the truest sense of the word, on Christmas Eve. She had restrained her desire to be with loved ones and had become entwined with the purpose of serving us, and she did so willingly and joyfully.

I wonder what would happen if we took the same approach with the Lord? What if we recognized that we are here for Him rather than the opposite? What if we learned to come into His presence as a waiter approaching a customer, truly longing to serve Him in every way? What if the nature of our relationship with Him changed so that, instead of the primary focus being our wants and our needs, it shifted to His desires and our willingness to play our part in the fulfillment of those desires? What if we acknowledged our need to be gathered unto Him in plan and purpose and cooperated with Him in His attempts to bring that about? Isn't it time we lay aside our soulish thinking that has stymied His life in us for far too long?

Jesus told His disciples to wait in the upper room for the baptism of the Holy Spirit. They tarried there for about ten days. Can you imagine waiting for something you've never experienced or even seen, for several days in a row? Think of the tension as their souls faced the temptation to give up after a few hours, and yet the promise of the Lord gripped their hearts. I'm confident that, as they waited, there was a very real preparation taking place within them. They were becoming entwined with the purpose and plan of God and were being primed to receive Him as life in an incredibly powerful way.

I also believe the same could be true of us. As believers, we've already been impregnated with the Seed of Christ and experienced some measure of the maturation of His life. Even so, what might happen if we learned to wait on the Lord in the truest sense of the word, recognizing that we are called to be His waiters? Instead of acting like Pharisees who invited Jesus over for dinner but did not offer to wash his feet (Luke 7:44), what if we got down on our hands and knees and said to him, "Lord, I exist to serve you. How may I wait upon you?" What measure of His life might He then release within us as we position ourselves rightly before Him as loving servants?

I'm not suggesting we lock ourselves in a room for ten days, however, I fear that we've lost the discipline of coming daily into His presence and making ourselves available to Him as any good waiter would do for his customers. It's no wonder that we're in a state of confusion as to what's on His heart, as we've spent so little time seeking it! Intimacy is never one sided, and the deeper we go into the Lord, the less we care about expressing soulish desires and the more we desire to know His heart. The pathway to readiness absolutely demands that we accept our place in this relationship. We exist for His pleasure, and we serve at His command! We have not been hired to work an occasional shift, but rather, we are His bondservants meant to be fully engaged in this relationship at all times. We must heed the message of the watchtower and embrace the long and sometimes lonely path of waiting upon Him.

There is no road to readiness that does not include the discipline of waiting upon Him.

CHAPTER 11

IT'S THE RELATIONSHIP, STUPID!

> I will stand at my guard post and station myself on the tower; And I will keep watch to see what He will say to me, And what answer I will give [as His spokesman] when I am reproved. Then the Lord answered me and said, "write the vision and engrave it plainly on [clay] tablets so that the one who reads it will run.
>
> Habakkuk 2:1-2 AMP

Watching and waiting are critical disciplines necessary for readiness, but let's be clear… they are not ends unto themselves. They are merely tools that facilitate the necessary intimacy with God which brings about our readiness. Remember John 15. Jesus was clear. The Father is the Vinedresser, and the Son is the Vine. We are simply branches. Fruit comes as we abide in Him. I know I'm repeating myself, but repetition is invaluable in countering the false messages that compete with the testimony of Christ which we've been bombarded with over the years. The abiding being spoken of in John 15 is not a doctrinal position. God doesn't deal in the realm of theory but rather in experience. He is after an actual abiding, manifested as an intimate relationship with Him. If we will engage in the divine relationship that He has initiated with us and remain steadfast, maturity will be the end result. We will be made ready, and He will get the fruit He is after.

A MEMORABLE MESSAGE!

One of the most impactful sermons I have ever heard was preached in 1996 when I was a young adult living in Atlanta. I don't remember the name of the guest speaker who had come to

Mount Paran that Sunday, but his message was concise and profound. Using Bill Clinton's 1992 presidential campaign as an illustration, the speaker highlighted the campaign slogan which helped President Clinton win the popular vote, which was: "It's the economy, stupid!"[25] Clinton was running against a relatively popular George H. W. Bush whose only susceptibility was the flailing U.S. economy, which was teetering on the brink of recession. Adopting this slogan with the label "stupid" aimed at himself, Clinton managed to successfully keep the economy as the primary focus during his campaign. It worked, and Clinton won. The speaker then exhorted the congregation to keep our relationship with Jesus as the singular focus of our lives. It's far too easy to get distracted by the cares and pleasures of the world, and it can be just as tricky to navigate the trappings of Christianity. These "rabbits" which we're prone to chasing are the secondary things of the faith such as ministry, blessings, giftings, etc. Yet at the end of the day, true intimacy with Him is all that matters. "It's the relationship, stupid!" he reminded us repeatedly. This simple but profound message stuck with me, and over the years I've often chided myself, "It's the relationship, stupid!"

While I may not know you personally, please know that I love you enough to say the same to you, hoping it doesn't bring offense. Perhaps it will help to know that I certainly don't mean to belittle you in any way. The opposite is true. I love you enough to say something so shocking that it stands a good chance of staying with you, as it has with me. Everything else, as we've already said, is at best secondary and at worst deadly. All the attempts at watching and waiting outside the boundaries of a love relationship with the Lord will do us no good. They will never bring maturity without us

25 I realize it's a bit risky to paint Bill Clinton in a positive light in a book on readiness, and I in no way endorse either the man or his politics. I also acknowledge there were forces far more powerful than a slogan that put him in the White House. The speaker merely was pointing out how this slogan helped to keep Clinton focused, and it was a powerful illustration. For this reason alone, I've referenced this sermon.

being rooted in an actual friendship with Him. They will never, in and of themselves, result in fruit. Only He can produce the fruit of His life, and He does so in those who learn to come to Him, sit at His feet, and learn of Him. So, without further ado, I remind you, "It's the relationship, stupid!"

This is illustrated so poignantly in the account of Jesus teaching in the home of Martha and Mary, two sisters who had a much different response to the presence of the Lord. Martha, the scripture tells us, "...was distracted with much serving," (Luke 10:40), while Mary sat intently at the feet of Jesus. Very much irritated that "the burden" of the work had fallen to her, Martha went to Jesus to complain openly about her sister. Jesus's response to her was both unexpected and clear:

> Martha, Martha, you are anxious and troubled about many things, but one thing is necessary. Mary has chosen the good portion, which will not be taken away from her.
>
> Luke 10:41-42

Evidently, the Lord was not in Martha's busyness. He never asked her to serve Him in the way that she was, and she never thought to yield to Him. Her foot was on the accelerator, and she was serving as she thought best at a neck-breaking speed. Jesus desired relationship with the women, and Martha's concept of "doing things" for Jesus was in no way facilitating the intimacy He desired. To the contrary, it was actually impeding it. Like a waitress presuming to serve food that had not been ordered and doing so in a way that best suited her, Martha failed to wait upon the Lord.

Mary, on the other hand, wanted to be near Jesus, listen to His words of life, and receive all that He would give of Himself. She recognized that the chores would still be there once He had gone, but for the moment, He was all that mattered. Let others see to the trivial concerns that seem so big to them! As for Mary, her place was with Him. She chose the better thing.

THE PERIL OF UNBELIEF

When I heard the "It's the relationship, stupid!" sermon, I was in a phase of my spiritual life known as "first love." Though I grew up in the church and had been "born again" as a boy, my heart hadn't truly been engaged in relationship with Jesus until my final year of college. It was then that the Lord moved me from a place of mental assent into an experiential love that forever changed the trajectory of my life. A painful breakup had triggered some pent-up emotional pain stemming from the loss of my father just before my birth, and I wondered if I would ever experience a lasting relationship. I cried out to the Lord in a desperate desire to know His love, and He showed up in a tangible way that shook me to the core of my being. God was no longer distant; He was with me. His love was no longer a vague concept. It was now the substance that held my life together and defined me. I became addicted to His presence and couldn't get enough of Him, and over the next year and a half, I developed an insatiable hunger for Him. As I pursued Him, He met me daily, and I came to know Him as a person.

But that first love season ended almost as quickly as it began. It wasn't because the Lord abandoned me, though it often felt that way in the months and years that followed. Rather, I wandered away from Him. I still loved Him and never fell away from my faith in Him, but I wasn't as engaged as I had been in that amazing first love season, and I couldn't understand why. I simply stopped sitting at His feet and quit listening to what He had to say. I neglected the pursuit of the person. Ironically, I got busy "serving" Him during this time, which became a substitute for true relationship. Like Martha, I was not choosing the greater thing. This lasted for years.

Eventually I reasoned that first love was only meant to be temporary, and while I continued to be faithful towards the Lord, I did so thinking I would never experience the closeness we had once shared. Finally, in the spring of 2021 (almost 25 years later!), the Lord began to bring back memories of first love in a way that haunted me. I recalled the joy of sitting at His feet and listening to Him speak, not just daily, but even multiple times each day. As I did, a geyser of longing began to spring up from deep within. I wept as if I'd lost the most precious thing I'd ever known, which is precisely what had happened. In that moment, I heard Him calling me back to first love.

A few weeks later, on Father's Day no less, the presence of the Lord came into my truck in a most unexpected way as I was driving to Chattanooga to have lunch with my son. He sovereignly delivered me from something in a most undeniable way, though at the time, I had no idea what it was. I felt a heaviness leave my body, and I trembled uncontrollably in His presence. In the days that followed, I noticed that it was suddenly much easier for me to come into the presence of the Lord, and I heard Him more clearly. Most of all, my heart was engaging in intimacy with Him in a way it had been unable to for a very long time.

A few weeks after being delivered, the Lord approached me and asked if I wanted to know what had taken place in the truck. I immediately said, "yes," and He responded by showing me that I had been delivered from a spirit of unbelief. He went back to the very moment when I had given that spirit legal authority to gain a foothold in my life many years before. I will share the full details as we go, but I will say now that I had misinterpreted some painful events that the Lord had allowed. As a result, I hardened my heart towards Him and fell into the very same trap that the Israelites in the wilderness did. The writer of Hebrews writes, "Today, if you hear his voice, do not harden your hearts as in the rebellion," (Hebrews 3:8). He continues on, "Take care, brothers, lest there be in any of you an evil, unbelieving heart leading you to fall away from the living God," (v.12). A hardened heart is an unbelieving heart, and while I did not abandon Him entirely as some did in the wilderness, there was certainly a presence of unbelief that overshadowed my relationship with Him. Because of this, I was unable to enter into the rest of sitting at His feet, feasting upon the Bread of life.

Belief, as we demonstrated earlier, is a function of the heart not the mind. It is the heart that must be engaged in this relationship, and so, it is with the heart that we must believe. Likewise, when we give way to unbelief, it is the heart that becomes sick, and unbelief is an opening for the demonic. The good news is that the Lord is our strong Deliverer (Psalm 18:2), and He's more than capable of freeing us from demonic entanglements. We simply have to repent of our unbelief, ask Him to deliver us, and choose to believe in Him. I want to point out the fact that, while my mind was fully convinced that I believed in the Lord, my heart knew better. Thankfully, the Lord sovereignly set me free. Since that time, I've been rediscovering the joy of first love.

It's the relationship, stupid! And for us to engage in the intimacy He desires, we must have a believing heart. Our minds will always be susceptible to occasionally wavering and so will our emotions. Nevertheless, we must learn to quiet the noise of our soul, choosing belief even when our souls would argue against it. David says, "I have calmed and quieted my soul, like a weaned child with its mother; like a weaned child is my soul within me," (Psalm 131:2). You and I must learn to do the same. The clamoring of the soul will eventually lead us into unbelief and inhibit intimacy with Him.

The soul is largely unconquered ground and is in no position to lead the way to the feet of Jesus. It is the heart that longs to believe, and if we can learn to submit to the Spirit of God, we can choose to walk in a belief that promotes fellowship with the Lord. If the heart is sick and bound by unbelief, it is quite easy to look to the soul for help. But belief is a function of the heart not the soul. At best, the soul simply counterfeits true belief in the form of mental assent and feelings. A feeling of belief will easily be undermined at the first sign of adversity, and mental assent will always lead to hypocrisy. Remember the Great Blondin! If we're not regularly climbing into the wheelbarrow of intimacy with the Lord, allowing Him the permission to carry us across whatever tightrope He has in mind, there is a good chance that unbelief is the culprit. And make no mistake: coming to Jesus out of desire for relationship involves risk in a multitude of ways. What if I don't hear Him clearly? What if He says nothing at all? What if He says something that's not very pleasant? What if He requires something of me? These are all legitimate questions and ones that reflect the risky nature of intimacy. But if we're willing to face those risks, we'll soon discover that the reward of knowing Him is far greater.

Please remember that belief is meant to be in the person not in an outcome. My faith is misplaced if it's in a desired answer to prayer. It is meant to be placed in the Son of God. That's not to suggest that I don't pray for specific needs as the Lord would lead me to. I do! It is to say, however, that I hold all things loosely before Him, much as Shadrach, Meshach, and Abednego did. Remember their story? When faced with the punishment of the furnace because they refused to worship the graven image, they told the king with great confidence,

> Our God whom we serve is able to deliver us from the burning fiery furnace, and He will deliver us out of your hand, O king. But if not, be it known to you, O king, that we will not serve your gods or worship the golden image that you have set up.
>
> Daniel 3:17-18

In other words, God is able to do what I'm asking, and I choose to believe in Him. If He doesn't save us, I still won't stop believing in Him! This is the faith that pleases the Lord. It is not placed in a secondary thing but in Him.

We must learn to come to Him just for the sake of being with the One we love. We should not be looking for or expecting supernatural experiences, heavenly encounters, visions, blessings, gifts, signs and wonders, or any other "thing." We should just be like

Mary who only wanted to sit at His feet and listen to all He had to say. It's the relationship, stupid! And our role is simply to believe it's available to us and seize it!

SHUT UP AND LISTEN!

Most of us have been taught a form of prayer that involves little to no relationship. In fact, many of us spend way more time talking to the Lord than we do listening to Him. Imagine if you approached your marriage in that way. How much intimacy would you share with your spouse if you were always the one doing the talking? How much love would be shared if you always had to be in control of the conversation? My year and a half experience with first love intimacy with Jesus was so incredible not because I showed up in the secret place with a list of things to talk about but because I learned to come before Him with an expectation that He would speak to me. And He did. Often. That doesn't mean that I never said anything to Him. I did. I shared my heart with Him. I spoke words of praise to Him, acknowledging His goodness, extolling His character, and thanking Him for all that He is and all that He's done. I learned to talk to Him about my day, sharing the specifics as if talking to a friend. In that way, I made myself more accessible to Him, inviting Him into the nitty gritty details of my life. At times, I asked for things, and at other times, I asked Him questions. But in all of this, I took the time to listen to what He would say in return. Without dialogue, we cannot truly experience relationship.

Moses tells us, "Man does not live by bread alone, but man lives by every word that comes from the mouth of the Lord," (Deuteronomy 8:3). If anyone understood this to be true, it was Moses. He once spent 40 days on a mountain without food or water, simply sitting in the presence of the Almighty listening to Him. Scientifically, that is an impossibility—like walking on water—but not for God. He sustained Moses through the words He spoke. I'm confident that each of us acknowledges this truth in our minds, but how many of us act on that belief? Do we recognize, at a heart level, that just as the body requires food, our true need is to hear words of God, "which are spirit and life" (John 6:63)? Do we come to Him daily, not just to mumble a few quick words and ask for "some stuff" but to hear what He has to say?

It's the relationship, stupid! And without it, we will never be ready to meet Him face to face. I believe it's way past time for some brutal honesty in the church. If we're stuck in a false system mentality, we'll be quite content running around serving busily as Martha did, doing a bunch of stuff all the while missing out on the better thing.

"Man, Ben! You sure hate works!"

No, I don't. I've just found that sitting with Jesus is far better than my running about acting like a waiter who refuses to take an order. When He wants something, those at His feet will be the first to hear and respond. Look at Martha's troubled and anxious state. There was clearly no life in her busyness. Life is in the Living Word, Who is a person. When He speaks, He gives of His life. How can we have true life growing within us if we're not taking the time to listen to all that He speaks?

"Yeah, yeah… intimacy. Got it. But we've got work to do! Didn't you read the Great Commission?"

But have you read the great commandment? "You shall love the Lord your God with all your heart and with all your soul and with all your mind," (Matthew 22:37)? If we do the stuff but don't have a relationship, where does that get us? (See Matthew 7 and the workers of lawlessness. See also 1 Corinthians 13 and the noisy gongs.) A quick survey of our lives should tell us all that we need to know. Who is seen in you as you go about your day? Is the patience of Christ coming through when you're running late for work? Is the joy of the Lord your strength when you've gone without sleep the night before? Are the kindness and humility of Jesus your defense when you've been falsely accused? Is love your response when you've been treated maliciously by one who's betrayed you? If you don't like the answers to these questions, more "busy serving" is not what is required. Time in His presence is.

"Well, that's harsh. You should be more loving."

I love you enough to tell you that you have no business serving Him outwardly when you repeatedly refuse to come and sit in His presence in a place of true intimacy. Mary chose the better thing, not because she was anti-service but because she understood her place. I fear we do not! The waiter exists for the one being served, and Jesus is not our waiter! We are His! Why is it such a stretch to suggest that we should ask the Lord before going about serving Him? Why is there such resistance, perhaps even now, within your own soul as you read this? What are you afraid of? Are you afraid that you won't hear His voice? Is your faith in Him, or is it in your own ability to hear? Are you afraid that you will hear but you won't like what He says? Is your faith in Him or in all the ways you think you measure up, in your present condition? Are you afraid He'll take away your ministry? Is your faith in Him, or in some calling you hold more dearly? Are you afraid that He'll lead you down a path you'd rather not go down? Is your faith in Him, or is it in your own ability to remain in control? Are you afraid that He doesn't need you? I have news for you. He doesn't. But He loves you! And His desire is for you to sit at His feet and learn of Him.

"But we have the scriptures! They are full of commands for action!"

Don't look now, but you're making the same argument as the Pharisees. They didn't need God telling them what He wanted of them. They had the law and the prophets, and they were quite comfortable interpreting those writings as they saw fit, and in the process, they completely missed the boat. And yet, like Martha, they looked quite good on the outside, always running around "serving" in the way they understood, never stopping to ask God what He wanted. The scriptures are a living, breathing testimony of Jesus. To approach them without listening to the Holy Spirit will always lead us into reckless, fruitless activity. I'm not suggesting that we throw out the Bible. To the contrary, we need the written word of God! But if we foolishly think we can understand them apart from a relationship with Him, we are deceived. The written word is all about the person, and we should always approach it from a desire to know Jesus. Inevitably, He will lead us into missional assignments as He sees fit, but service always flows out of intimacy—never the opposite. Fleshly service only leads to more service. It will never usher us into greater fellowship with Him.

In all my years in the church, I've heard countless sermons and teachings, participated in numerous Bible studies, classes, and conferences, and participated in more outreaches than I care to remember. They all placed "doing stuff for God" as the primary focus. Not once have I ever had someone teach me how to foster relationship with Him. Not once. And yet relationship with Him is the primary goal! It's the relationship, stupid! What is wrong with this picture? Is it not at least remotely possible that we have not only put the horse behind the cart, we may well have unhitched it and shot it in the head? We must get back to basics!

Forget the church building and the programs, the worship services and the praise sessions, the Bible studies, radio programs, and the livestreams for just a second. We were tasked with the simplicity of knowing Him. Somewhere along the way, we lost our way! And if we're ever going to be made ready for eternity, we must not skip this foundational truth. It's the relationship, stupid! The whole purpose of God in creating us in the first place is precisely that!

A PRACTICAL APPROACH

What I'm about to share with you I did not receive directly from the Lord but indirectly through someone else's writings. I felt led to share this with you as I have both received and put into practice these disciplines in a way that has helped reawaken a hunger for His voice within my heart. If you want to take a deep dive into the following principles, you can find them in the book *Four Keys to Hearing God's Voice* by Mark and Patti Virkler. These disciplines, which I reference below, are taken directly from his book.[26]

I'm sharing specifically because so few of us have ever truly been taught how to hear the voice of God for ourselves, and these keys are fantastic tools for learning. As with most of what I have discussed in this book, they should not be used as a formula. Instead, they are merely tools for learning how to cultivate intimacy with God. As you learn to hear His voice with greater regularity and clarity, don't be bound by these steps. It's a relationship, stupid! The Holy Spirit will inevitably lead you into spontaneous times of fellowship with Him, so don't revert back to a four step method. This is merely a beginning point for those who've never been taught the basics.

I would remind you of Habakkuk 2:1-2, which we discussed earlier.

> The prophet says, "I will take my stand at my watchpost and station myself on the tower, and look out to see what he will say to me, and what I will answer concerning my complaint. And the Lord answered me: 'Write the vision; make it plain on tablets, so he may run who reads it.'"

There are 4 disciplines revealed in this passage which can help us hear the Lord on a daily basis.

---

26 Virkler, Mark & Patti (2010). *Four Keys to Hearing God's Voice.* Destiny Image Publishers, Inc.

KEY #1—STILLNESS

"I WILL TAKE MY STAND AT MY WATCHPOST AND STATION MYSELF ON THE TOWER..."

We must learn to be still before the Lord. Notice the mention of the watchtower. Think back to our discussion on watching and waiting. If you want to hear what the Lord has to say, you must still your soul and come before Him in the Spirit. As David quieted his own soul like a weaned child, you must learn to do the same. You have the authority to choose to do just that, and as you seek the Lord, tell your soul to shut up! The unregenerate mind is hostile to God, so it's okay to give some hostility back to it! The soul has no place making noise when you're trying to hear the Lord in your spirit. As you come before Him, say to your soul, "Shut up, mind! Shut up, feelings! This is not the time for you to speak! You be silent until I've heard all that the Lord has to say to me."

This key is much like the waiting we have already spoken of. It is the very process of denying the soul and learning to focus intently on the Lord's desires. We come before Him to minister to Him, seeking to hear His voice and desiring to obey all that He commands. It is not a "hurry up and wait" process. It may take time to get into the Spirit, particularly if you've been operating out of the soul for most of your day. Don't rush. Carve out enough time to prepare yourself to enter into His presence and allow Him to say all that He wants to say to you. You may even spend some time choosing to becoming aware of Him in your spirit, which may well lead you into a time of thanksgiving and praise. The Psalms can be incredibly helpful to us. They were given to us as prayers and songs of praise to the Lord. Praying through them can engage us spiritually with the Lord.

KEY #2—FIX YOUR EYES ON JESUS

"...AND LOOK OUT..."

The second key is watching Him. Again, since we've discussed the watching dynamic at length, there is not much need for further explanation. Silencing the soul—waiting upon Him—is only part of the equation. You must exercise your spiritual vision, intently looking towards the Lord. As we lock our spiritual gaze upon Jesus, we desire to "see" what He's speaking. Ask the Lord to bring clarity of sight and keep you from deception. It's helpful to take authority over the enemy, asking the Lord to keep him out of the equation. He is a deceiver, and he would love to provide counterfeit revelation that leads away from the Lord.

We must learn to consistently choose not to depend on the eyes of the soul. Remember, this is a discipline, and your soul likely isn't very good at following orders, since it's been in the pilot seat for most of your life. It's likely to try to interject. When it does, don't fall into condemnation and thoughts of despair. Those are weapons of the enemy. Simply rise up and take authority over your soul again. I don't care if you have to do it 15 times in a 30-minute meeting with the Lord. As often as it takes for your spirit to emerge and the soul to be subdued, take your place of authority and assert your will over the flesh.

Bear in mind, spiritual vision isn't necessarily extra-ordinary. In other words, don't look for visions or angelic visitations or some sort of supernatural manifestation. Your spirit is simply in need of focusing on the Lord, listening to all He has to say. I find it helpful to use the scriptures as an anchor to keep me grounded in the testimony of Jesus. I will often read through them until the Holy Spirit highlights something to my spirit. As He does, I often put down my Bible and meditate on His Word (Psalm 1:2), making His Word my own, praying through it. I have found this to quickly open my ears so that I can then begin to hear what He has to say.

KEY #3—SPONTANEITY

"...TO SEE WHAT HE WILL SAY TO ME..."

The third key is spontaneity. Now that we've entered into stillness with eyes and ears that are fully engaged and open, it's time to listen. We must never come before the Lord with expectations of what we want Him to say. If we do, the soul will most assuredly hijack the conversation. Instead, we must be prepared to hear whatever is on His heart. Relinquish any impulse to dictate the conversation. God cannot be manipulated. While there are certainly times for us to have a conversation with Him, the purpose of going through this discipline is to teach me how to hear Him consistently. For that reason, I would encourage you to concentrate on listening during this time. I am finding that if I'll do that He'll direct the conversation onto His ground, and I'll know how and when to respond in a way that's pleasing to Him.

In His interaction with the Samaritan woman at the well, Jesus offered living water to her, revealing that it would, "...become in him a spring of water welling up to eternal life," (John 4:14). There is a flow of the Holy Spirit that is neither forced nor planned. Hearing the voice of the Lord requires that we tap into that flow. As we ask Him to restrain the enemy and choose to silence our souls, fixing our gaze on Him, we are now on safe ground to listen to the spontaneous impressions, impulses, thoughts and pictures that He would speak to us with. By faith, we must trust that He will speak when given the opportunity. As He does so, go with it. Believe that what you're "hearing" is Him, and trust Him to lead you and to teach and correct you when you get it wrong. Don't be afraid of failure. Think of a toddler learning how to walk. If a fear of falling holds us back, we'll never learn to walk in the maturity of hearing Him on a regular basis!

KEY #4—JOURNALING

"AND THE LORD ANSWERED ME: 'WRITE THE VISION; MAKE IT PLAIN ON TABLETS...'"

As those thoughts, impressions, impulses, and pictures come, write them down. Write them down! Write them down! I can't stress this key enough. As the Lord speaks, just write. Don't think about what He's saying. Don't try to make it seem more "reasonable" to your mind or more applicable to your present situation. Don't attempt to interpret or even understand for that matter. Just follow Him where He leads. Stay spontaneous and simply act as a scribe while He speaks. Write down what you're hearing without judging it, studying it, or dissecting it. That time will come later. For now, just write. And don't stop writing until He stops speaking. If you have a question, ask it, but don't be rude and interrupt Him. As you ask, write down your question along with His response. Remember, it's the relationship, stupid! And that is a two-way street.

Once you've gone through the process, submit what you've written first and foremost to the written word. Nothing God ever speaks to your heart will violate the scriptures, so if you've heard something contradictory to the Bible—any of it—it's not the Lord! If that happens, don't get frustrated. You are learning! Remember, this is a discipline. The more you do it, the better you'll become at it. Next, submit what you've written to one or two people that you trust to help you gain confidence in the Lord. Ask them for discernment in determining if what you heard is from the Lord. These should be proven, spiritually mature friends who have an interest in helping you learn to hear the voice of the Lord with confidence. Their role isn't to nitpick your grammar or your writing style, but rather to prayerfully exercise discernment. As you do this, you'll find yourself becoming more assured of His willingness to speak, as well as His ability to open your spiritual ears.

You may start out hearing things you already know. That's OK. You have to start somewhere, and the Lord would encourage you in the process. The more you progress, however, the more I'm certain that He will begin to address some things that need to be dealt with in you. Maybe it's a sin issue or a need for deliverance. Maybe it's an area that's not submitted to Him or an area where you're currently demonstrating a need for discipline. The beauty of journaling is that you have a written record that you can refer back to as a point of prayer going forward. If we learn to come before Him in this way—listening to His heart and then praying according to what He has shared—I assure you, we will begin to progress down the path of readiness at a much greater pace than we've ever known.

As we close this most unusual chapter, let me just end by saying this. It's the relationship, stupid! And don't you forget it.

CHAPTER 12

THE DIFFICULT WAY

> Because narrow is the gate and difficult is the way which leads to life, and there are few who find it.
>
> Matthew 7:14 NKJV

As I've allowed the Lord to teach me in the process of writing this book, I've come to see watching and waiting as the means by which we open the door of the vineyard to the Vinedresser. As He comes in, we have opportunity for intimate fellowship with Him. It is not a religious exercise akin to saying a quick prayer, going to church, or reading your Bible, but rather, an engagement of heart and spirit in the presence of the Lord out of desire to be with Him. Yes, there is a discipline involved since the flesh will often be unwilling to cooperate, but we are not simply going through the motions so to speak. As we spend time before Him sitting at His feet, His words are meant to become actual spiritual food to us.

This is right out of the scriptures. Jesus said, "Whoever feeds on my flesh and drinks my blood abides in me, and I in him," (John 6:56). The language He uses here can be quite difficult for us just as it was for many who abandoned Him when they heard it. As the Living Word, He is the manifestation of the spoken or written word of the Father. The Father, in all things, is speaking of His Son. Eating of Him, then, is partaking of the word that God is speaking. That's not a soulish study of whatever scriptures you choose but rather a "now word" spoken by the Holy Spirit, whether it comes through the written word or something He's speaking directly to your heart. Simply hearing, however, is only part of the process. His word must become spiritual food that nourishes us. In other words, we must choose to receive it, believe it, and obey.

A NECESSARY PRUNING

Without a doubt, the Vinedresser comes into the vineyard, motivated entirely by love. John writes this in his first epistle:

> We have come to know [by personal observation and experience], and have believed [with deep, consistent faith] the love which God has for us. God is love, and the one who abides in love abides in God, and God abides continually in him. In this union and fellowship with Him, love is completed and perfected with us.
>
> 1 John 4:16-17 AMP

What a beautiful picture! God, who is love, has come to abide in us in a rich, life-giving relationship. As we then experience union and fellowship with Him, He is able to bring about the deep transformational work necessary to perfect His nature within us. This is speaking directly of readiness. But, while He is deeply in love with us, we must not kid ourselves about a very important function He's come into the vineyard to perform. In the context of relationship, He has come with pruning shears in hand.

The Vinedresser mentioned in John 15 prunes, and we are the branches He's actively cutting. God is not careless with His imagery, and it was not given without careful consideration to what is being communicated. In love, He has come to cut away dead tissue with the precision of a surgeon, aiming to remove all that is a part of our lives yet not useful for bearing fruit. A wrong understanding of this process may lead us into thinking there are certain parts of our nature that are Christ-like and others that aren't so much, and that it's the not-so-Christ-like parts that He's diligently working to prune. But such thinking is devoid of any scriptural footing. He has not come to accentuate our positive characteristics by simply cutting away that which we deem to be negative. The fall resulted in the total depravity of mankind, and the fact is, the self-life is completely devoid of anything Christ-like.

For the Apostle Paul, even that which he deemed to be positive prior to knowing the Lord was a detriment to relationship with Him in the inner man. In Philippians 3, he identified several of those seemingly "good" characteristics of his own flesh. He had been raised "in church," so to speak. He was there every time the door was open and never missed a service, prayer meeting, or outreach. He had done everything he had been commanded to do, and as regarding the commandments, he was outwardly flawless. He talked about God all the time and knew more about His ways than pretty much everyone around him. He was the one who was constantly correcting other people's bad doctrines. He was an expert in all that the Bible had to say and wasn't afraid to let others know! In terms of boring, lackluster testimonies, his was at the top of the list, and I mean that in the best way possible. And yet, in no uncertain terms, he proudly denounced all of this "accomplishment" as rubbish for the sake of knowing Christ (Philippians 3:9).

Paul rightly discerned that no good can possibly come from the self-life, including that which we deem to be godly in our limited understanding. He bore witness that, even when those positive traits came forth, they did so entirely out of self-interest and self-reliance, which are the antithesis of the life of Christ. Paul knew by revelation from the Lord that God's answer for the flesh was not to transform it and make it better but to crucify it so that we could be free to live by another source of life—His alone (Galatians 2:20).

The nature of our journey in the Lord, then, is not a discovery of "our true selves," as some present teaching can easily lead us to believe. It is the journey of discovering Him. As we do, two very important things happen. Firstly, and rightly so, we become enthralled with Him. To see Him is to know Him, and as the old song goes, to know Him is to love Him.[27] As my spiritual eyes are opened so that I become aware of Him, I cannot help but to be overwhelmed by His beauty and fall more deeply in love with

27 Spector, Phil. "To Know Him is to Love Him." (Single) Dore Records, 1958.

Him. His glory cannot be compared with anything else we have known or will ever know. He is the exact likeness of the Father and represents Him completely in every way (Hebrews 1:3). God's wisdom, power, kindness, love, holiness, and all the rest of His amazing attributes are all fully expressed in the person of Jesus, the only begotten Son. We will spend an eternity getting to know Him in a first-hand, intimate way, and we will never even come close to scratching the surface of His goodness.

But, as the light of His life radiates into our innermost being, it exposes all the darkness of the self-life by contrast. Self, as we just said, is the exact opposite of Christ in every way. It is the absolute absence of His light and life. It is death. It is rebellion against God and has nothing to do with Him. So, as I fall in love with Jesus, I become increasingly aware of and disgusted by my own flesh, and that is an ongoing process so long as I am still on this earth. As Christ is selfless, so then, flesh is utterly consumed with "me, me, me." Even in my best moments, when I appear outwardly to be operating in a mode of kindness and humility by serving those around me, if I'm doing so from the flesh, you can bet there is a self-centered, self-serving, hidden agenda involved. If it comes from me, there is no life in it, nor can there be. There is only death. It may seem right to me in the moment, and it may even feel like it's the Lord. But flesh can never produce anything acceptable to God. On my best days, all my best efforts are as filthy, dirty rags (Isaiah 64:6).

This seems harsh, especially if it's never been presented to us in this way. But it's precisely what Jesus was addressing in Matthew 7 when He spoke of many who would stand before Him on the day of judgment, clinging to their own good works as evidence of their faith in Him. His response is both chilling and clear:

> And then will I declare to them, 'I never knew you; depart from me, you workers of lawlessness,'
>
> Matthew 7:23

Paul hit the nail on the head in 1 Timothy 1:15 when he said,

> The saying is trustworthy and deserving of full acceptance, that Christ Jesus came into the world to save sinners, of whom I am the foremost.

Paul said this towards the latter part of his life after he had undergone the severe pruning of the Lord, and there was no false humility or condemnation in his assessment. He maintained that his flesh was just as depraved then as it had been when he met Jesus on the road to Damascus. The only difference was that he saw it more clearly since he had journeyed with the Lord.

The deeper we go into Christ, the more we behold Him. The more we behold Him, the more the light of His glory provides a stark contrast to the utter depravity of our flesh (Philippians 3:3). This should lead us to the rightful conclusion that we should put no confidence in it. The Lord, on the other hand, is worthy of all our trust. He is absolutely sufficient; we are sorely lacking in every way. He is powerfully strong; we epitomize weakness. He is glorious light; we are utter darkness. Yet in our lack, He is proven sufficient, and in our weakness, His power is perfected. The essence of our progression into maturity is in learning to yield to Him and ceasing from our fleshly efforts.

"Well, what of transformation?" you might ask. "Aren't we new creations once Christ has come to live inside of us?" What I have just described is precisely the process whereby we are being transformed. Faith in Christ does not transform the flesh into a new being. Rather, it initiates a spiritual work within, whereby we have been given a new spirit and a new heart (Ezekiel 36:26). Spiritually, then, we are a new creation. But this is true simply because He has come to live within us. What we call transformation is the life of Christ being "worked out" (Philippians 2:12) from the spiritual realm into the soul. As tenant farmers charged with stewarding the vineyard, we determine who has access to the soul. The Vinedresser would come in for the purpose of pruning away the self-life influence, thus renewing and regenerating the soul to be a vessel of His life alone.

There is only one source of life—Christ Jesus. Everything else that emanates from man is of Adam. Adam represents the flesh and all that is wrapped up in the self-life. Paul refers to him as the "man of dust" (1 Corinthians 15:42-49)—a perishable, weak vessel who is only capable of producing that which is also perishable and susceptible to death. But there is another Adam—the life-giving Spirit, Christ, who was not sown of perishable seed but of imperishable. He is the only source of life, and all that flows from Him is not only impervious to death but radiates with His divine life. My friends, we are either in Adam or in Christ, and I am not referring to a doctrinal position. God help us in our tendencies towards mental assent to doctrines! I'm speaking of an experiential, relational reality of God living within us. The Vinedresser's desire is to prune away the death and disease of Adam within the soul, putting away his thinking and his dependence upon feelings, paving the way for the life of the true Vine to come forth bearing life unto transformation.

All that is of me must eventually be pruned. My thoughts. My plans. My hopes. My dreams. My ministry. My calling. My fame. My destiny. My strengths. My gifts. My talents. My time. My relationships. My possessions. My comfort. My security. My life.

Think with me for a second here. Prior to the fall, when Adam and Eve were still in right relationship with God, they were so devoid of any thoughts concerning "me and my" that they didn't even notice they were naked! What an absence of self! I'm in no way suggesting that the goal is to shed our clothing, but I am saying that He would shed us of the "me and my" beast known as the flesh. As long as we're asking, "but what about me and the transformation He's done in me?" we're still beholden to the monster of the self-life. This has nothing to do with us and everything to do with Jesus. This is His story not yours and mine.

In the modern identity teaching, we rightly want to break off condemnation that stems from a legalistic understanding of Christianity. But in doing so, we've allowed the pendulum to swing too far in the opposite direction, putting the focus on self, which is precisely what the flesh craves. Whatever measure of transformation has taken place in us is because another Being has come to live in us. It's all because of Christ, thus the praise, accolades, and focus should be on Him not on the transformed or redeemed parts of us. If we're going to talk about transformation, let's make sure we remain focused on the source; otherwise, we misunderstand the nature of being a new creation—which is a direct result of having the Creator living within us. His regenerating life is being worked out within us, redeeming the soul and changing its very nature. But we demonstrate a severe lack of discernment as to what's been renewed and what remains unregenerate soul.

I've come to embrace the truth that very little of my mind and emotions have been renewed after decades of walking with Him. That which we all too often think is emanating from the renewed mind is really just flesh, but we're too blinded to tell the difference. I'm not trying to beat us up with criticism. I'm simply making the point that, in our humanity, we are far too weak and limited to spend our time trying to play God in our lives, assigning titles to ourselves, making judgments about what's been renewed and what hasn't, and boasting of ourselves in any way. If we're going to boast, let it be in Him (1 Corinthians 1:31).

If the Lord is given His way, He would prune all that is rooted in the Adamic nature of the flesh. It doesn't take long perusing the list of "mys" mentioned earlier (my will, my comfort, etc., which is by no means an exhaustive list) to understand that when the shears begin to slice and dice, it will be quite the painful process. The Vinedresser does not use anesthesia. If we idealize the nature of our journey with Him, we may be doing ourselves a serious disservice, since it is guaranteed to be one marked with pain and suffering (Philippians 3:10). A failure to grasp this foundational truth has led far too many to fall away into disillusionment when the Vinedresser's blade pierces their flesh. Others put up a fight, seeking to preserve Adam and defend the desires of the flesh.

In large part, this is directly related to false assurances given by those who prop up a fantasy-based Christianity devoid of the cross. I don't mean one where the physical cross of Christ is omitted. We're quite comfortable with the idea of someone else being nailed to a tree on our behalf, but the gospel that Paul preached also included the cross that Jesus spoke of when he said, "whoever does not take his cross and follow me is not worthy of me," (Matthew 10:38). Each of us, in accepting Christ as Savior, has been assigned our own cross which we are to bear. That cross is not His cross. It's ours, and we are meant to be crucified upon it. Jesus said it this way, "Narrow is the gate and difficult is the way which leads to life, and there are few who find it," (Matthew 7:14 NKJV). Tragically, too many, even within the church, know nothing of this difficult path and fail to respond rightly to the Vinedresser as He prunes in the way He told us He would.

RIGHTLY DISCERNING THE PRUNING AS IT COMES

When I was 23, I quit my full time job and joined YWAM, choosing to "serve the Lord" in full time, foreign missions. It is obvious to me now that, while the Lord was leading me in this decision, my expectations as to what He was after were clearly not in line with His ways or His thoughts. I had fallen in love with Jesus and wanted to serve Him by "doing ministry" for Him. Such was my limited understanding of our relationship and what He was doing within me. I enrolled in a Discipleship Training School in Switzerland in hopes of receiving some hands-on training. As one of the older students in the school and having natural leadership ability, I was asked to consider leading a team of nine students into the former Yugoslavia on a three-month outreach. Again, the Lord was in this opportunity, and He confirmed it in multiple ways. So,

I agreed thinking that this was my chance to "do something great for Him."

Off I went into the war-ravaged nations of Croatia, Bosnia and Serbia unable even to speak the language. Perhaps even more foolishly, I thrust myself headlong into a spiritual battle zone with little understanding of the Lord's desire to prune away my flesh. In retrospect, I'm grateful for the experience, but that short, intense season proved to be a baptism of fire I was not expecting.

Throughout the outreach, our little team of nine experienced internal conflict on a daily basis. The source of much of it revolved around my relationship with Heather, which had just begun prior to outreach. Several members of our team wrongly believed that I cared more for her than I did for obeying the Lord. Over time, their suspicions of my motivation led to a deep mistrust in me as their leader, and tensions began to build. Being keenly aware of what was going on yet lacking the wisdom to deal with it, I became resentful of those who put my character on trial. Day after day, mounting undercurrents of division would bubble up to the surface through snide remarks and sarcastic jabs disguised as humor, and finally, after weeks of dysfunction, we attempted to hash it all out as a group. Rather than the peaceful resolution I had hoped for, we walked into a spiritual ambush—a mud-slinging flesh-fest of criticism, bitterness, and resentment that ended in a major rift in our little team.

We were, perhaps, the most fragmented group of people I have ever been a part of, and that's quite the statement considering I've youth pastored in two churches with major splits in the congregations. In retrospect, I'm dumbfounded at the level of soulishness and lack of discernment I personally walked in. I literally stood on the ground where a spirit of division had led to a war and genocide, causing a nation to be splintered into six new countries following years of bloodshed and murder, yet I was blinded as to how that same spirit was manifesting within our team and completely powerless to deal with it.

Very little, if any, of the life of Christ was seen in any of us during that outreach, and I'm speaking primarily of myself. As we ended this period I affectionately refer to as "my three-month journey through hell," I was in a complete and utter funk and walked away with my tail tucked between my legs. I had set out to "prove my worth" to the Lord, and I took this failure especially hard. He had chosen me to lead an outreach, and I was confident that I had failed Him. I was supposed to be one of the more mature ones in our school, or so I was told. I should have been more prepared. I shouldn't have given way to accusation and petty quarreling. I should have recognized the spiritual battle. I should have stood strong, calling others to do likewise. I… I… I…

In all of the introspection, what I had failed to grasp was that the Lord hadn't led me into that outreach to do some great work for Him. In fact, though He's prepared good works for me to walk in, some of which were there in those nations, His desire has always been to do those works through me and not simply hand me a to-do list and send me on my merry way. On this particular trip, He was leading me into the wilderness for the primary purpose of doing a deep work inside of me.

It was during this outreach that my first love season came to an end, and I hardened my heart towards the Lord, wrongly believing that, because of my failure, He had abandoned me. That was not true, by the way, and I see that clearly now. Prior to this season, I had been regularly showered with the kisses of heaven, daily hearing His voice with clarity, but in the wilderness of Bosnia, He seemed to have stopped speaking altogether. I had no grid for understanding this new and difficult portion of the journey. By the end of the outreach, I was seriously questioning the nature of my relationship with Him, wondering why His amazing grace, which had been so tangible in the months before, was no longer being extended to me. What I couldn't see was that this outreach marked the beginning, in many ways, of my journey into maturity.

From Yugoslavia, we headed to Greece, where we met up with the rest of the school for a chance to pray through and process our time on outreach. I remember sharing my failures and disillusionments with one of the school's staff members, hoping that he could offer some hope of redemption, as all I could see was the negative. After I whined for several minutes, my friend thought deliberately and intently with furrowed brow as the silence hung in the air for an uncomfortable period of time. Then he looked at me and said, with his thick, endearing Australian accent, "Oh yeah, mate! I reckon that's how it is with God, eh? He throws us right into the fire and squeezes us so that we can see all the junk and rot that comes out of us. Doesn't mean He's okay with it, but it also doesn't mean He's disappointed in you. He already knew it was there. He just wanted you to see it, so He can deal with it. Along the way, He proves His commitment to us, teaching us that we can trust in Him. He's our sufficiency, not us!"

The word of the Lord in that moment brought clarity and a much-needed change of perspective. I limped into Greece, consumed with my pain and my disillusionment. But as the Lord broke in, I caught a glimpse of Jesus once more. And in the beauty of His light, He exposed the gunk of my own flesh in a way that led me to repentance. The pressure situation He had designed literally caused a measure of self to bubble up to the surface. I witnessed, first-hand, just how utterly awful my self-life is, even on this side of salvation. That in no way justifies my poor choices or alleviates my personal responsibility in making them, but it helped me see what He was after. He was revealing the stark contrast between His ways and mine, calling me to repentance and into a place of trusting Him in a deeper way.

EMBRACING THE CROSS

The trials of life are not a sign of God's rejection of us, with no apologies to the thieves and foxes of the American prosperity gospel and all of its many iterations. When the Vinedresser draws near with pruning shears in hand, it is not because He is casting us aside or because we're being punished for some unconfessed sin. It is, rather, a sign that we have garnered His attention in a good way. Something within us, at some point in time, has said to Him, in some way, shape, or form, "Lord, I want to know you. Deep in my heart, I truly desire to be close to you. I was created for this. Please do not withhold yourself from me!" And He has taken us up on that invitation. He will every single time.

History, by the way, bears this up. The seed of the gospel as given by the Holy Spirit to the apostles was sown through tremendous adversity. The Apostle Paul himself was shown at the outset of his journey not how much he would accomplish for the Lord but how much he would suffer on His behalf (Acts 9:16). As the seed was received into good soil, it endured the process that Jesus described in John 12:24—it fell to the earth and died so that it could bear much fruit. That death came in the form of persecution, famine, hardship, division, and intense, direct opposition by the kingdom of darkness. At no point did the good news go forth without being accompanied by a backlash of intense suffering.

Not only was it true of the early church, but it was also true of the Old Testament type and shadow of the church, Israel. Having been birthed in the wilderness of modern-day Arabia, this new nation of priests was engulfed in trials on almost a daily basis, including hunger, lack of water, civil unrest, plague, and the threat of conquest. Yet through it all, God was preparing them for something. They were being made ready to go up against the most fortified city in existence and to dispossess its inhabitants who stood as giants among grasshoppers (Numbers 13:33). There was method to the Lord's madness in dealing with our spiritual forefathers, just as there was method to His madness in dealing with me in the former Yugoslavia. He was not punishing them, and He certainly hadn't led them into the wilderness to die. He was exposing their weaknesses while proving His power. He was exposing their faithlessness, while proving His faithfulness. He was exposing their foolishness while proving His wisdom. Through it all, He desired to gather them into a place of greater fellowship so they could learn to trust in Him. Instead, so many failed to cooperate and never entered into the place of rest He had prepared.

The lesson that we must learn from Israel is this: if we fight Him in the wilderness, we'll miss the benefit of the cross. Most of Israel rebelled against Him, and their 40 years of hardship were wasted. The value of the cross is not in simply enduring painful circumstances but in the brokenness and humility that is meant to be gained in the process. Such surrender to the Lord requires a choice to be made in the midst of suffering—a choice to hold all things loosely before Him for the sake of knowing Him. Too often, we fail to connect the wilderness seasons with the hand of God and His process of preparing our inner man. We wrongly believe that He's against all suffering and seek to avoid it at all costs. When we're forced into the desert, we often get mired down in introspection, trying to figure out where we went wrong and vowing not to let it happen again. We may also reach for consolation in the midst of our pain, grasping at idols that promise momentary relief such as relationships, work, entertainment, or religious activity. Or, we may seek a premature escape from our condition, wrongly focused on contending against the enemy until our circumstances change. When we find ourselves in the wilderness, what we actually need is to fully embrace the cross and recognize that it is the only way to truly know the Lord.

There is no pathway to preparedness that does not involve difficulty. We must decrease—plain and simple. Consider His end time bride, in whom the measure of Christ will come to a level of fullness never before seen. He will use the Great Tribulation to do a tremendous preparatory work in her. The fires of that season will literally be used to forge her into the vessel He has destined her to become. She will not escape the hardship and the suffering through rapture, just as our church fathers did not escape the cross as it was manifested in their lives. If she endures to the end, she will be the bride without spot or wrinkle that we see in Revelation 19.

The purpose of hardship is refinement. As gold is purified in fire, so too, must the life of Christ within us be shed of the dross and impurity of our self-life. The fires are not meant to make you more pure—they are meant to remove the impurities that cling to that new creation Christ-life that has come to live within you. The distinction here is subtle but profound. Again, the emphasis should always be on the Lord, else we too easily empower the flesh. It is the burning of flesh on the brazen altar that created a pleasing aroma to the Lord in the wilderness, and it is the burning of our flesh in the fires of adversity that delights Him today. It represents the costly sacrifice of a life laid down and a mature love.

Paul writes, "For this light momentary affliction is preparing for us an eternal weight of glory beyond all comparison…" (2 Corinthians 4:17). A little perspective is warranted here. For Paul, light affliction meant receiving 39 lashes five times, being beaten with rods three times, getting stoned and left for dead outside the city, living through three different shipwrecks including 24 hours adrift in the open sea, multiple imprisonments, countless sleepless nights, fasting often, and a whole host of trouble directed at him by robbers, fellow Jews, various Gentile groups, and worst of all, false believers (2 Corinthians 11:24-27). And yet, there is no record of the man ever complaining about how hard things were for him. He understood something we fail to grasp. The Lord is in the fire, and if we want to know Him, we must be willing to get burned. That said, the fire was not his focus. Christ chose, in the midst of hardship, to keep the prize for which He was being nailed to the cross always before Him. This is not only realistic but attainable as long as we continue to abide in Him even when the temperature around us starts to heat up. We can experience Him in the fire, and the very point of Shadrach, Meshach, and Abednego is that we're meant to! We're never alone when the suffering kicks in. The great question is this: Can we see Him, or are we too busy being fixated on self?

I'm appealing to you, as I sit here and write, to allow the Holy Spirit to impart fresh revelation to your spirit. The great truth of life is that you cannot insulate yourself from suffering. You're going to experience heartache, loss, and pain on some level. Why not let the God of Creation use those things to shape you into the vessel He's created you to be? Why not look for Him in the midst of the trials that He sends your way, getting to know His nature and learning to hear His voice? Anyone can hear the Lord when He's shouting encouragement into our souls, but only those who are led of the Spirit can hear the faint whisper of His voice in times of hardship. Don't fall into the same trap that Israel fell into. Their murmuring and complaining against God opened the door to unbelief, and their hearts became stony. Don't look for escape in the things of this world, and don't resort to an inner strength and a positive outlook to keep you going. Let the hammer of God break you and cause you to walk with a limp for the rest of eternity so that you come up out of the wilderness leaning on your Beloved (Song of Solomon 8:5). To do so, you're going to have to learn to find Him in the fire.

If we circle back to Buster Douglas, we'll find that the real key to his success going toe-to-toe against one of the most dominant heavyweight fighters of all time was in his willingness to endure an inordinate amount of pain. I'm not simply speaking of the blows he absorbed from Tyson, though that alone would have deterred most people. I'm also referring to the countless hours of training, the pushing of his body to its limits and beyond, the building of his endurance and stamina, and the toughening of his mental resolve. I'm speaking of every adverse circumstance that helped make the man into the champ. All of it served to create the fighter who was able to beat the unbeatable. Through all he endured, James Douglas the nobody boxer that few people cared about died, and Buster Douglas the heavyweight champion of the world came forth.

God is forming His own champion in this hour. And He's doing so through fire. Are you willing to endure? Will you cooperate with Him as the temperature heats up?

CHAPTER 13

THE HEART OF THE FATHER

> My son, do not make light of the discipline of the Lord, and do not lose heart and give up when you are corrected by Him; For the Lord disciplines and corrects those whom He loves, and He punishes every son whom He receives and welcomes [to His heart]." You must submit to [correction for the purpose of] discipline; God is dealing with you as with sons; for what son is there whom his father does not discipline... For the time being no discipline brings joy, but seems sad and painful; yet to those who have been trained by it, afterwards it yields the peaceful fruit of righteousness [right standing with God and a lifestyle and attitude that seeks conformity to God's will and purpose].
>
> Hebrews 12:5-7; 11 AMP

> Behold, I will send you Elijah the prophet before the coming of the great and dreadful day of the LORD. And he will turn the hearts of the fathers to the children, and the hearts of the children to their fathers...
>
> Malachi 4:5-6 NKJV

Back in the late 90s and early 2000s, I remember hearing and reading much about "the Father's heart." Having lost my biological father to death, I always carried a deep yearning within me to know what it is to truly be fathered. As a result, I devoured every book and teaching I could find on the subject in an attempt to connect with God as Heavenly Father. During this time, the Lord did some much needed inner healing in me, and I came to experience a measure of deliverance from a spirit of rejection that had been with me since birth. I also saw, for the first time, that His heart towards me is one of absolute acceptance and unconditional love instead of the condemnation and constant feeling of inadequacy that had been my unwelcome companion for so many years. No longer seeing Him as a distant Deity likely to abandon me the instant I disappointed Him, I realized that He is a good Dad who has every intention of being with me for eternity. In addition, I experienced Him in a firsthand way as my provider who was faithful to meet my material needs. It was a rich season of revelation and encouragement and one in which the Lord healed me of much of the pain I had experienced through the loss of my dad.

OF INSECURITY AND BROKEN DRYERS

But just as steel must be hardened in the furnace, so must truth become solidified in the testing. Simply reading a book, listening to a message, or even receiving a direct prophetic word wherein the Lord publicly lavishes His kindness upon me could not solidify my belief in the love of the Father towards me. I didn't know this at the time, but God doesn't teach in a classroom setting through empty words or abstract theories. The school of the Spirit is in day-to-day life, as evidenced by Jesus' three-year sojourn with His disciples. Though I had received much from Him, I was still in the habit of questioning His love for me whenever I encountered hardship.

Like the children of Israel who relished the love of God on the heels of the miracle of the Red Sea and when they received the provision of water from the rock, I accepted the truth of the Father's love as long as my circumstances seemed to offer proof of it. But also like the children of Israel who grumbled and complained every time they didn't get what they wanted, I quickly questioned His love every time hardship came knocking at my door. It's amazing to me how quick we are to cast judgment on those ex-slaves in the wilderness while failing to recognize how similar we are to them!

This went on for about eight years or so. It was a seemingly endless roller coaster of questioning God's love, having the Holy

Spirit confirm it time and time again, even receiving a measure of understanding of the trial I had just come out of, then encountering some other set of circumstances that would cause me to question His love all over again. Just as the Hebrews had done for so many years, I was circling the same mountain over and over, never seeming to get anywhere in my journey of readiness.

One day, the Lord absolutely nailed me and put an end to the insecurity with finality. I don't remember all the circumstances surrounding that moment, but I do recall that it was in a time of tremendous financial stress during which I was in a job that was barely providing for our needs. Several years prior, the Lord had spoken a clear prophetic word to us regarding His "oceans of provision," which He intended to make available to us. When I first heard this, I imagined a great sum of money coming my way, which is not at all what He was referencing. In retrospect, my Father has always taken care of every physical need we've had, and then some. Even though things have seemed quite lean for us at times, we've always had enough. And on this particular day, in the midst of planning for a fourth child on the way, while fixated on the ever-growing stack of bills, Heather informed me that our dryer had just stopped working. And being the hot-headed jerk I tend to be in my flesh, I quickly mumbled something I instantly regretted. "Thanks a lot, Lord!" I fumed in arrogance. "Where were you and your oceans of provision when my dryer quit working?"

You're probably as amazed as I am that I wasn't struck dead right there on the spot! All poor Uzzah did was reach up to stop the ark from falling, but I had openly challenged the Most High God in my own stupidity. What audacity to make such an accusation! But instead of killing me, the Holy Spirit did something much worse and much better all at the same time! No sooner had the words rolled off my tongue than I received my answer in the form of a vision. I saw the Lord, bloodied and beaten with his flesh torn apart, hanging on the cross. And while beholding His face, I saw His eyes, piercing into my soul. He then spoke to me with tremendous clarity, "I was here! I was right here, hanging on this cross!" In that moment, a lightning bolt of revelation hit the core of my being, and I understood that the question I had mumbled was not the real question I was asking. What I truly wanted to know was, "Lord, in light of all that's happening, have you stopped loving me again?" And it was that question that He, in His patience and mercy, was addressing.

In a firm but gentle way, the Lord was saying to me, "Son, why would you still question the truth of my love? Don't you see it has nothing to do with circumstances? This cross forever proves that I love you. Can't you see that I've written my love letter to you in my own blood? Settle it in your heart and move forward because this is the only proof you need, and it's the only proof I'm offering! I owe you nothing!" And just like that, the correction of the Lord put me in my place. It stung, and it was beautiful!

FRIEND OF GOD?

Since that day, I've come to recognize that there is an aspect to fatherhood I had never fully connected to God's fathering of me. Oddly enough, few of the books I had read on the Father's heart even mentioned this critical role let alone expounded upon it. It was not until I connected the dots between this conversation with the Lord and my own experience as a Dad that the light finally went on for me. I used to tell my older children whenever I had need to discipline them, "I'm your father, not your friend." By that, I certainly wasn't saying that I didn't love them, nor was I saying, "We can never be friends." What I was communicating, however, is that my commitment to them is, first and foremost, as a father. I have an assignment from the Lord to help them mature in all aspects of their lives, and walking out that call in love must be my top priority. To that end, I am the disciplinarian in my household.

It's strange how blind we can be to something only to wonder, once we finally receive sight, how we ever functioned in our blindness! Up to that moment, all I had heard about the Father was how affirming and loving He is and how He'll never abandon or reject us. All of that is certainly true, but if we don't frame that love and acceptance within the context of His role to push us to maturity, we're left with a namby-pamby, mushy sentiment with no real substance to it. The Father's great purpose isn't simply to make us feel good, yet that's what I had come to expect from Him until the day my dryer broke down. When He finally took me out to the woodshed in a way that brought revelation, I began to appreciate the He is a disciplinarian, fully committed to my maturity. In fact, let me take this even further. He's not initially concerned with a friendship relationship with us, but one called Fatherhood. There will come a time for friendship as we cooperate with Him in the readiness process and move onto the ground of maturity, but for now, His primary desire is to Father us. In that role, He is pushing us—many times against our will—into spiritual manhood so that we might become *huios* sons of His. Now, in saying that God isn't firstly concerned with being your friend, I'm confident I just pushed every religious button within you, so let me explain.

A few years back, there was a popular worship song that went like this, "Who am I that you are mindful of me, that you hear me when I call? Is it true that You are thinking of me? How you love me! It's amazing! I am a friend of God." Then it basically just repeats itself a bunch of times. And I like the song, so this isn't meant to be a criticism. But I sometimes have this weird thought that, before we go throwing around statements about God in song form, we should probably make sure they are biblically sound. It would seem, based on these words, that the only real qualifications God has for friendship are that: He thinks about them, He hears them when they call to Him, and He loves them. This pretty much means that everyone who's ever lived is His friend, and I daresay that's what many may actually believe. But the scriptures show us something quite different.

The phrase "friend of God" is taken from James 2, where it is said of Abraham. But James mentions the patriarch in the context of faith being demonstrated through works. What he's actually saying here is that Abraham demonstrated his faith by laying Isaac on the altar (2:21), thus his faith was perfected. He then refers to Abraham as the friend of God two verses later. God didn't just flippantly throw out the title of friend just because. Abraham trusted God so much that he obeyed Him even in the incredibly costly act of sacrificing his own son. Because of that proven commitment, he was considered by God to be a friend.

Likewise, in John 15, Jesus says of His disciples, "No longer do I call you servants, for a servant does not know what his master is doing; but I have called you friends, for all things that I heard from My Father I have made known to you," (v. 15). If this verse were written in a vacuum, then it would seem to apply to all those who follow Jesus or possibly even beyond. But it wasn't written as a standalone statement. In the verse before, Jesus literally says to them, "You are my friends if you do what I command you," (v. 14). Obviously, the common thread between James 2 and John 15 is obedience. What is the ultimate end of a Father's discipline? True spiritual maturity always leads us into greater obedience to the Lord. There will come a time for friendship with Him once we've first been Fathered into maturity, and consequently disciplined by Him into a place of submission.

Again, please don't misunderstand me. Am I suggesting that friendship is for those of us who have mastered all fleshly desires and defeated the temptation of sin and disobedience in all forms and with finality? Absolutely not! I don't believe such a person exists in the natural realm, which would severely limit God's friendship selection pool! I am simply saying that friendship is proven through obedience. Too many live as though they have a claim to rewards that have not yet been attained to. To do so is to fail to understand that the Father is offering us rewards which are meant to encourage us in the midst of His rigorous process of discipline.

Friendship with Him is one of those rewards! If we simply hang on to Jesus and allow Him to instruct us as He desires, then friendship with Him (and far more!) will be eternally ours! We don't have to wait until this life is over to begin to experience that either. Jesus called His disciples friends after three years of learning obedience from Him. We can experience friendship with Him while still here on earth. I'm not here to tell you if and when you reach the point of friendship with Him; I'm simply saying that we have need of maturity in so many ways, and if we learn to submit to the Father, He will see to it that we get there.

DISCIPLINE, REPROOF, AND CHASTISEMENT

As stated in Ephesians 4, maturity is the end goal of the Father towards His true sons: "…until we all attain to the unity of the faith and of the knowledge of the Son of God, to mature manhood, to the measure of the stature of the fullness of Christ," (Ephesians 4:13). A mature branch will produce the fruit the Vinedresser is after, but an immature branch is incapable of producing fruit. The same is true of children in the natural. Without proper discipline, a child will never develop the character needed for godly living, and if there is any measure of perceived success in that child's life, the underlying character issues will be exposed as insufficient to handle what little "fruit" is produced. Of course, God is not primarily interested in our idea of success. That, to Him, is the same as wild, sour grapes. He's aimed at the eternal fruit of the life of His Son, and He has every intention of moving us from spiritual babes to mature men who have been conformed to His likeness. He does this through the process of discipline.

One of the breakdowns that exists within our current western church culture is that we no longer have an understanding of or appreciation for the role of sound discipline. This is, to no small degree, directly tied to the societal breakdown of the home, the feminist movement, and the emasculation of men. I could devote an entire chapter to those issues alone, but this book is already long enough! Suffice it to say, however, that the role of men within the home has been greatly diminished over the past five decades or so to such a degree that we have multiple generations of people who have gone largely undisciplined. In our confusion, we somehow consider this trend a good thing or even a sign of enlightenment, and we celebrate the fact that we no longer embrace the "outdated, barbaric" practice of corporal punishment. But God has something much different to say in the matter.

When discipline is removed, there is no restraint. The Amplified Bible says this,

> Where there is no vision [no revelation of God and His word], the people are unrestrained; But happy and blessed is he who keeps the law [of God]. A servant will not be corrected by words alone; For though he understands, he will not respond [nor pay attention].
>
> Proverbs 29:18-19 AMP

Catch the wording of those verses. Being "unrestrained" is likened unto a state of being unteachable. And the discipline of the Lord, which is there to teach us and correct us, does not come through words alone. In our rebellious state, we are not prone to responding or paying attention to mere words.

There is need, then, for a mechanism by which we can learn obedience. Such mechanism exists. It is called "pain and suffering." And rather than being completely averse to it, we should recognize that it is a powerful teacher. Even the Son of God (who by our way of thinking had no need to be disciplined) still had to "[learn] obedience through what he suffered," (Hebrews 5:8). The mature *huios* Son of God was fathered in a way that led Him into complete obedience, and that process of learning was not one of being subjected to words alone. Mere positive affirmation might feel like a better alternative to those who are more nurturing in their flesh, but it will not get the job done. A servant will not be corrected by words alone. Nurturing doesn't bring about obedience; discipline does.

Drawing from several Old Testament scriptures, the writer of Hebrews presents it this way:

> My son, do not regard lightly the discipline of the Lord, nor be weary when reproved by him. For the Lord disciplines the one he loves and chastises every son whom he receives,
>
> Hebrews 12:5-6

There are three distinct Greek words being used in these verses. *Paideia* is translated as discipline, and it literally means "the training, discipline and rearing of a child."[28] It includes chastisement or correction for the sake of teaching. *Elegcho* is translated as reproof, and its definition is "to expose or convict."[29] The connotation is to convey a sense of guilt over wrongdoing. The final word, *mastigoo*, literally means "to scourge," as in the flogging of a victim being strapped to a pole.[30] The implication is God sends severe pain in the eternal best interests of the one being scourged. So we see here that the Father has a sort of "holistic" approach to instructing us that includes not only verbal instruction but also conviction over wrongdoing and foolishness as well as pain.

I want to be crystal clear here and not give anyone any ground to misinterpret me. Obviously, there is a form of pain which is often inflicted on children that is contrary to the heart of the Father. I am in no way advocating for or excusing abuse. A measure of pain can be quite helpful in teaching us, but if we go too far or if we punish out of anger and cruelty, the impact can be absolutely devastating, alienating a child from the love of God and stifling his maturity. That's not what's being pointed to in the reference to scourging here in Hebrews. It is certainly not a pleasant process and one in

---

28 Strong, J. (1890). Strong's exhaustive concordance of the Bible. Abingdon Press.

29 Strong, J. (1890). Strong's exhaustive concordance of the Bible. Abingdon Press.

30 Strong, J. (1890). Strong's exhaustive concordance of the Bible. Abingdon Press.

which the pain often seems quite severe at the time, but it's carried out in a very controlled and measured way by our Heavenly Father with eternal reward in view.

Simply hearing a word from the Lord without enduring a measure of pain will never result in the proper training that the Lord is after in us. Yes, we must be instructed, but we must also be reproved by Him. As we are, then we can see our need for His instruction and accept our guilt so that we can repent and be restored to fellowship with Him. That is an ongoing process. When necessary, we must also endure the scourging of the Lord, which I'm convinced is simply whatever trial drives His instruction from a place of head knowledge into a belief of the heart. I'm confident in the fact that He is God, and I am not. Therefore, He well knows just what I need in order to learn what He's trying to teach me. Whether I respond or not is my choice. Thankfully, if I don't respond the first time, He'll march me right back out to the woodshed again as often as He needs to. Around and around the mountain we go until I finally yield to Him in the way He desires. This is where cultivating a lifestyle of watching and waiting upon Him is so key. I'm a little less prone to having to circle the mountain so many times if I'll just get clued in to what He is speaking to me.

Like any dad, He doesn't particularly enjoy inflicting pain on His kids. He simply knows that it's the best teacher. Because we've lost a healthy appreciation for discipline in the home, God's discipline of us has become quite a foreign concept. In sparing our kids the pain of proper discipline, we essentially afford them the freedoms of adulthood without first subjecting them to the training needed to handle those freedoms. And by peddling teachings and doctrines that undermine the discipline process of God, the false system has spoiled the flock into thinking it has a right to all of the promises associated with maturity without any of the discipline required to teach them how to handle those promises wisely. Make no mistake, God is not going to hand out rewards to people who aren't mature enough to handle them. It would be less destructive to hand a loaded gun to a 5-year-old than pour out blessings that cannot be contained onto a self-centered, undisciplined, so-called disciple. Just to be clear, I'm not advocating for either!

Our false understanding of the grace of God has caused us to miss the connection between our circumstances and His desire to mature us. He is oftentimes using events in our lives to speak to us, teach us, reprove us, and even scourge when necessary. Instead of seeing adversity as simply being a result of fallenness or a function of the enemy, we must understand that the sovereignty of God means that He will use all things for our maturity. Isn't that precisely what He's promised to do in Romans 8:28? So we can be guaranteed that, in every situation, God is teaching. But our deafness has become an insurmountable wall, keeping Him out of the vineyard at all costs. What's needed in the church, perhaps now more than ever, is a recovery of the love of the Father manifested in His loving discipline. The sad reality, however, is that the recovery cannot come in mere words alone. We must be jolted out of our slumber.

AN INVITATION TO FRIENDSHIP

The Vinedresser's pruning, while unpleasant, is quite strategic in nature. A grapevine, if left to its own, will put off growth in all directions. This may seem quite nice at the advent of Spring when the dormancy of winter fades and new leaves appear on the surface of the vine, but, if left to its own, the vine will produce so much growth that it could ruin the harvest. Grape leaves need adequate exposure to sunlight. It is in the leaves that photosynthesis—a process by which water and carbon dioxide are combined to form sugars—takes place. This process is triggered by energy from the sun, so it is vital to ensure that there is maximum exposure of the leaves to the sun. Without pruning, the vine will begin to crowd out the light from the sun resulting in a shortage of the sugars needed for fruit development.

Typically, a vinedresser will accommodate for the growth of four major branches: two sets of two in opposite directions, one above the other. Anything else produced by the vine is cut off. This process is known as "training the vine," and it is a picture of the Lord's discipline process. He prunes that which emanates from Adam—the new growth that sprouts in whatever direction seems right in our own eyes. This wild cacophony of vegetation emanating from the flesh would be quite cut off from the light of the Son, thus those branches would only produce the sour, wild grapes of Isaiah 5. In love, then, He trains. In love, He reproves. In love, He scourges. How does He do this? He leads us into a wilderness experience, also known as a trial, where he exposes our true nature which always wants its own way. At the same time, it's in the wilderness that He speaks tenderly to us (Hosea 2:14), revealing Himself as the solution to our utter depravity, offering to restrain our wild growth so that what is produced in us comes from Him and not the self-life. Through it all, we have a choice in the matter. Will we grant Him access to the vineyard where He can prune us, or will we keep Him at bay?

The trial itself is not the pruning. The surrender He desires is. Simply abiding hard times is not akin to brokenness any more than passively enduring of the passage of time is true waiting. Through the hardship, the Lord is making us aware of our need for Him, as well as pointing to Himself as being sufficient to meet that need. Whether we heed Him or not is entirely up to us. The sad reality is that far too many of us have suffered great hardship and tremendous loss over the years only to fail to yield to the Lord in the way He has desired. I've watched friends and loved ones pay the ultimate price only to then resist the Lord in His attempts to prune, thus negating the purpose of some pretty severe trials. What a tragedy!

Again, this is where being a watchman to the Lord is so key. It is all fine and dandy to learn how to watch and wait during seasons of peace and comfort, but it is a different matter entirely to continue on in that vein when the Lord sends the turmoil for the sake of pruning. In those seasons, we very often get disoriented and submerged in the chaos of our circumstances so that we lose sight of Him. But we must settle it in our hearts that discipline, reproof, and scourging are an integral part of the journey, and when they come, we must quickly get into a posture of watching and waiting upon Him.

I'm convinced that the most valuable thing you could possibly do when the storm hits is to draw near to the Father and ask Him, "What is it that you're doing in this season, Lord, and how can I respond rightly?" Know that it will likely take some time to hear clearly what He says. This is, in part, by design. He's after a yielded heart in us, and that takes time. A quick, manipulative attempt to put an end to suffering won't cut it. We're also meant to learn how to endure as He teaches. There is no rushing that process. That said, we needn't prolong things unnecessarily. Allow Him to make you a watchman. Be intentional about waiting upon Him in the truest sense. Let your priority be the relationship, and learn to come before Him with a quieted soul to hear what He has to say to you. Imagine if your children responded to your discipline in this way. How pleased would you be to have not only captured their attention but also to have gained their full and complete submission and cooperation?

Keep in mind that the Father doesn't owe us any explanations. Our desire to understand in the arena of our soul can potentially become a stumbling block to us. Sometimes the only answer He gives will be, "Are you willing to trust me when I withhold understanding?" A friend of ours was in Serbia in 1999 when NATO forces carried out extensive airstrikes there. She described the nightmare of living through the nightly attacks holed up in her home with other believers, and crying out to the Lord as the explosions drew near. She shared with me that the one thing she kept before her in that season was this phrase, which she repeated to herself: "When I don't understand His ways, I can trust in His goodness."

That must always be our posture. At the end of the day, He is Dad. And when we're incapable of understanding Him, we must see the Son hanging on the cross for us and know that He can always be trusted. He doesn't have to give us understanding to get what He's after. If it's surrender that He wants, I don't need to understand. I just need to surrender to Him.

There is a legend from the life of Teresa of Avila in which she and some companions set out to follow the Lord as He led them to minister in a small village some distance away from their convent. As they set out, they encountered a host of obstacles including heavy rain and severe weather. Upon reaching a river crossing, the driver of their carriage determined that the current was too strong to continue. Instead, Teresa convinced her companions to wade across the river. At one point, she lost her footing and was nearly swept downstream, but through the help of the Lord, she managed to regain her legs. As she stood, she asked Him, "Lord, when will you cease from scattering obstacles in our path?" His response was simple, "Do not complain, daughter. This is how I treat my friends." She immediately replied, "Ah, Lord. It is on this account that you have so few!" Whether this story is true or not, I don't know. I am confident, however, that the sentiment is entirely accurate.

It is the discipline, reproof, and scourging of the Lord that present us with the opportunity to be pruned. It is the pruning of the Lord that produces obedience. It is obedience to the Lord that leads to friendship with Him. And it is friendship with Him that causes fruit to come forth. Knowing this, are you willing to open up the vineyard to the Vinedresser?

CHAPTER 14

THIS MEANS WAR!

> And I heard a loud voice in heaven, saying, "Now the salvation and the power and the kingdom of our God and the authority of his Christ have come, for the accuser of our brothers has been thrown down, who accuses them day and night before our God. And they have conquered him by the blood of the Lamb and by the word of their testimony, for they loved not their lives even unto death.
>
> Revelation 12:10-11

The Lord confronted me several years ago, showing up in the middle of one of my pity-parties and presenting me with a question. "Do you know what your problem is, son?" He asked. I had been complaining about the difficulty of pastoring a church and all the warfare that surrounded it, and the Lord had had enough of my griping. He went on without hesitation (thus prohibiting my soul from unwisely interjecting itself), "Your problem is that you want to be an overcomer, but you don't want to face Goliath." In an instant, the word of the Lord once again pierced me, revealing the distinction between my soulish understanding and His true ways, and I was able to see as I had not before.

I wanted the spoils of battle without the sacrifice, risk, and pain associated with engaging in combat. I wanted the blessing of knowing Him without feeling the bite of the enemy's blade on my flesh. I wanted the satisfaction of victory without paying the price for it. I wanted to quote scriptures as inevitable truth when I had no willingness to contend for them to be made manifest in me. I wanted to be an overcomer without putting myself into a position of vulnerability where I would need the Lord to show up on my behalf. As He reproved me, I not only saw my own condition, I also recognized that much of the way we view spiritual warfare in the present-day church is along these same lines.

Before He brought that correction, I had come into a strange place of mixture where I put way too much emphasis on a wrong understanding of both God's sovereignty and the nature of the victory He obtained at Calvary. This lead me to think that warfare was unnecessary in many instances and too perplexing to know how to stand in others. How easy it is for the soul of man to become utterly confused! Rather than taking the time to seek the Lord as my Teacher, I opted for the path of laziness and simply let others engage in warfare while I just focused on what I had been "called to." Looking back, I'm ashamed that I simply checked out of the fight while so many others faithfully stood in the gap for years. I am, furthermore, extremely grateful that the Lord exposed my foolishness and brought some much needed correction! Since that time, I've been learning how to fight the right kind of warfare even though much of it has come through mistakes. It would be impossible to give a thorough how-to guide on spiritual warfare in just one chapter, so please don't take this as such. There is much I don't know about this subject. I am by no means an expert. Nevertheless, I've felt the need to share a few basic principles I've picked up in recent years.

THERE IS AN ENEMY

The first truth of warfare is simply the fact that **you do have an enemy who stands between you and the scriptural understanding of readiness**. This may sound obvious, but so many believers live completely unaware of Satan's strategies and oblivious to his tactics. The quicker we can acknowledge that he is a very real and dangerous foe the better. He is not a defanged serpent as some have referred to him. Yes, Jesus overcame the devil at the cross and guaranteed the ultimate victory over the kingdom of darkness, but the war is not over by any stretch of the imagination. Christ's guarantee of victory is much the same as the promise to give Canaan to the Israelites. They still had to go to war, and so must we if we want to see the manifestation of final victory in our day.

Just as the Canaanites fought back with real swords and spears, so too will the demonic resist you as you press into readiness. In saying this, I am in no way trying to evoke fear. Quite the opposite, I would rouse you to courage, knowing that the Lord has promised us the victory if we'll simply engage in the battle in the right way. We just need to be realistic about the nature of our warfare. Too many wrongly believe that God's just going to show up at the end and sovereignly put away all evil for us without realizing that we are meant to play a part in the realization of His promised victory. A bride making herself ready is what will trigger the end. That will involve a serious fight from those willing to be a part of the bridal company, and they must be dedicated to standing firm amidst the relentless onslaught of the enemy.

Too many wrongly think that a quick and easy prayer "in Jesus' name" is all that is needed to send the devil running in fear, but that belief likely comes from the very one who least wants you to assume your place on the battlefield as a warrior ready to take him on. The truth is that all warfare is a violent and bloody affair, and while we can trust in the Lord to bring about the ultimate victory, we have no guarantees of a quick or painless outcome. Three times in the first chapter of Joshua the Lord told the commander of Israel to "Be strong and courageous," (Joshua 1:6, 7, 9). We're going to need the strength and courage of the Lord to endure the battles of our day, and He will be that in us if we'll simply stand. When we face the Lord at the final judgment, we will not be allowed the luxury of saying, "Well, I didn't know you meant a real war," or "Nobody ever taught me how." He will demand an account as to whether we stood resolutely against the evil one in our day. Warfare is not optional!

THE NEED FOR CLARITY

That leads to the second truth of spiritual warfare: **we must have clarity about what we are fighting for and why**. I ran across this quote and thought it was quite applicable:

> War is an ugly thing, but not the ugliest of things. The decayed and degraded state of moral and patriotic feeling which thinks that nothing is worth war is much worse. The person who has nothing for which he is willing to fight, nothing which is more important than his own personal safety, is a miserable creature and has no chance of being free unless made and kept so by the exertions of better men than himself.[31]

There is, without a doubt, much confusion in the present-day body of Christ as to what exactly we're fighting for, as pertaining to the scriptures regarding spiritual warfare.

Many believers have been taught the necessity of engaging in spiritual warfare against the devil yet fail to discern the outcome God desires. Far too often, our battles are disjointed and seemingly more tied to circumstances than they are to an overarching theme or an ultimate military end. Whether we understand the ultimate goal is irrelevant to the issue of obedience. We've been commanded to stand firm, and stand firm we must! But if we're aware of our ultimate objective, we're much more likely to fight with purpose and wage a more successful campaign against Satan. I am also convinced that, to endure the fight ahead of us, we're going to have to understand that we truly have a cause worth laying down our lives for, or else we'll too quickly succumb to the pressure to stand down or flee in the day of battle!

As I've come to see it, there are many peripheral things that often draw us into the fight, for example, a physical sickness, a loss of a job, or any number of adverse circumstances. These are not bad

31 John Stuart Mill - https://www.bartleby.com/73/1934.html

things to contend for, and doing so may even eventually line up with God's plans, but there is something far greater that our warfare must ultimately be centered upon. God is Himself a Warrior, and His warfare is not merely concerned with altering events or circumstances in a realm that is passing away. Standing with Him means that we're fighting for the same thing He is. If that's not happening, we'll eventually find ourselves fighting against Him.

If our understanding of warfare is confined to circumstances alone, we'll have to be drawn into battle as a response to the enemy. Thus, our fighting will be mostly defensive in nature. But as we come to understand the Lord as the aggressor in this spiritual war, we must see that He has a specific outcome in view. The Israelites were led by the Lord into a physical showdown with specific instructions to conquer the land of Canaan and destroy its inhabitants, thus fully possessing it as a lasting and permanent homeland. There was little to no obscurity as to their ultimate objective, since the fight was entirely surrounding physical and literal ground. But they are a type and shadow of a spiritual truth. Canaan represents a spiritual reality called sonship, a bride made ready or as we've referred to it throughout this book, the harvest. Canaan has nothing to do with temporal circumstances and everything to do with coming into a mature, intimate relationship with the Lord whereby He becomes our life in the measure of fullness He envisioned when He created man. It is the increase of Christ's life within us to a measure that surpasses even what was seen in the apostles in the New Testament. Canaan is God's eternal purpose, and our warfare on this side of eternity should always be fought with that end in mind.

We are fighting for the harvest to be realized, as we've come to know and understand the true meaning of the word. That is the desired outcome, and we must see that it will not happen without battle. We've become far too passive regarding our eternal inheritance in the Lord, failing to connect the dots between what He has promised us and what He promised the Israelites. Neither were meant to be gained without directly engaging in warfare. Jesus

Himself tells us, "From the days of John the Baptist until now the kingdom of heaven has suffered violence, and the violent take it by force," (Matthew 11:12). God's eternal purpose, like Canaan, is for those who see it by faith, discern rightly that an enemy stands in our way of securing it, heed the invitation of the Lord to take up arms and dispossess the land of the giants that resist, and believe that He will cause us to stand victorious in the end. If we want to be the bride He's created us to be, it must be tested in the throes of out and out warfare. As the bride steps into that arena, the love of God will be proven within her as she becomes willing to lay her life down towards the ultimate objective of being His forever.

Don't you think it's high time that we stop wandering around in the wilderness refusing to fight for the ultimate goal of possessing Christ as our eternal reward? Haven't we had enough of purposeless living, and treating the Lord as if He's an add-on to our temporary lives here on earth? Aren't you sick of an aimless Christianity where everyone gets a trophy so there's little need to actually obey the command of the Lord? God would put an end to all the needless sin, death, and suffering here on this planet just as soon as a generation rises up and marches towards our spiritual Canaan with the intent of possessing it in full. It will be a violent, bloody affair, but if anything is worth fighting for, this is. It is worth dying for, and we may in the process. We are given no guarantees as to our length of days except that we are here temporarily. Our church fathers laid their lives down in pursuit of this end, and why shouldn't we? Do you suppose you'll have any regrets in eternity if your life is laid down unto that end? We've let false doctrines, bad teaching, and unappointed leaders emasculate Christianity, and we need a revolution. Canaan is literally within sight for those who have eyes to see, and I am convinced that a remnant is coming forth to go in and take it.

UNDERSTAND GOD'S OBJECTIVES

The next truth, which is closely tied to the previous one is this: **there must be clearly defined strategic military objectives in our warfare, and we must learn to discern them rightly from the Lord**. A military objective is defined as follows:

> An object which by its nature, location, purpose, or use makes an effective contribution to military action and whose total or partial destruction, capture or neutralization, in the circumstances ruling at the time, offers a definite military advantage.[32]

One of the things that made the Vietnam war so bloody was a lack of clearly defined military objectives. Combat operations often resulted in an area being cleared of enemy combatants one day, but back firmly under their control the next once American troops moved on advancing a front that was nonexistent. As units made their way through the jungles, they often faced a barrage of ambushes from Viet Cong guerilla forces, booby traps, and conventional attacks from the North Vietnamese Army.[33] The U.S. military was ill-prepared for this heavily guerilla-style warfare that was being waged on them by an enemy who was not nearly as concerned with incurring casualties as the U.S. military and political leaders were. Though the U.S. had superior technology and weaponry, their refusal to adapt to the nature of the warfare eventually led to defeat, as the Communist forces prevailed in the South. I'm convinced that the Vietnam war is a picture of the current state of spiritual warfare in the present-day church.

Many are fighting skirmishes with the enemy over unclear, undefined objectives, simply reacting to his ambushes and booby

---

32 Article 1(f) of the 1999 Second Protocol to the Hague Convention for the Protection of Cultural Property

33 https://alphahistory.com/vietnamwar/vietnam-war-soldiers/#Uncertain_objectives

traps, while much of the church is safe at home proclaiming peace and prosperity or simply unwilling to engage. We have incredibly superior weaponry which, if properly utilized, would put a relatively quick end to this war—namely, the Lord Himself! But our aversion to casualties is literally prolonging death on this planet. We care more about our own lives than we do winning this war! We must stop trying to fight the enemy on our terms, cherry picking targets and rules of engagement that are not part of a cohesive, well-defined strategy, gaining ground one day only to surrender it the next, all the while advancing a non-existent front.

It is quite normal to get drawn into a direct conflict through a secondary issue, such as the type of circumstances we mentioned earlier. But we must have wisdom in keeping secondary things in their place and God's eternal purpose as our ultimate objective. If, in the midst of a battle where the enemy disrupts my sleep at night, I fight him on the ground of recovered sleep and nothing else, then even if I'm able to transition out of adverse circumstances, no ground directly related to God's ultimate objective has been attained. I've simply, selfishly recaptured my sleep—something that will be irrelevant in the age to come. And incidentally, that ground, even if gained, is just as likely to be surrendered down the road. But if I resist with the harvest in mind, I recognize that even in the less than desirable wartime circumstances, there is something of eternal value that the Lord would accomplish, and I come into agreement with that objective.

He is fighting for fruit, which has to do with internal ground. There will come a time, as He comes for His bride, when He'll secure the physical ground and establish His kingdom here on earth. But until then, He's waging war for the souls of man—the vineyard of God. He is fighting to conquer the unregenerate soul of man within a corporate vessel. Remember, the harvest is synonymous with maturity not salvation. I'm not at all against born again experiences. The truth is, however, far too many are willing to contend for salvation on behalf of others but see little need to fight for the Lord to gain ground in their own souls. Both are important to the Lord, and as our Commander, He has the prerogative of defining objectives. Our job, then, is to learn to listen to Him and obey His command. When we find ourselves engaged in a spiritual battle, it is imperative that we get before Him and ask Him to show us what those objectives are as well as the strategy for securing them.

Job is a tremendous example to us. The Lord drew Job into a spiritual battle when he brought up his name directly to Satan (Job 1:8), who then had permission to attack Job and his entire family. Why would God do such a thing? Doesn't He love Job? Why would He sanction such tragic circumstances? The wrong answer to these questions is that Job was old covenant and thus this story is no longer relevant to us. Such thinking negates the testimony of Christ embedded in the 39 books that Jesus referred to in John 5:39. Remember, the ground God is taking is internal, and He's doing so with eternity in mind. So, God is out to deal with Job's soul.

A right posture for Job as the battle came to him would have been to get before the Lord and ask, "What is this unto, Lord? What ground are you desiring to take within me?" In saying this, I'm not putting Job on trial or suggesting somehow that he handled this battle poorly. Not by any means. Job is a forerunner in spiritual warfare, and he never had the benefit of the scriptures to teach him. It is his life that has been given to us to teach us a thing or two about battle, and yet few have had ears to hear!

The issue of the attack was over the question of the fear of the Lord (1:8, 2:3). Satan claimed that Job feared God, and thus loved and served Him, because of the physical blessings God had provided and his physical health (1:9, 2:4). Said another way, Satan accused Job of having a shallow relationship with God based on amenable circumstances. The fear of the Lord comes as we rightly behold the Lord—seeing not with our physical eyes but with the eyes of the inner man. Job feared the Lord as much as he knew to, but he did in fact have a blindness he was not aware of. That blindness manifested itself throughout the book in Job's comments and had to do with the projection of human wisdom and human attributes onto God. In that way, Job had reduced God to something much less than that which He truly is. Put another way, Job's relationship with God was not nearly as deep as he thought it was because he did not see God rightly. When the Lord breaks into the battle, speaking directly to Job in His inner man, He confronts and easily obliterates Job's limited understanding of His nature. The end result is that Job openly confesses, "I have heard of You by the hearing of the ear, but now my eye sees You," (42:5). In other words, I thought I knew you, but now I see you clearly.

Job illustrates this concept: There was unconquered territory in his inner man fully under the control of the flesh and thus producing wild, sour grapes for the Lord. This unconquered ground was directly related to a shallow understanding of God. The Lord then initiated a battle designed to conquer that territory. As Job wrestled with Satan throughout the battle, his limited, human understanding came out into the open. Then the Lord showed up and arose as light and opened Job's eyes—both so he could have deeper revelation of the nature of God and so he could rightly see his own brokenness and weaknesses. Job saw both and repented (42:6), coming into a deeper fear of the Lord. As the battle ended, ground was gained in the inner man, and thus Job's story became a blueprint for us. He never resisted the enemy on the ground of the temporal. He kept the primary thing the primary thing, and the Lord eventually restored all that was taken from him in the natural.

It is the same with you and me, friends. The enemy may have authority from the Lord to bring an attack against you, and such an attack may manifest itself in a number of ways. But the military objective is never a physical circumstance alone. Remember, in all of God's dealing with us, He holds His eternal purpose in view. He's interested in gaining a definitive military advantage towards that ultimate objective. Simply working a miracle or healing someone or providing financially for a need doesn't provide that advantage to Him. Again, please don't misinterpret me. I'm not suggesting He's against miracles or healing or provision any more than I have suggested He's against works. He does all those things, but His military objective in any fight is to take ground in the inner man.

As He is able to conquer ground in you, He will, at times, lead you into a place of intercession where you'll be called on to contend for the taking of ground in others. The primary need, then, whether it is on someone else's behalf or ourselves, is a greater seeing of the Lord. When He arises as light, He can expose the flesh and reveal His nature in a deeper way, bringing about both a greater level of repentance and surrender to Him.

Watching and waiting, thus, come into a place of great significance within our warfare. As we assume our places as watchmen, we ask for eyes to see as He would cause us to see. If the battle is for ground in someone else, we are contending not only for increased vision in us so that we may wage the right warfare, but also increased vision in that person so that he or she can behold Him. We both need increased revelation of the Lord and exposure of the ground the Lord would take within us. In that way, we are countering the enemy's tactics of perpetuating spiritual blindness (2 Corinthians 4:4). He is a deceiver, and even the saved have very prevalent blind spots within our souls. We are called to contend for eyes that see the Lord, standing firm against the blindness that results from being aligned with the enemy, and trusting in the Lord to bring about that victory. As He speaks to you as a watchman, you then have the responsibility of obeying Him in the specific prayers and declarations He would lead you in.

Understand that it is flesh that is empowering the enemy on this earth. When Adam fell, Satan gained entrance into the soul of man, obtaining a measure of manipulative influence over both his thinking and his emotions. Every time we come into agreement with his manipulation, the flesh becomes further enslaved to his influence (Romans 6:16), and I am speaking specifically about believers. As the Lord deals with our flesh through His process of exposing it and leading us into true repentance, the enemy loses a strategic foothold within us. At times, his foothold is so secure within a believer that they need deliverance before they can ever truly get free. In such cases, there must be both deliverance and repentance, which is both turning both from sin and self-sufficiency and choosing instead to trust and obey the Lord in that area. If there is not both, there is still a potential open door for the enemy and a chance to regain and strengthen his foothold.

LET GOD DEFINE YOUR WARFARE

The fourth principle is this: **make sure that God is defining not only the military objective, but also the enemy combatant you're called to resist**. Every spiritual battle you encounter, no matter how severe, is an opportunity for God to gain an advantage towards His readied harvest and the casting down of Satan to the earth in preparation for His ultimate defeat (Revelation 12:10). It's way too easy to think others need more conquering than you, but this belittles the significance of unconquered ground in you if you even admit it exists. I promise you, it exists, and the Lord has every intention of targeting it because it has tremendous strategic significance to Him. Always remember that He is our Commander, and He defines the targets. Thus, our fighting is at His command not our whim.

The battle is the Lord's not ours. That should be clear to us, but far too often presumption and self-centered ambition becomes our downfall. Consider Israel in going up against Canaan. The Lord designated Jericho as the initial objective, and in the natural, this seems counter-intuitive. This little fledgling nation of ex-slaves with no prior military experience went up against the most fortified, walled fortress in existence. Common sense would have suggested that maybe they take on a smaller, more vulnerable target first. But God had another strategy in mind, and it was executed quite beautifully so long as the people adhered to it. As they found out at Ai, the slightest deviations from His plan will lead to defeat and only serve to make things more difficult in the long run.

You don't get to tell God what ground needs to be taken in you or in anyone else. First of all, He knows far better than we do what ground is secured and what ground is unconquered. Also, He's both the strategist and the one that empowers us in our warfare. If you decide to go on a crusade when He's not initiating a battle, you're only going to stir up a hornet's nest you don't have the authority to deal with. Such was the case with me, when I went into the former Yugoslavia on an intercession outreach thinking that our little team was sent to pull down strongholds of hatred and division that had been in place for centuries. We not only didn't have the authority to pull them down, but we were also clueless as to the many openings those spirits had access to within our own unconquered souls. The end result was a spiritual butt whipping for myself and the rest of my team. Looking back, I do believe we were there on assignment by the Lord, but we operated largely outside of His mandated mission. Had we sought Him with greater fervency and humility, I'm confident things would have been much different instead of turning into a painful learning experience.

All authority flows from the One to whom all authority was given (Matthew 28:18), and He gives us authority to carry out the missional assignments He delegates. We do not have authority outside the parameters of those assignments. This is true in any endeavor but certainly as it pertains to warfare. Our source of strength in the battle is the life of Christ within us, and if we endeavor to fight an enemy He's not presently targeting, we'll find ourselves resisting a supernatural being with our own natural strength. Trust me, that's not a place in which you want to find yourself. Few know the difficulty of wrestling against principalities, but the more you are made readied for the Lord, the more you'll face them. When you do, don't presume you're called to take them down. In most instances, you're simply called to secure internal ground—either in yourself or others—that is under their direct influence, thus diminishing their power. They will be taken down according to His timing in this war, so leave that notion where it belongs—in His hands.

FIGHT TO THE END

The final principle is simply this: **once we engage in the battle, we must do so until the victory is recognized**. I mean this both as it pertains to a battle and to the war. There are too many stories in the Old Testament of half-hearted attempts to cleanse the land or execute a battle plan as directed by the Lord, and none of them ended well. We must learn to stand as He instructs us to stand until He says the battle is over. To end prematurely, even when the circumstances have changed and the feeling of urgency has waned, could have the end result of failing to secure the strategic objective God desires, thus making the whole thing nothing more than a giant learning experience. We fight until the day the Lord allows us to step on the necks of kings. Whether that's dealing with a demonic influence within you or within someone else, it makes no difference. Fight until the Lord says to stop. This is where we have such a tendency to get formulaic, but even in battle, the Lord is very much relational with us. He doesn't just give us instructions to carry out, He is in us and with us, leading us in the fight. All eyes are on Him. We must maintain a position of watching and waiting. While that's important all the time, in warfare it is absolutely critical.

Know that the results that the Lord is after may not be seen for some time afterwards. We had a number of extended battles surrounding the will of God for one person in our fellowship in Georgia, and that person was my brother-in-law Rob, who I mentioned earlier. For several years, we went toe-to-toe with the enemy, crying out to the Lord on Rob's behalf. In our final year in Edison, we saw the Lord do miraculous things in conquering ground within him, and it was not only worth the wait but worth the fight as well!

When the battle ends, don't look to jump into another one prematurely. My experience is you don't have to tell people this. If they've truly been in a spiritual battle, they quite appreciate the R&R that the Lord allows. But don't get too comfortable there either. The Lord has another battle on the horizon, and such is our lot until this war is over or the Lord calls us home.

The enemy is primarily concerned, as we've said multiple times, with the harvest coming forth. That means that as you progress in this journey, you become more of a threat to him. He responds to that threat and will then concentrate more of his resources on resisting you. This is not to scare or deter you, but to prepare you for the reality that battle is our lot until the war has ended. Remember, as was the case with Job, the Lord gives limited authority to the enemy for the ultimate objective of gaining ground in His people. He is a good God, and we can trust Him to be our Shepherd.

We must learn to approach this war with a full desire to end it. General Patton is quoted as saying,

> There is only one tactical principle which is not subject to change. It is to use the means at hand to inflict the maximum amount of wound, death, and destruction on the enemy in the minimum amount of time.[34]

Such ought to be our resolve in these end times. God has all the resources necessary to finish this war with the possible exception of one thing. That one thing is the wildcard in this whole discussion. It is not a question of strategic or tactical wisdom necessary for outmaneuvering and outsmarting the enemy, as the Lord Himself is our Commander. It is not a lack of superior firepower, as He Himself is our weapon and more than capable of pulling down strongholds. It's not even a question of numbers, as there are twice as many angels fighting with us as there are demons fighting against us. The wildcard in this fight is you and me. Will we rise up in this

34 Patton, General George S. (1944) Instructions to the Third United States Army

hour, knowing that the fields are ripe and ready for the harvest? Or will we maintain the status quo of modern Christianity? Will we be numbered among men like Joshua and Caleb who pressed Moses to go right into Canaan, or will we fall away into irrelevance and obscurity like the other 10 who failed to seize upon the grace of God for full victory? So much is at stake in this critical hour, and while you have no say in whether or not someone else rises to the occasion, you must recognize the clear choice that is front of you.

How about it, my friend? Will the Lord find such faith in you?

We few, we happy few, we band of brothers;
For he to-day that sheds his blood with me
Shall be my brother; be he ne'er so vile,
This day shall gentle his condition:
And gentlemen in England now a-bed
Shall think themselves accursed they were not here,
And hold their manhoods cheap whiles any speaks
That fought with us upon Saint Crispin's day.[35]

God make us warriors in this hour!

35 Henry V by William Shakespeare, Act IV, scene III

CHAPTER 15

FINAL THOUGHTS

> Where there is no vision [no revelation of God and His word], the people are unrestrained;
>
> But happy and blessed is he who keeps the law [of God].
>
> Proverbs 29:18 AMP

The story goes that President Ulysses S. Grant once attempted to take up golf while on a trip to the British Isles. After setting up on the first hole tee box, he pulled out a club and attempted to drive the ball down the fairway. But instead of connecting with the intended object, his club simply threw bits of turf and dirt into the air. After multiple such failed attempts, he finally turned to his caddie and said, I have always understood the game of golf was good outdoor exercise and especially for the arms. I fail, however, to see what use there is for a ball in the game."[36] He never picked up a club again.

Like President Grant, too many within the church have failed to grasp the purpose of Christianity, wrongly confusing the personal benefits they derive with the Lord's ultimate intent towards humanity. Our lack of vision has caused us to fail to connect with the foundational truth of Christ as life, and as a result, we have not only misunderstood the primary purpose of the cross, we've also misallocated and mishandled the things of God. The true prophetic, which is the testimony of Christ (Revelation 19:10), has been forsaken, much like Grant's golf ball, and in an unrestrained state, the church has become drunk with the pleasure of pursuing the random exercise associated with a form of godliness that offers no power to transform us within. Put another way, we like the idea

---

36 https://www.insidehook.com/article/politics/presidents-golf-short-history

of being known as disciples of Christ, but few have understood and heeded the true nature of His invitation, which is expressed beautifully in Dietrich Bonhoeffer's sentiment, "when Christ calls a man, he bids him come and die."[37]

But God, in His steadfast love for the Son and His absolute commitment to securing a bride for Him, longs to unveil His full purpose for all who will listen. In so doing, He would move us off the ground of random, self-centered, self-sourced living and drive us right down the fairway of bridal readiness, ridding us of the shackles and limitations of the old man and filling us with the life of the Son. I am able to share a tiny bit of revelation in this area simply because the Lord has been revealing Himself to me. In the process, I have witnessed first-hand that He is stirring in the hearts of others as well. And while we are most likely just a remnant within the church, I am convinced that this present stirring is a world-wide movement to awaken His bride unto full readiness. I, for one, am convinced that she is arousing from her slumber.

I once had a dear friend tell me that his greatest aim was to somehow by the grace of God find himself in heaven once his life on earth is over. And while I appreciate the fact that such a sentiment is a much higher aim than that of most of the world, it is a severe short-changing of the ultimate desire of the Father, and it undermines His invitation to participate in a wedding ceremony. We have been entrusted with a precious, awe-inspiring gospel message whereby the God of creation has announced His intent to become one with us. Yet, far too often, we have navigated through life as if we're content with the distant promise of a place called heaven. But entrance into heaven is not the standard upon which we will one day be judged.

The Parable of the Talents in Matthew 25:14-30 likens the Lord to a wealthy man who entrusted his servants with a measure of his wealth expecting that they would invest it wisely and

---

37 Dietrich Bonhoeffer, The Cost of Discipleship (London: SCM Press, 1948/2001), 44.

yield an acceptable return. With eternal purpose in sight, this parable becomes quite clear as to what the Lord is after in us. Having deposited a measure of the life of the Son within us, He's expecting that life to increase. To be clear, we're not talking about the increase of doctrine or the increase of book knowledge or even the increase of behavior modification. It is the life of the Son of God that He is desiring to multiply within us. That will only happen as we go down this path of readiness—the inward journey of embracing the cross and living by the Faith of the Son of God as He reveals Himself to the inner man.

We will give account for the increase of His Son within us or the lack thereof. That is an inescapable, harsh reality that we must own up to. We don't like such difficult statements in today's church because we've opened the door to the squishy subjectivity that emanates from the spirit of the age. Thus, the messengers proclaiming objective truth are often castigated as being legalistic relics of a darker time in church history when believers weren't as open-minded and tolerant as they are today. But the truth is, the voices proclaiming Christ and nothing else are paving the way forward down the narrow and difficult way, not harkening the church to the past.

If you've made it this far into this book, you will not have the ability to say, "No one ever told me about this, Lord," on the day of judgment. You have been warned. But more than a warning, you're being lovingly summoned into a place of responding to His invitation. I think often about the story of the man on the side of the road on a dark and stormy night, soaked to the bone, flagging down motorists in an attempt to warn them that the bridge ahead had been washed out and was therefore impassable. Many protested at his admonitions, going so far as to ridicule him for his direct and foolish message, boasting that they had traversed this road their whole lives and never once encountered problems crossing the old bridge. What would compel a man to speak so boldly and so confidently about what lay ahead? What would cause him to risk being misunderstood and rejected? Is it not the kind of love that says, "I would lay my life down for you, that you might not make the mistake of driving off into danger?" I am, by no means, perfect in the delivery of the message, but please know that there is great danger ahead for most of the church. We need a course correction like never before. That is the very purpose of this book. It is, I believe, an affirmation of the invitation given in the So, and a small encouragement from one who is learning to heed that invitation.

What is needed from us—from you—is a choice. We don't go down this path without great intention. Likewise, we don't go down this path without great sacrifice. I refuse to lie to you or sugar coat the message as so many have done over the years, thus leading the masses into error. Saying "yes" to His invitation will cost you everything, and by that, I do mean everything. Nothing is sacred to the Lord in this journey except our commitment and dedication to Him. All else will be tested and must be laid upon the altar. I'm sharing this not from a place of doctrine or theory but from personal experience. I've had to lay down my career... more than once. I have sacrificed friendships and even relationships with family members who do not understand my pursuit of Him above all else, opting to obey the Lord instead of doing what seems right in the eyes of others. I've endured assaults from the enemy upon my health multiple times, and I am learning to continuously hold my plans, my expectations, and even my doctrines loosely before Him. I've even had to lay my own children on the altar, entrusting them to Him. This is not a boast, nor am I complaining. I'm simply sharing with you the nature of the journey that is required of us. Through it all, I am learning what Paul meant when he said:

> I count everything as loss compared to the priceless privilege and supreme advantage of knowing Christ Jesus my Lord [and of growing more deeply and thoroughly acquainted with Him—a joy unequaled]. For His sake I have lost

> everything, and I consider it all garbage, so that I may gain Christ, and may be found in Him [believing and relying on Him], not having any righteousness of my own derived from [my obedience to] the Law and its rituals, but [possessing] that [genuine righteousness] which comes through faith in Christ, the righteousness which comes from God on the basis of faith. And this, so that I may know Him [experientially, becoming more thoroughly acquainted with Him, understanding the remarkable wonders of His person more completely] and [in that same way experience] the power of His resurrection [which overflows and is active in believers], and [that I may share] the fellowship of His sufferings, by being continually conformed [inwardly into His likeness even] to His death [dying as He did]; so that I may attain to the resurrection [that will raise me] from the dead.
>
> Philippians 3:8-11 AMP

The ultimate question that is being asked of you—as should be asked of any bride in the natural—is simply this: "What is your Beloved worth to you?" The answer must never come from a place of words alone, but it must be answered in life. Friends, we may not particularly like that we are being asked such a pointed question, but it is the very question upon which we'll one day be judged. God is forcing us, in His mercy, to acknowledge it today, giving us opportunity to do something about it before it's too late. That is why this message is blunt and hard and why it evokes a strong reaction within our souls. Most of us will bristle to some degree, taking offense over the idea of a God who has the audacity to confront His own creation with such pointed candor. But it's only because we're insisting that the bridge ahead, which we cannot see, is still very much intact. It is not, and to persist in the way that seems right to us will lead us to death (Proverbs 14:12), even if it's a way that is widely accepted within a wayward church.

There is a movement taking place in our day. You won't hear about this movement on the radio, and you won't read about it in Christian magazines. It will never be promoted on TV or even proclaimed from many of the pulpits of the mainstream church, and there will even be prominent and powerful ministries that will viciously attack those that are a part of it. But make no mistake, this movement is being birthed by the Lord Himself. The movement of His Spirit goes directly against the current of the present church system, but if we'll embrace it, we'll find that it leads us directly to Him. That is the whole purpose of this book, and if, in some small way, you find yourself being stirred by the Lord to get off the ground of the wisdom and strength of the soul of man and put your trust entirely in the right Man, Christ, then this book will have been an overwhelming success.

Today is the day of choosing, and you must understand that not choosing is a choice in itself. We must choose, today, whom we will serve (Joshua 24:15), and, again, the Lord is forcing the issue in our hearts. I beg of you, my dear brother or sister, do not make the mistake of failing to respond to Him as He desires. If you're offended, I invite you to do what I've had to do repeatedly over the past several years (and I say this in love)... "get over yourself." We will never find Him as long as we're clinging to our own sense of self-importance.

This book was written with you in mind, and I pray that you'll hear the voice of the Holy Spirit as one crying in the wilderness saying, "Prepare the way for the coming of the Lord!" Such preparation won't come through passivity. It won't take place by trusting in our wisdom or in our own strength. And it won't happen through the rapture. It will only happen if and when you choose to journey down this path of readiness.

What are you waiting for? Time is short!

Made in the USA
Middletown, DE
17 August 2024